The Science of Why

This page intentionally left blank

The Science of Why

Decoding Human Motivation and Transforming Marketing Strategy

David Forbes

First published in 2015 by
PALGRAVE MACMILLAN®
in the United States—a division of St. Martin's Press LLC,
175 Fifth Avenue, New York, NY 10010.

Where this book is distributed in the UK, Europe and the rest of the world,
this is by Palgrave Macmillan, a division of Macmillan Publishers Limited,
registered in England, company number 785998, of Houndmills, Basingstoke,
Hampshire RG21 6XS.

Palgrave Macmillan is the global academic imprint of the above companies
and has companies and representatives throughout the world.

Palgrave® and Macmillan® are registered trademarks in the United States, the
United Kingdom, Europe and other countries.

ISBN: 978–1–137–50203–2

Library of Congress Cataloging-in-Publication Data

Forbes, David L.
    The science of why : decoding human motivation and transforming marketing
strategy / by David Forbes.
        pages cm
    Includes bibliographical references and index.
    ISBN 978–1–137–50203–2 (hardcover : alk. paper)
        1. Consumer behavior. 2. Motivation (Psychology) 3. Marketing—
Psychological aspects. 4. Consumers—Research. I. Title.

HF5415.32.F67 2015
658.8'342—dc23   2015002535

A catalogue record of the book is available from the British Library.

Design by Newgen Knowledge Works (P) Ltd., Chennai, India.

First edition: June 2015

10 9 8 7 6 5 4 3 2 1

Contents

Preface

This page intentionally left blank

This book is a result of nearly three decades of conversations with people—about their everyday lives, about the choices they make in those lives, and about the thoughts and emotions that lie behind those choices. My colleagues at Forbes Consulting and I have been fortunate to have an exceptionally wide range of topics in these conversations as we pursued commissions from clients ranging from health care to home care, banking to breakfast cereals, colas to convertibles. I want to begin this book with a heartfelt thanks to all those consumers who gave us their time and let us into their lives.

The ideas about motivation in this book have been distilled from themes that emerged time and again in our work. We searched naturally for a common set of core motives behind behavior and for a map of motivational space that would help us "put legs" on our motivational insights so that a business manager could actually use these insights to do a better job. The structured model of human motivation we call the Forbes Matrix was developed to assist us in that task. It helps clients to reach a broader overall understanding of motivation and also gives them a compelling vision of how to speak to and leverage the specific motivations operating in their market. I would also like to thank each and every one of those clients whose business interests led us to examine a wonderful diversity of windows on everyday life and whose business challenges became for us a passport to deep emotional learning.

I hope that your passage through the pages of this volume lets you experience a small portion of the excitement and wisdom that comes from a lifetime of consumer research and marketing consulting.

This page intentionally left blank

Acknowledgments

This book would not have been possible without the assistance of my colleagues at the Forbes Consulting Group whose collective efforts helped bring a theoretical vision into scientific reality. Jeremy Pincus, in particular, gave generously of his counsel and spent countless hours of his time working out the details of the MindSight research tools. My writing assistant and coach, Julie Penfold, transformed this manuscript from an academic monologue into an interesting and accessible narrative. My good friend David May supported my efforts from the very beginning and provided me with real-world opportunities to refine and perfect both the theory and practice described in the book. My editor at Palgrave Macmillan, Laurie Harting, has given both support and guidance as I moved from a loose draft to a completed manuscript. My copy editor Sabine Seiler did a stellar job taming my sometimes unruly syntax and more. My children Emma and Duncan offered endless hours of patient listening as sounding boards over the years in which I developed my ideas. And my wife Ginny Sherwood as critic, editor, and all-around giver of support was nothing short of essential to my actually getting the work done, getting it right, and staying sane throughout the process.

This page intentionally left blank

Introduction

Why *do* consumers do what they do?
What's *really* behind the choices they make?
What moves them, what delights them, what do they love?

Questions like these have probably vexed marketers since the days when shells and spears were the most popular fast-moving consumer goods. Yet, as pressing as those questions are, we haven't really made much headway in answering them since noted advertising executive David Ogilvy lamented back in the 1960s that people don't really think the way they feel, or say what they think, or do what they say.

So, why has our mission stalled here?

It's not because we haven't invested the time, energy, and resources we need to learn about our consumers, far from it. According to the Council of American Survey Research Organizations, US companies spent $ 6.7 billion in efforts to learn more about their consumers in 2013. Worldwide, almost $19 billion is invested annually to discover what consumers really want. Neither of those figures takes into account expenditures from smaller companies that don't report them to media, and both figures are expected to grow.

It's also not because we don't value the opinions of our consumers. We take great care and use an extensive range of methods to engage consumers along every step of the product life cycle from concept development to use in the home.

It's certainly not because we labor under the delusion that we already know it all when it comes to our consumers. To the contrary, in my experience, the longer and harder we search for true consumer insight, the sooner we realize we are in Einstein's dilemma: "the more we learn, the less we know."

Instead of any of these hypotheses, I'm willing to wager that the real reason we still share Ogilvy's lament is that we've yet to discover the tools we need to truly understand our customers, including the right questions to ask, the right way to ask them, and the right answers to be looking for.

Those are things that we're going to discover in these pages.

Interesting Times

"May you live in interesting times" is reputedly an ancient Chinese blessing that can also serve as a curse, depending on who's offering it and under what circumstances. This double-edged message does a good job of characterizing the current status of our profession.

As hyperbolic as it may sound, it is nonetheless true that the challenges we marketers face have never been greater. The very nature of the consumer marketing/research world has tilted on its axis as societal and technological changes have reinvented what it means to "consume." And on the heels of that, inevitably, are radical changes in what it takes to understand and market to today's consumers.

Suddenly, our consumers are not where they've always been. They are not doing what they've always done. They are not buying what they've always bought. And they're not buying *anything* the way they've always bought it. It's no exaggeration to characterize the great, sweeping changes in media venues, in product development, in messaging, and in popular culture itself as anything short of revolutionary.

One result of all this is that today's consumers and the process of consuming bear little resemblance to what the entire market research industry evolved to understand way back in Ogilvy's day. New and emerging alternative media mean consumers no longer need to watch or to listen to traditional advertising at all. In addition, powerful, consumer-driven movements make it easy for today's consumers to opt out of all the direct mail, e-mail, and telemarketing efforts we've so painstakingly—and expensively—put in place to reach them.

"Where are they now?" we'll soon be asking, if we're not already. "How can I get them to hear what I have to say?"

As our marketplace becomes more and more diverse, changes in the difficulty of reaching and attracting our new consumers make understanding what really, deeply motivates them more critical than ever. Products that don't promise real fulfillment and messages that lack the emotional impact to break through the clutter haven't a chance of moving consumers.

As a result of all these market realities, the way we do business will inevitably change. It's changing already. The question for each of us then becomes: do we want to anticipate that change or to react to it? In other words: as we encounter the "stampeding elephant" of changing consumer behavior, will we be tossing spears at it from behind, or will we be out in front of it, digging a big hole?

New Realities: New Challenges

To succeed in the fast-approaching marketplace of *tomorrow*, we need to get up to speed *today* on who our new consumers are and what they really want. It's time to own the fact that our new and emerging market realities require new research methods to address them.

It's fair to say that we as marketers haven't done a great job so far of finding the key to consumers' hearts and minds (despite the billions we throw at the problem), and surely we'll need to do better as that job grows increasingly more difficult. Changes in the lives and lifestyles of our consumers, coupled with changes in the media and marketplaces where they buy products and services, require changes in the way we learn about them and market to them. And the intensity of competition means we're likely to fail unless we can finally find our way to the hearts of our consumers, understand their inner frustrations and aspirations, and craft products and messages that reach out ot them. And at the crux of that challenge lie the *emotional* motivations of consumers.

This book brings together up-to-the-minute details of the new market-place; advances in consumer research methods; and new information on uncovering, understanding, and targeting the emotional motivations that drive the actions of every consumer, all of the time. In the pages that follow, we'll uncover a new way to understand motivational theory and a new way to apply this understanding in the consumer-empowered marketplace that's emerging as we speak.

The best route to learning about consumers' deep seated emotional needs—the ones we'll explore here—requires new research methodologies for learning about them and a new approach to decoding the information we uncover in that pursuit. In the new marketplace, it's essential that we bring to light the emotional forces that drive the behavior of our consumers; these

are the emotional forces powerful enough to pull consumers from their arm-
chairs at home, move them to their automobile, drive them to the store, com-
pel them to search for a particular product (yours, we hope), and part with
money they've worked hard to earn; or powerful enough to make them reach
for their computer mouse, navigate to a seller of your product, and enter all of
the personal information necessary to place an order online using that same
hard-earned money. Nothing but a firm and reliable understanding of those
motivational forces will allow us to harness their energy and use it to inspire
consumers with products and product messaging that will move them to take
those products and brands into their lives and ultimately to include them in
their vision of who they are as individuals.

For a fortunate few products and brands that discover and best fulfill the
emotional needs of their customers, this sequence of behaviors will happen
over and over again, and customers who feel truly and deeply fulfilled by
these products will make owning and using them a part of their lives.

That's how you build a brand.

And that's what *The Science of Why* is all about.

Think of it as a map to guide us as we set out on the journey to discover
who our consumers are and to learn why they do what they do. That journey
begins and ends with an understanding of consumers' deepest psychological
motivations and how these play out in the marketplace.

Motivations Are Everywhere

The term for these deep-seated emotional forces that drive our behavior is
"motivation." And as you'll discover in these pages, motivations are at work
wherever you find people.

Here's an example: When you picked up this book, you acted on a motivation. Turning to the title page: motivation again. In fact, every action
you've taken today—and nearly all the actions we all take every day—have
been prefaced, primed, and punctuated by the emotional motivations pre-
ceding them. In the case of this book, you somehow consciously "knew"
you were interested in the topic, you were attracted by the title, and you
were drawn in by the ideas in the first pages. But lurking beneath these
conscious thoughts, your emotional and mostly subconscious urges are what
really put the book in your hands.

Motivations come in a lot of different "flavors." You may be reading these sentences now out of a desire to feel smarter (the empowerment motive) or based on a need to stand out from the crowd of your colleagues (the identity motive), or perhaps you are driven to perform your job at your highest ability (the mastery motive). Whatever mix of motives caused you to read this sentence at this moment, your choice is a facet of who you truly are at your deepest emotional core. And, if this book does a good job of fulfilling your primary motives for picking it up, it will have succeeded in its mission to become a part of who *you* are.

Every action you and your consumers take has a psychological motivation underlying it. Without the drive of motivation, there would be no impulse buy at the checkout stand, no incentive to reach past an inexpensive generic product to choose the name brand that "feels" safer, smarter, and better even if it contains the same ingredients and costs twice as much. We all buy because we are first motivated by what we feel that product will do for us emotionally. Always.

Marketers who understand consumers' deep emotional motivations, who uncover unmet and possibly even unknown customer needs will have the opportunity to blaze amazing new paths of innovation and to create dazzling new product successes that seemed unimaginable before. Cultivating a deep understanding of what moves your consumers emotionally also opens the door to new and effective marketing messages that literally *move* them into their vehicles or onto the Internet to bring your enticing product into their lives.

Understanding this level of consumer motivation also enables you to create the kind of loyalty that exists only when consumers feel they are deeply understood and appreciated. Over time, effective motivational marketing could even take you to the ultimate goal of marketing when it elevates your customers' relationship with your brand to the point where it becomes a part of their identity, a meaningful component of their way of being in the world.

Need proof? Just think of Harley-Davidson riders. Or look at Nike customers, wearing their swooshes on their shoes and shirts, proudly proclaiming with their badges that they're part of a team whose mission is to "just do it." Harley-Davidson and Nike didn't get that kind of loyalty just by making motorcycles or shoes.

What would the chance to have a relationship like this with your customers be worth? The possibility of such an outcome is probably at least part of what motivated you to pick up this book in the first place.

Motivations versus Goals and Plans

Our first step in this journey is to distinguish between two uses of the word "motivation." The first, the "motivation," we casually refer to when we're talking about our goals in life or the items we place on our to-do lists, including our need to "get motivated" to tackle them, is a planful construct of the conscious mind. We can reflect upon, discuss, or alter that motivation easily and any time.

For most of us the plans and goals that "motivate" us provide an overall direction to our lives. From our earliest days, as we seek to develop a flight plan for life's journey, these conscious motivations help us map out: "I want to be a fireman," we say, or a teacher or a doctor or a princess.

As we progress along each life stage in our development, we always have an eye on a prize (though that prize alters along with us). "I want to graduate with honors"; "I want to be a parent"; "I want to see the world," or even: "I want to write a book." Conscious motivations, then, are about plans, strategies, and tactics. They are the atlas we use to consciously guide our lives, the compass we use to stay on course. For our purposes here, I'll refer to these mental entities as goals or plans.

The second use of the word "motivation" refers to the deep-seated, typically subconscious emotional forces we'll be discussing in this book. These psychological motivations are continually at work behind the scenes of our consciousness and drive us to do the things we do, always pressing us toward actions and choices that will make us feel good in some way and pushing us away from actions that will make us feel frustrated or fearful. These deep, emotional, and primitive motivations are responsible for all of the worlds and worldviews we create. They are the driving impetus behind each of the thousands upon thousands of decisions we make to move our lives along; they influence the mates we choose, the cars we drive, the media we consume, and the way we feel about them all.

Think of it this way: if day-to-day plans and goals are the maps and compass of life's journeys, then psychological motivations are the reasons we set out on the trip in the first place.

Aspirations and Frustrations

The usually subconscious emotional motivations we're learning about here come in two forms. The first refer to motivations that "pull" us toward things we want; we are driven by our emotional "aspirations," our yearnings for positive things in our lives. We experience these aspirations as "urges," for example, the urge to be more powerful, to be more caring, to be more accomplished, and so on.

This act of aspiring is a uniquely human trait, one that separates our species us from the rest of all life on the planet. We humans are inherently dreamers, hopers, seekers. We've built cathedrals and skyscrapers; we've climbed mountains because they were "there." We have taken giant steps on the moon and have held beating human hearts in our hands (remarkably, this is almost routine now), and we all work on an amazing Internet (what did we ever do without it?) that instantly connects any of us with nearly all of us, in fractions of seconds.

As the opposite of aspirations, the second type of motivations are those that "push" us away from things we don't like; we are driven by the emotional "frustrations" in our lives, including our longings to feel less weak or less emotionally isolated or less like a failure. We become frustrated when something we want isn't available to us, when a skill we seek to acquire eludes us, or when a relationship we want to establish proceeds too slowly or doesn't proceed at all. In the end, the root of all frustration is a shortfall in some aspect of our aspirations.

Almost every action we take is driven by one or the other of these twin emotional forces that urge us to move toward pleasure or to move away from pain. Thus, beneath every consumer's visible behavior lies a complex symphony of unconscious emotional forces that shape every urge they have to acquire, use, own, and display whatever helps them change the way they feel about themselves and change as well their expectations about how others will see them.

If we agree that aspirations and frustrations are the fuel that feed our consumers' dreams and desires, it follows that marketing tactics that promise to fulfill these twin emotional yearnings are the surest route to consumers' hearts. That's why it's so important to learn the language of the truest, deepest desires of the people we want to connect with. How we coax those desires to speak to us in a language that reveals the truth is what *The Science of Why* is all about.

We will be fluent in that language before we are done with this book.

I Drink (Coffee), Therefore I Am

You can witness the upside of an emotionally connected relationship the next time you're in line at a Starbucks store. Take a look at the patient customers waiting in line with you. They are not there because the quality of the coffee is far superior to that of the competing stores (although that might be what they tell themselves or how they'd respond in a survey). They are certainly not there because the coffee prices are so low that they're a bargain compared to other alternatives. In fact, they are not there for any reason that has to do with those brick-and-mortar, rational justifications at all.

Instead, many of those customers are there with you because the Starbucks coffee *experience* has become *a part of who they are*. Not only does it figure into how they want to see themselves in the world, but it also—and this is just as important—contributes to their vision of how they'd like to be seen by *others*.

In that way, the ritual of that Starbucks coffee purchase fulfills the emotional needs of its customers. Perhaps it's important to one customer that he can count on how that experience will unfold every time he visits (the security motive), or maybe it supports another's self-image as a discriminating coffee consumer (the mastery motive), for still others, the appeal may lie in the way the Starbucks staff treats them (the esteem motive).

The customers you're in line with are not just buying coffee, they are engaging in an extremely fulfilling social ceremony. Starbucks nurtures its relationship with its customers to a point where this morning coffee interaction feels a bit like family time.

Starbucks does clever things to drive this impression home. The staff members ask for names and write them on the cups they use, so that they can publically announce when the customer's exclusive, customized beverage is ready. Those customers always know that their personal cups of coffee—those lattes with three shots, extra hot—are like no other and have been formulated just for them. That level of personalized attention is a testament to their social status in the store, and a powerful signal to others and to themselves of how important they are to Starbucks.

So close are their consumers' emotional bonds with the brand that Starbucks no longer even mentions the word "coffee" in its logo. Founder and CEO Howard Schultz famously sums up his company's success, in part, this way: "We are not in the coffee business selling to people," he says. "We are in the people business, selling coffee."

Reinventing Business Processes

As the example of Starbucks demonstrates, many things need to change if we are to make the journey from "business as usual" to a motivational marketing program. The first is the fundamental approach to doing business. Most companies get started because somebody is really good at something or because somebody has a great idea. Quite naturally, established businesses proceed along the path that got them started; they take their ideas and turn them into products. Marketing for this type of business means taking the products and services that flow naturally from the energy of the company and convincing the consumer public to learn about and appreciate these products. In other words, marketing in these cases involves persuading consumers to buy what you as marketer are selling.

But if you commit to becoming a company that is dedicated to a process of motivational marketing, you have to turn this process on its head. Instead of the consumer appearing at the end of the production process as a "target" to be persuaded, you must put the consumer at the start of the process, as a source of information and inspiration you can turn into products.

My colleagues and I see this most strikingly in our pharmaceutical clients. It was once the case that scientists developed new products for those suffering from diseases based on the natural process of scientific discovery. Pharmaceutical marketers then set out to convince or persuade patients that they needed whatever benefits the new drug provided. Today, pharmaceutical manufacturers and marketers begin by talking to the people who suffer with an illness or condition, and learn from them what kinds of lifestyle improvements these consumers wish for most. Only then do the scientists get busy with a drug development agenda, now guided by what consumers want most.

Of course, not all products start from scratch, nor should they. But a consumer-driven, motivation-driven business process means trying to build a connection to consumers at their psychological core. We have to start discovering consumers' aspirations and frustrations to craft messages that help them find our products and envision how these products might help them fulfill their inner motives. We have to stop putting the products first and then looking for a way to persuade consumers to buy (into) them.

In other words, rather than trying to drive consumers toward a goal we devise, we need to put our consumers' desires, wishes, and fears in the forefront of our relationship with them; we need to make the products that they want us to make and create the messages that lead them to discover the value of our products on their own terms. In this way, they can, eventually, be inspired to buy our products because they believe those products might help them realize at least a part of their innermost desires.

That kind of deep, emotional resonance is what transforms a motorcycle driver into a Harley driver, a computer user into a devoted Mac user, a beer drinker into a "Bud man" (or "woman"). As an added bonus these spectacular brand identity campaigns have led to loyal users who've embraced "their" brand as a part of "who they are" and therefore will generally not even attend to messaging from other, "lesser" brands. How's that for a return on your investment?

Uncovering Insights about Motivations

Let's face it: You can't rely on a traditional question-and-answer dialogue with consumers if you're looking for insights into emotional motivations they are not aware of themselves. To align our business processes with consumers' emotional needs and wants and to work toward fulfilling consumers' sub-conscious emotional motivations, we need to be able to reach and understand these motivations. And that calls for a change in how consumer research is conducted.

We'll spend time in this book looking at the challenges of researching emotional motivations and outline the current state of the alternative methods being used to overcome them, including an overview of MindSight, the innovation my colleagues and I developed that uses rapid exposures to validated emotional images to open a dialog with the consumer's emotional subconscious.

Understanding and Applying Motivational Insights

Another challenge of motivational research and motivational marketing is that we have lacked a common language for talking about motivation. Theorists have worked in the area for centuries and intensively so for the past one hundred years. The work of several of these theorists has made its way into conversations about consumer psychology and marketing. But no single compelling vocabulary exists that will let us identify the full range of human motives, contrast and compare them with one another, and systematically translate motivational concepts into marketing strategies.

The Science of Why will answer those challenges and change your vision of consumer marketing in the meantime. Toward that end I've created a simple, easy-to-understand and easy-to-apply model of human motivation, a kind of periodic table of motives that identifies, organizes, and explains the nine core motivations, one of which is behind every action of every consumer.

The Forbes Matrix, which we'll get to in the next chapter, contains all we need to know about why consumers do the things they do in the way they do them. The nine core motives in this matrix are all you'll need to craft motivational marketing strategies that link consumers' innermost desires with the emotional benefits your product can deliver. The matrix will explain the subtle differences in the emotional makeup of different consumer groups in your market; it will provide alternatives for your approach to motivational marketing, and it will help you understand the consequences of the choices you make between these strategic alternatives. These nine core psychological motivations are all you need to know to answer the questions that opened this chapter: Why *do* consumers do what they do? What's *really* behind the choices they make? What moves them, what delights them, what do they love?

As you get into this book and proceed toward answers to those questions, you may find you begin to "think in motives." You will instantly be able to evaluate advertising you see by the nature and quality of its motivational impact, whether intended or (often) unintended. And you will consistently think in new, systematic ways about your business and the fundamental kinds of emotional fulfillment your products can deliver. You will be on the road to a whole new way to do business, and you will have a handbook for surviving and thriving in the radically new marketplace that is emerging around us.

To drive those insights home, each story unfolds actionable information with clear connections to the bottom line. Each motivation chapter uses real-world case studies to demonstrate the motive in practice. Consumer profiles in each motivation chapter provide a comprehensive but simple real-world image of how each motive can come alive as a set of beliefs and values, tastes and styles. To move those case studies and profiles into your "real world," I offer targeted marketing messages designed to break through the clutter and bring your message home to the hearts of your consumers. To keep it all in top-of-mind awareness and actionable, each chapter concludes with a list of the most important takeaways, so you never need to reinvent the wheel.

So without further delay, let's begin your journey into the world of motivational marketing.

CHAPTER 1

Marketing to Motivation

The drive to persuade and to sell is part of what makes us human. We are, if nothing else, a social and a political species. From early childhood, we seek to persuade and to influence the situations and people around us. If you've ever seen a child working though sixteen reasons why it's not yet time to go home from the playground, you know exactly what I mean. Ever since we've had something to sell, trade, or barter, we've been trying to persuade someone else to buy it.

From Lascaux to Twitter

We have taken a long strange trip from the caves at Lascaux to the welter of communications in the bold new world around us today. The clutter we navigate every second far exceeds anything we could ever have imagined even a generation ago. In fact, it's probably not an exaggeration to characterize the great, sweeping momentum of that change—in media, in communication, in popular culture—as transformational.

A big part of that change manifests in the way we consume media and messages today. When I was a kid, in the late fifties, there were only three channels available on TV. Everyone watched the same three channels. We all absorbed the same messages, available for the same amount of time, night after night. At 11 p.m., the three channels signed off. It was time for the country to go to bed. And so we did.

We consumed most of our other media in collectively standardized fashion as well. Our favorite musical artists regularly released standard-length albums, complete with catchy liner notes and mesmerizing cover art. We listened to them—in real time—with our friends, from beginning to end, day in and day out, until their grooves literally wore away. Then we taped quarters to the stylus of our record players and kept right on listening.

Like everyone around us, we knew those lyrics by heart and used the most personally meaningful of them to create a soundtrack for our lives. As we faithfully listened to that music and watched those shows, we progressed through a succession of predictable life stages together. We didn't all like the same things, of course, but we shared a basic understanding of the options available to us. We saw those options as paths to reject or embrace as we made our way in the world. They embodied the zeitgeist of the era, the social bonds that held my generational cohort together.

The world began to change for my generation when Ted Turner created a fourth option to compete with our beloved three networks. CNN and the 24-hour news cycle stormed the scene in 1980, and the world would never be the same again. Suddenly we could consume media around the clock—and suddenly it was less of a "given" that we'd all watch or hear the same things.

Of course, Turner's revolutionary concept and the offerings of subscription television quickly evolved further still, and now these too are becoming quaint and obsolete. Faced with this tsunami of stimuli, we fall back on the psychological mechanisms that have served us well since the time of the cave drawings. Our ancient brains are filters. They continuously pay attention to some things and shut out others. They tell us when to turn a glance into a gaze; they filter out the important signals from the cacophony of noise going on around us. They tell us when to start paying attention, and they tell us when to stop.

Foremost among these filters are the *emotional* filters. With every stimulus that comes in as a candidate for our attention, our emotional filters almost instantaneously ask these questions: "How do I feel about this?" "Will this be useful to me?" "Should I run away from this, or should I attack it?" Our emotional brain asks these questions over and over as we move through our day—and it does so faster than the speed of light and almost always below the threshold of our consciousness. This emotional processing lets us take action in situations that matter to us, helps us take advantage of situations that can benefit us, and keeps us safe in city crosswalks just as it once kept us safe from predators on the savanna.

Our brains still start the emotional processing of every new stimulus with the amygdala and its "fight or flight or freeze" judgment. But this is just the beginning of the complex emotional filtering that occurs with every new thing we encounter. Our emotional brain evaluates the emotional significance of what our senses bring to our attention. At this point, our core motivations—the ones we'll be exploring in this book—come into full play. The question about "Will this be useful; can this help me out?" is answered foremost by reference to the core motivational forces that drive us all. These questions become "Could this represent a chance to fulfill any of my aspirational yearnings?" or "Might it give me a chance to overcome some of the frustrations that nag me as I move through my life?"

If a particular stimulus passes the threshold of emotional relevance, then we move on to the intellectual evaluations that will help us take best advantage of the opportunity—and get the most emotionally fulfilling outcome: "Should I react to this now or later?" "Will this go well with what I'm doing at the moment, or will taking advantage of it require a change of plan?" All these and many more intellectual questions need answers before we fully formulate how we will respond to a new situation that our senses present to us.

As we perform these evaluations, in thousandths of a second, we determine whether what we perceive represents something we feel good—or bad—about and whether it gives us an opportunity to change our lives for the better. And so it is that the very first questions we will ask are linked to the aspirations and frustrations we carry along with us as we move through life. These psychological motivations not only drive what we do but literally form a set of lenses through which we perceive the world around us.

Marketers widely complain about the clutter of messages in the marketplace today, but that's really just the half of it. The clutter of marketing messages is only a subset of the broader clutter of stimuli that surround us in the world in which we now live. That's why marketing messages—if they are to stand any chance of gaining access to our brains—must first pass through our emotional filters by communicating immediately and on a visceral level. They must be redolent with the promise of positive emotional experience. And they must arouse one of our core emotional motivations. Otherwise the print ad will lose out to the article on the facing page or to the child in the room asking about breakfast. The television advertisement will lose out to the vase of flowers that needs watering or to the rumbling of our stomachs that signals it's snack time. The billboard advertisement may lose out to the attractive person passing in front of us or to the cute kid in the stroller just ahead. Likewise, the pop-up ad may lose out to the video link. And so it goes with every stimulus we encounter. The process of making these almost continuous emotional evaluations is largely instinctive – a function that is as old as or older than our first recorded steps toward motivation and persuasion in those "advertorials" on the ancient cave walls.

A Brief History of the Marketplace

Starting with trading beads like those discovered in the earliest human cave dwellings, the market has both created and answered consumers' needs for products and services. Since those first primitive exchanges, "manufacturers" have scrambled to improve their products and to invent new ones at a dizzying pace, always chasing the signals and signs of what people want. Of course, unlocking the secrets behind what consumers really want is the province of motivational theory and emotional research—a journey we're just beginning.

We can trace the early beginnings of marketing as we now practice it in the business world back to the beginning of the agricultural revolution. In the eons before we learned sedentary agriculture and animal husbandry, humans were nomadic, living hand to mouth and always engaged in the pursuit of food, safety, shelter, and the primal directive to reproduce.

In those early days, staying alive took up all of our time and all of our energy—calorically, physically, mentally, emotionally, and even culturally. In fact, before we invented cooking food over a fire, we literally spent more than half of our day just chewing our food.

We didn't have the luxury of downtime to drive production, consumption, and ownership, and we didn't yet have permanent homes to fill with the things we cherished. Only after our basic physiological needs were met did we begin to have the freedom to consider less urgent concerns. Only then did we become able to dream of and build a better life.

Through a series of pivotal developments, the agricultural revolution took hold, allowing members of those nomadic groups to put down literal and metaphorical roots. Over the course of many generations—again, in terms of evolution, just the blink of an eye—we became experts in planting and harvesting food and inventing and using tools. Cereals and grains were among our first domesticated crops. Gourds were reimagined as bowls. We kept our own animals as helpers and tamed them for use as food (like cattle and pigs and other livestock), as providers of commodities like wool (provided by sheep and llamas), transportation (horses, mules, camels, and elephants), protection (dogs), and eventually as companions. We made pottery and learned food preservation techniques. At last, we became comfortable enough to feed our minds as well as our bellies. And all of this steadily increased our capacity to look beyond our physical selves and our immediate needs to imagine and yearn for a veritable host of ways we could improve our lives and make ourselves happier.

As we built permanent homes, they became spaces we could improve over time, places our children could live and play in, and places to protect us, to house our possessions, and to preserve our legacies. We filled them not only with items of necessity, to be sure, but also with things that meant something to us on emotional and spiritual levels. As the significance of these items grew, we began to treasure them and to struggle to preserve them.

Not too far into this process, the day came when we found ourselves with significant excess time and excess provisions. This left us with the building blocks of the first "products" we could now trade with our neighbors, who were also newly able to produce more than they needed to survive. As time passed we devised methods to produce more and better products—sturdier shoes, clothes that fit, and felt better, and soap that really got things clean. Meanwhile, our neighbors were also hard at work and devised systems and innovations that let them produce their products at a higher quality as well. And in this freest of free markets there were naturally redundancies in what everyone was making, and that's what gave rise to competition.

This also led to the beginning of marketing ("Hey, look," said John, "my soap is better than the other guys'!"). As insights, inventions, and new products sprang up to populate the marketplace, new options only succeeded over competing ones if they delivered a better way (or the perception of a better way) to improve the lives of the people who bought them. That is, to prevail in the market, products and services had to possess a compelling ability either to bring consumers closer to their aspirations and hopes or to help them move farther from their frustrations and fears.

The idea of "branding" began to emerge, asspecialization, innovation, and word-of-mouth endorsements propelled generations of fortunate craftsmen to develop the reputation for making the best shoes (or clothes or soap) possible. (See sidebar) Whole neighborhoods and whole villages became expert in making a small number of products.

A Brand to Trust

The name recognition and reputation of early craftsmen marked the beginning of what we now know as branding. That term developed, as you might guess, from the practice of branding livestock, particularly cattle. First used some 4,000 years ago, brands were symbols burned onto the animal's haunches that served two important purposes

The first and most obvious job of branding was to differentiate one "product" from another: this cow is mine, that cow is yours. But in a more subtle way the brand symbol also came to indicate the skills and reputation of the "producer" as well. That cow is the property of an excellent businessman, the brand insisted. The person who wields this symbol has great worth, status, and value.

Gradually, as we learned to advertise and deliver a wide range of goods across a widening range of communities, the brand mark evolved into a kind of shorthand for marketers who wanted to spread awareness of their products among a growing number of consumers most of whom were still unable to read. That's how the concept of the logo as a signal of provenance—a "brand mark"—as we know it now was born.

For many generations at the beginning of our marketplace culture, we did business with our neighbors and friends in our own general neighborhood of small villages where people were well acquainted with each other. Most of those exchanges occurred in homes or commons. We knew the quality of products because we intimately knew the producers and the users of them, and we had known their parents and clan for all our lives. In this society of consumers and producers, reputations were made and lost on the basis of how well our products performed; everyone knew firsthand or heard from trusted friends and neighbors that John's (and John's son's) soaps, for example, really worked.

As increasingly efficient methods of manufacturing evolved, a growing surplus of goods outstripped the needs of people living within the boundaries of the known neighborhood area. Marketers needed ways to increase their reach. This gave rise to another game-changing shift.

Growing the marketplace beyond the local neighborhood of villages and engaging in trade with more distant and larger audiences ushered in a new era of sales-driven business practices as we looked for new ways to compete. To succeed we had to motivate new consumers to buy our products— customers that we'd never seen or met and who did not know us and our goods at all. To reach consumers at a distance beyond word-of-mouth reputation it became necessary to broadcast, and that's how product advertising was born—and the business of consumer persuasion began.

The Evolution of Motivational Marketing

These early forays into the art of persuasion still focused on the reputation of the individual or the craftsmen. And presentation of the products from these master craftsmen focused on the functional benefits, and a reputation for quality and value was everything.

But with a steadily increasing barrage of products, manufacturers, and advertisers working for them, it quickly became apparent that many excellent brands of almost any product type were available. Faced with the inability to compete simply on quality and value, manufacturers needed a way to persuade their customers to buy their brand even without an obvious or provable advantage.

Meanwhile, inventors and entrepreneurs used their brainpower to create new products that had never existed before, and they needed to create a need in consumers' minds where there previously had been none. In these new marketplace contexts, the idea of "higher-order benefits" and the activity of "brand positioning" became an inexorable part of global commerce. Thus, a manufacturer of products competing with other brands of equal quality and value could appeal to his long and caring relationship with customers

("Johnson's Soap—helping you stay fresh since 1892"), an example of the nurturance motivation in action (see chapter 13), or he could talk about his brand as "the one to trust" if a security motivation (see chapter 4) was more appropriate. And for the entrepreneur with the previously unknown product, new rhetoric aimed at the marketplace identified the "unmet need" as a topic of advertising: "Wouldn't you love to stop struggling with the buttons on your pants? Now there's the zipper!" In all of these cases, consumers first needed to be sold on what was lacking in their lives and then had to be convinced that their life would be much better if they had the missing "it." All of these changes in how brands were presented to consumers and especially the increasing references to "higher order benefits" in positioning and new product advertising created a new need for businesspeople to think about their consumers' lives by looking at the big picture. They had to focus on what people "really" needed or wanted and identify the kinds of product promises that might truly motivate them at their emotional core. Brand marketers who had until then just talked about products needed to start talking about how consumers might feel if they used a particular brand or tried a particular new product and how the item might change their lives for the better. The need then arose for marketers to get to know consumers and their motivations in a whole new way.

The Medium and the Message

At the same time when these changes in the landscape of production and promotion were happening, the ways to get the message out to the masses changed as well. Word of mouth was the dominant form of advertising in the earliest marketplaces, even after Gutenberg rolled out his printing machine and produced the first printed Bible in 1455.

And word of mouth worked. As we travelled, we spread the word to the people we encountered that Johnson's soap was indeed the best in the world. Later, merchants hired dedicated salespeople who travelled to consumers and attempted to sell them their products. The job of the traveling salesman, the Fuller Brush man, and the Avon lady started there.

Over time, as people continued to migrate to cities, everyone began to have access to public notices and newspapers. These papers in turn became cheaper, appeared more frequently, and became accessible to all. Very slowly, literacy rates improved, and the public no longer had to wait for information to come from an educated minority who consumed it first. As literacy and readership of media grew, the media itself transformed, and illustrations and the first grainy photographs appeared to communicate more vividly (and one hoped persuasively) the indescribable qualities of products—and the feelings consumers could get from using them—that words alone could not do justice to.

Remarkably quickly then, innovations in printing and transportation meant that newspapers could be delivered almost anywhere quickly and reliably. And inside each of those issues, tucked between the news and the opinions, were messages about products. The era of print advertising had arrived.

Thus, changes in methods and capabilities of production, development of new modes of distribution, and transformation in the technologies of communication all came together to radically transform the little village marketplace where John's son had built his shop (and where the demand for his soap had grown to a point where his wife kicked the business out of the house). National product brands became the new marketplace norm, and products were advertised to national audiences by way of sophisticated print media with national reach. The need to talk about products evolved into its own special discipline as people who were exceptionally clever at devising persuasive ideas joined with people equally clever with words and other people equally creative at design. Together, they put themselves to work creating messages for multiple companies and product brands. Advertising agencies emerged as businesses in their own right, and brought with them their own culture, jargon, and values. And eventually, consumer research came into being, and experts in this new science developed ways of learning more about consumers and the effectiveness of messages designed to reach and persuade them. Not coincidentally, these first forays into the science of consumer behavior were called motivational research. From the very beginning, there has been an (unfocused) awareness that consumer activity began with the motivation to imagine, try, and buy.

Consumer Motivation and the American Dream

As people returned from the Second World War, changes in the worldview of the average household began to take place that would revolutionize consumer culture. Class barriers were breaking down among soldiers who had been united in the fight for freedom, and economic status became defined by what one could afford to buy instead of by inherited social class. And we rapidly began to develop a fantastic material culture for consumers: marvels of engineering (television, the automatic transmission!) and miracles of "Better Living Through Chemistry" (plastics!) that promised continuous changes for the better in our lives. The ideal of the American Dream became a dominant life aspiration not just in the United States but around the Western world, based on the conviction that we were entitled to a better life than the one our parents had, namely, a life filled with opportunity and options. Soldiers returning from war were often given loans that put more families into homes of their own. College tuition was provided for every veteran who could gain admittance, and levels of education and upward mobility led to the creation of a new culture focused on getting ahead in life.

This vision of ever expanding possibilities for progress took hold of our imagination, and the ideal of living up to our dreams and outstripping the successes of our parents took hold. The ambition to "keep up with the Joneses" became widespread, and a culture of material success blossomed. Almost all of us came to feel sure that with the requisite Buick in the driveway, the washing machine, and the new television set we could be really happy.

By this point, almost all of us could read and newspapers arrived daily at our doors. Radios sat in the living rooms of every home, and televisions were rapidly entering most homes. Electricity was no longer just about light. We wanted electric appliances to improve the quality of our lives, to amuse, distract, and enlighten us.

At the same time as this "perfect storm" of events that brought us into the modern age of consumer culture and that transformed the marketing world, the largest and most sweeping population surge in history took place. A single age group that was to dominate the landscape for decades was born in the demographic earthquake we now know as the baby boom.

This generation became the first to grow up completely under the sway of omnipresent communication, continuous innovation, and relentless consumerism. When the baby boomers were children, TV dinners, fast-food restaurants, and the commuter lifestyle of suburbia shaped a new perspective on domestic life. As adolescents, baby boomers embraced snack foods and soft drinks and changed the way we fed ourselves. College years of war protests and rock and roll changed the mores of our social lives. Young, upwardly mobile boomer yuppies took on Wall Street, acquired luxury cars and created the condo. Today, as retirees, they're driving a revolution in leisure activities and retirement planning. The boomer generation was the first generation that was thoroughly marketed to, and their response to this ever attentive marketplace reshaped the world as we know it today.

The process will continue with coming generations. While none of them may have quite the impact of the first real market-driving generation, each forthcoming generation—their values and attitudes, their behaviors and styles, and the needs and motivations linked to these will continue to reshape the culture as marketers continuously scurry to adapt to and adopt the perspective of emerging consumers.

And through all of this, success in the world of business will continue to depend on the ability to understand the psychological big picture of consumers' wants and needs, their deep emotional motivations—and the capacity to translate these insights into messages about how products can change the experience of living for the better.

Takeaways

1. One impact of our "connected" revolution is that we are engulfed in media stimuli whose complexity outstrips the processing capacity of our brains.
2. This complexity makes it necessary for us to filter incoming stimuli to pay attention to those that promise to be most important or meaningful to us. The most powerful of these filters focuses on emotional relevance.
3. The realities of consumer filtering and the complex and crowded information marketplace set a high standard for effective consumer communication—and much of what is out there will simply not get through to consumers.
4. For marketing messages to penetrate the media cacophony, they must make it past consumers' perceptual filters.
5. The surest way to do this is to appeal to the consumers' strongest emotions, that is, their dominant psychological motivations.

This page intentionally left blank

CHAPTER 2

Introducing the MindSight
Motivational Matrix

To understand consumers' motivations and build products to fulfill those motives we need a comprehensive playbook, a detailed map of the emotional landscape of human motivation. As in any map-making exercise, we first have to identify the names of all the places on the map, and then we need to understand where each is located in relation to the others. In this chapter we will provide the first look at our motivational marketing playbook—the MindSight Matrix.

But before we get to the heart of the matter and begin to uncover the powerful emotional forces that are the key to our business success, we have to get clear on three very basic issues:

- What kind of emotion qualifies as a motivation?
- How do motivations work for us as marketers?
- How can marketers create a successful motivational marketing strategy?

Let's briefly look at these in order:

What Kind of Emotion Qualifies as a Motivation?

First, it's important to acknowledge that not all emotions have the same force. Motivations are very specific emotions that fulfill very specific needs. Plenty of scholars of emotion have written broadly on the topic, and their works can guide you through its complex depths. (For a solid overview, try the textbook written by Paula Niedenthal and colleagues: *Psychology of Emotion: Interpersonal, Experiential, and Cognitive Approaches.*)[1] For the sake of business thinking about consumer emotions, however, we need to distinguish only between two types of emotions.

1. *Experiential Emotions*: these are transitory emotional states that arise in reaction to events happening around us as we move through our day. They are the feelings that make up the continuous emotional "music" of our lives, and they are as numerous and diverse as our life experiences.

2. *Motivational Emotions*: these are emotional forces that are fueled by the aspirations we hold for ourselves in our emotional "hearts" and by the frustrations that develop when those aspirations go unfulfilled. Motivational emotions are fairly permanent, "trait-like" predispositions created by our constitutions and our personal histories; they are not fully dependent upon things going on around us at the moment.

The aspirations that motivate us range from the sweet stuff of childhood dreams ("I want to be an astronaut") to the more practical hopes of adulthood ("I want to retire by 60"). They can remain latent for years ("I always wanted to go to Paris") only to reignite when circumstances make them possible ("now that I am retired..."). Aspirations can also be tied to life's frustrations ("I've got to get rid of this job, this rug, this brand of detergent"). The emotional forces related to these aspirations and frustrations are constantly with us: we are always looking for opportunities to make positive change in our lives, to realize our aspirations, or to escape our frustrations.

A healthy catalogue of aspirations is critical to our life experience. Aspirations make things interesting and keep us moving forward, constantly on the lookout for opportunities to improve our lives. Aspirations provide us with things to reach for in our lives, reasons to get out of bed in the morning, a foundation on which to build our dreams. Of course, not all aspirations involve "reaching for the stars." Some of our aspirations are aimed toward getting less of something bad, which is still a great way to improve our life experience.

As we move through life, some of our aspirations fade as they become more unlikely ("I'll probably never climb Mount Everest or play in the NBA"), and this is a good thing. Unrealized aspirations can become a burden if we let them rule our lives. A lifelong yearning for wealth or for fame, for example, can diminish the pleasures inherent in our lives as they are lived.

Our aspirational emotions become "activated" when circumstances emerge that promise to make their fulfillment possible ("Since I won the lottery, got a new job, or invested wisely, I can help my parents buy a nicer house"). Whenever the circumstances of our lives inspire us, when we see a chance to make some progress regarding our life aspirations or frustrations, we jump at the chance. That's because we are motivated—*moved*—to take action and reach for positive change. Creating this kind of activation, this inspiration to move, is our job as marketers.

In sum, motivational emotions are the forces that drive us to take action and pursue positive change in our lives whenever we see the opportunity; these emotions pull us toward realizing our life's aspirations and push us away from our life's frustrations. Emotional motivations are thus not reactions to situations or to behaviors. They are instead the psychological *causes* of behavior.

How Do Motivations Work for us as Marketers?

To put it as clearly and succinctly as possible, motivations close the sale.

Motivations are at work behind every purchase a consumer makes. Most of us walk around throughout our lives with a set of aspirations we are constantly looking and longing to fulfill, along with a set of frustrations we are constantly longing to escape.

To move consumers to act, to turn aspiration into the specialized emotional energy of motivation, we first have to *inspire* them. We must persuade consumers that now is the time to "go for it," to make that move, to reach for that desirable change. Next, we need to persuade them that we—represented by the product or service we offer represent the best chance of reaching their dreams.

In essence, the job title of any marketer could easily be "inspiration developer." We are in the business of moving people toward their dreams. If your product message is well crafted, if it delivers the promise of attaining aspirations or escaping frustrations, you will inspire your consumers, get them excited, and make them hopeful about good changes that can happen in their lives if only they buy and use your product. These feelings motivate—literally, *move*—consumers to make that purchase. To understand what consumers really want in the first place, to trace consumers' interest in a product back to its roots, means to understand the dynamics of human aspiration.

This understanding will yield insights that can put marketers far ahead of the competition.

How we can understand consumers' motivation at its roots, how we can coax consumers' dreams to speak to us, is the central focus of this book.

Creating a Successful Motivational Marketing Strategy

To tap into your consumers' latent emotional energies and transform them into motivational emotions, you first need to figure out two things:

- What is the range of motivational emotions that can drive consumers' decision making and behavior in your product category?
- Which of these motivational emotions is your product uniquely suited to fulfill?

After you have developed a portrait of all the motivational emotions that operate in your product category and you have selected the motivations your specific product is best equipped to fulfill, then you are off to the races and on the road to creating a motivational marketing strategy. Of course, it's not as easy as it sounds. I'm reminded of my childhood friend's plan for a lunar mission: "We'll just build a rocket, and then we'll turn it on and go!" It would be wonderful if life were that easy and if motivational marketing were that easy, but that's seldom the case. That's where the MindSight Matrix comes in. This matrix will help you visualize where your product's emotional benefits and your consumer's emotional interests intersect.

You Can't Tell the Players without a Program

The challenge of understanding consumers' motivations and linking them to products that can provide fulfillment of those motives led me to develop the conceptual roadmap I am about to share with you. It's a structured model for organizing human motives, a model that I call the MindSight Matrix. The matrix can help marketers identify and locate motives on a strategic map of consumer motivation, which shows how the motives compare and contrast with one another, and it can help marketers choose among motivational marketing strategies with a clear understanding of the relationships between the alternatives, and the implications of a particular choice.

"For the first time I saw a medley of haphazard facts fall into line and order. All the jumbles...seemed to fit into the scheme before my eyes— as though one was standing beside a jungle and it suddenly transformed itself into a...garden."

—C. P. Snow, describing the periodic table[2]

Our map of motivations doesn't really look like a map but more like a tablet. It is very much like the periodic table of elements. And just as the periodic table helped chemists identify elements and the relationships between them the MindSight Matrix can help researchers identify the important motivations driving our consumers and trace how each of them relates to the others.

The MindSight Matrix

The MindSight Matrix is built around two fundamental properties that all motives share. We identified these two properties by starting from the recognition that all motivation is a search for change and then identifying two basic questions we consider when we search for change:"Where do we want the change to have effect?" and "What kind of change would we like it to be?"

It turns out that there are three compelling answers to each of these two questions about motivation and change. And these answers generate the three-by-three grid of the MindSight Matrix. Since the matrix will be the foundation of everything we're about to learn about motivations and motivational marketing, it's important to look at it in some detail.

The *columns* of the Matrix represent the three most basic answers we can have to the first question about motivation, "Where do we want the change to have effect?" The three answers to this question are: (1) we can seek to create change internally, centered on how we think and feel about *ourselves*; (2) we can seek change directed outwardly, toward the inanimate things that populate our worlds, the bricks-and-mortar of our lives and lifestyles; and (3) we can seek change directed outwardly toward people and other living things we can have relationships with.

The first column of the matrix contains the motives that focus on internal change, and we call these intrapsychic motives. The second column of the matrix contains the motives focused on the inanimate objects populating our world, and we call these the instrumental motives. The third and final column of the matrix contains motives that focus on people and relationships, and we call these interpersonal motives.

The *rows* of the Matrix represent the three answers to the question "What type of change is sought?" and essentially represent the three distinct time frames in which we can experience change. The first row contains the motives that are focused on changing what our futures will look like. These are the motives focused on "expectations." The second row of the matrix contains motives focused on changing our experience of the present moment. These are the motives focused on "experiences." The final row of the matrix includes motives that focus on being satisfied with the results of our choices and actions in life, and it is thus focused on the past. These are the motives focused on "outcomes."

The nine cells in the MindSight Matrix defined by these rows and columns represent a highly structured and strategically organized portrait of human motivation, that distills and organizes insights on motivation from psychological literature over the past hundred years (for details, see the review of this literature in Forbes, "Toward a Unified Model of Human Motivation").[3] For each motive, it's important to note that its emotional force can either be positive (aspirational "desires for more" of an emotion) or negative (frustrations that drive us to "want less" of an emotion.)

	INTRAPSYCHIC The self	INSTRUMENTAL The object world	INTERPERSONAL The social world
EXPECTATIONS For the future	Safe, Confident **SECURITY** Insecure, Afraid	Free, Powerful **EMPOWERMENT** Trapped, Frustrated	Accepted, Belonging **BELONGING** Isolated, Lonely
EXPERIENCES In the moment	Unique, Interesting **IDENTITY** Ordinary, Boring	Involved, Absorbed **ENGAGEMENT** Passive, Indifferent	Sharing, Caring **NURTURANCE** Selfish, Unloved
OUTCOMES From past behavior	Talented, Exceptional **MASTERY** Incompetent	Victorious, Productive **ACHIEVEMENT** Defeated, Pointless	Proud, Respected **ESTEEM** Ashamed, Disgraced

The result is the first and most complete system for uniting consumer psychology, the full scholarship of human motivation, and emotion-based marketing.

At first glance, the matrix may seem like a lot to take in. But as we look at each motivation in detail in the coming chapters and discuss the best marketing approaches to take with each motive, you'll see that—like its cousin in chemistry, the periodic table—the MindSight Matrix offers a simple and systematic way to be sure, for the first time ever, that you've got all the bases covered when you seek to understand what truly motivates consumers to do what they do.

To give a good overview of the matrix and its motives I am going to give you a real-world scenario for each column in the matrix, illustrating how the three motives of that column might come into play in the scenario. One thing is very important to note as you read through my examples: each of them presents the motives as if they *form a sequence* in a person's life.

This kind of motivational sequencing can certainly take place (as indeed it does in our real-world examples). However, most of the time the motives crop up in our lives in no particular order, and in any given situation in life we may experience our emotional energies being directed toward any one of the nine motives. This is why marketers typically target just one or perhaps two of the nine motives in a marketing message without needing to connect to the rest of the motives in the matrix.

Starting with the first column, the intrapsychic or internal motives, let's look at the occasion of becoming a new parent, a major transition moment in how we think and feel about ourselves, as shown in table 2.1.

Then let's move to the middle column of the MindSight Matrix, which focuses on motives that influence how people want to feel about their interactions in the material world. In this case, I can draw upon an example from my own experience, namely, that of tackling the task of building a stone wall in my backyard. Over the course of this project, I experienced the force of all three motives in the instrumental column, as shown in table 2.2.

Finally, to illustrate the interpersonal motives, imagine that you've relocated to a new neighborhood—perhaps for a new job—and do not know anyone in this new place. The sequence of changes you would strive to make in how you thought and felt about your social interactions with others in your new location might look something like what is shown in table 2.3.

Table 2.1 Intrapsychic Motivation and Parenting

Intrapsychic Motive	How I want to think/feel about myself as a parent
Security (Expectation focus)	As I first become a parent, I'm worried about the future, about what's going to happen and what will be expected of me. I want to feel confident that I'm doing things right, that I can handle whatever comes up, to feel I *don't have to worry* about the seemingly daunting task of taking care of a child.
	As I become comfortable with the responsibility of taking care of a completely helpless infant, I gain the conviction that "everything will be all right" and I begin to know *what to expect.*
Identity (Experience focus)	I've always wanted to be a parent, and now I can't imagine life without my baby. I make choices about parenting strategy; develop my own personal "parenting style" that defines my particular approach to the process of parenting. My *personal, personalized experience of parenting* gets better and better.
Mastery (Outcome focus)	I can master this parenting thing and actually be a really good parent who has really great kids. I want to feel proud when I look at the *outcomes of the choices and strategies I have chosen.* I could even give advice to other new parents who might appreciate my help.

Table 2.2 Instrumental Motives and the Stone Wall

Instrumental Motive	How I want to think/feel about my project of building a stone wall
Empowerment (Expectation focus)	I first had to convince myself that building a stone wall was even possible. I talked to a stonemason friend, I went online, and I read articles on how to build that wall. As I gradually gained a sense that *I can do this,* I became empowered to build the wall. The project comes to fruition because I now believe that I can do it—I *expect to succeed.*
Engagement (Experience focus)	I wasn't really having much fun at first. I was self-conscious at every step, second-guessing every decision. But as the work progressed, I began to get the hang of it. And *my experience of doing the work got better and better.* I began to get the fulfilling sense of getting into it— being fully and pleasurably engaged in the process of building the wall.
Achievement (Outcome focus)	As the project came to completion, the wall was finished, and I had to admit that it wasn't bad. I could now proudly point to the *very positive outcome of my project* and enjoy the pleasure of achievement.

Table 2.3 Interpersonal Motives in a New Neighborhood

Interpersonal Motive	How I want to think/feel about my social relationships in my new neighborhood
Belonging (Expectation focus)	I enjoy being part of a group, and I start out knowing nobody. So I invite neighbors over for dinner and look for connections with some of the folks in my new neighborhood. When I discover a neighbor who also likes diving, I gain a sense of *positive expectations about my social life*: that I can fit in, I can belong in this new place.
Nurturance (Experience focus)	At first I miss the comfort of my old social network. Then I have a wonderful experience of neighbors coming over with a bottle of wine to welcome me. I'm invited to join a book group. These and many other *positive social experiences* allow me to feel that there are people here who will care about me and whom I can care about.
Esteem (Outcome focus)	It's important to me that my new neighbors see me as a positive addition to the neighborhood. I pay attention to keeping the yard neat and my car in the garage. After about six months my neighborhood association asks me to take photos for a brochure to recruit new residents. I now feel that I have achieved the *great social outcome* of being accepted as a member of the community.

Using the Matrix Structure

Just like the periodic table of elements, the MindSight Matrix is organized to help its users understand relationships *between* motives. For example, understanding how the motivations in your category (or the motives that drive people to choose your brand) are *distributed* in the matrix can provide its own form of guidance for your marketing strategy. In the pages that follow, we will see how information about the *distribution patterns* of your consumers' motives in the matrix rows and columns can inspire your thinking about emotional marketing for your product above and beyond the specific motivations you may target.

An overview of how patterns in the columns where your target motives fall can shape motivational marketing strategies is provided in table 2.4.

When we look at the rows of the matrix, we can see again how patterns in the matrix location of your key consumer motives can help shape your planning and execution of your plan (see table 2.5).

Table 2.4 Working with the Matrix Columns

If your category/ brand motivation is focused on:	Column One: Intrapsychic motives	Column Two: Instrumental motives	Column Three: Interpersonal motives
Then your marketing strategy should concentrate on:	Portraying your consumers reflecting, thinking about themselves. Portraying the consumers' confidence, independence, and pride	Portraying your consumers interacting with the material world: moving and changing things, getting things done. Portraying the consumers' competence and effectiveness	Portraying your consumers together with others, at work and at play Portraying the consumers' capacities for sharing and caring and the appreciation of others who share these traits

Table 2.5 Working with the Matrix Rows

If your category/brand motivation is concentrated in:	Then your marketing should:
Matrix row 1: Expectations for the Future	Present a vision of possibilities that your product will open up for the consumer, the "bright future" that your product makes possible. Portray the consumer in terms of hope and excitement.
Matrix row 2: Experiences in the Moment	Create detailed narratives about the "great moments" that are made possible by your product. Portray the consumer as caught up in the moment, "into" life as it is happening.
Matrix row 3: Outcomes	Depict the excellent results the consumer will see from your product—show how your product will result in a better outcome. Show how this will generate feelings of pride and satisfaction and cause others to feel good about the consumer.

By the time you finish this book, you will have a wealth of information about how to market to each of the nine motives in the matrix. You'll also be able to identify motivational marketing strategies based on the ideas that organize the matrix rows and columns. With your mastery of the underlying structure in human motivation, you will become in turn a master at motivational marketing.

CHAPTER 3

Introducing the Intrapsychic Motivations

INTRAPSYCHIC
The self

EXPECTATIONS
For the future

Safe, Confident
SECURITY
Insecure, Afraid

EXPERIENCES
In the moment

Unique, Interesting
IDENTITY
Ordinary, Boring

OUTCOMES
From past behavior

Talented, Exceptional
MASTERY
Incompetent

There is no more crucial relationship for us humans to develop than the one we have with ourselves. That's why intrapsychic motives are a gateway to other areas of our study. The ability to distinguish ourselves from the world around us is an early, critical developmental task that helps us establish our place in the world, discover and form our relationship to it and the people in it, and finally, build a positive, lifelong relationship with ourselves. Cause and effect, action and reaction, inside and outside—all of our most basic ideas about how the world works rest first on our ability to recognize what is "I" and "me" and what is not. Only after this distinction is made are we free to enter into a lifelong pursuit of protecting, understanding, evolving, expressing, and improving our vision of ourselves. All of the strivings in regard to the critical sense of self belong to the first column of the Forbes Matrix, the intrapsychic motives.

On the one hand, our intrapsychic motives function as healthy, supportive, and empowering generators of missions soon accomplished, creating the satisfaction of a life well-lived and speeding us on our way to deep, intrinsic satisfaction with who we are, how we are, and what we stand for. On the other hand, intrapsychic motives could be distorted by unhealthy, outdated feelings that hold us back and make our dreams more difficult to realize. In all ways, for better or worse, our relationship with ourselves forms the basis of our worldview, and has a significant impact on how the world views us. Since every action we take is in some sense an expression of self, our intrapsychic motives play a role in how we interact with the world in all situations; they shape the personal tastes, styles, and values that we bring to every moment of our lives.

Cogito ergo sum

Normally translated "I think, therefore I am," René Descartes's famous statement addresses the nature of existence and consciousness. Descartes concludes that the act of thinking about ourselves—introspection, a purely human capability—proves that we do, indeed, exist.[1]

That's why the understanding of our intrapsychic lives and the motivations that stem from them is one of the most fascinating subjects in psychology. The journeys we take to explore those questions are fundamental to who we become. And getting to know ourselves as individuals is at once the most familiar of our life experiences and the most mysterious.

Attempts to get a handle on what exactly is "I" or "me" have been with us since the dawn of philosophy and probably since long before written records began. In Plato's *Allegory of the Cave*, in his book *The Republic*,[2] for instance, we learn that what we see before us may not be reality at all, but rather shadows projected on the wall of a cave, with each interpretation and experience of those shadows as intricate and subjective and unique as the person viewing them.

Despite all the research and discussion regarding this topic, we still don't yet have a full understanding of the totality of our consciousness.

Who's that?
Infants don't understand that the reflection they see in a mirror is an image of themselves.

Becoming Self-aware

Most psychologists agree that consciousness of the self, or self-awareness, is initially very limited and must be developed over time. One of the most common yet reliable demonstrations of initial limitations in our sense of self is the mirror test. It's just what it sounds like. We put a small amount of cosmetic blush or some other harmless substance on the noses of babies and place them in front of a mirror to see what happens. Very young babies don't see the mirror as holding any image at all, and they show only moderate interest in it as part of the visual field in which they are placed. But somewhere around one year of age, babies become aware of the image in the mirror as something special to look at, as another person, and they'll reach out to try to remove the blush from the tip of the nose of the "other baby" they see in the mirror. Then something fascinating happens between the ages of 18 and 24 months when infants cross a line toward becoming self-aware. At this point, they recognize that the baby they see in the mirror *is them*, and so they wipe the blush off their own noses. This is a simple but profound demonstration of this first milestone in the intrapsychic journey we all must take.

Our self-concept continues to evolve, ceaselessly, from that point on. At around age 7 or 8, children become developmentally able to understand themselves as unique psyches with unique feelings and abilities. Around this age kids become capable of describing and identifying themselves beyond their concrete physical attributes ("I am tall, I am fast, I have brown hair") to more psychologically sophisticated and less concrete traits that describe their personalities ("I'm a good friend, I like to learn new things, I'm honest/ kind/ funny"). Just a bit further along this path of self-awareness, we become capable of introspection, the metacognitive activity of reflecting on who we are, how we think, and what we value.

Our self-concept ultimately comes to influence our behavior, our thoughts, and our feelings, everything from how well we achieve academically, to the number and kinds of friends we make, to our levels of happiness, anxiety, self-esteem, and overall life-satisfaction.

The Intrapsychic Journey

The development of our intrapsychic capabilities and the emotional motives that arise from them are prerequisites for success in fulfilling every other motive in the Forbes Matrix. Only with a well-developed sense of ourselves can we hope to move on to the motives that influence how we interact with objects and instruments in our world or how we influence and enjoy our interpersonal relationships. For this reason (and many others), the discovery of ourselves is the most significant journey of our lives.

As with all of the columns in the matrix, the intrapsychic motives take three distinct forms, and though any of these three can be active at any time, they can also be viewed as developmental stages that unfold from childhood through adulthood. We can also see the three intrapsychic motives as a set of "microgenetic" (small developmental) stages we pass through any time we acquire a new identity for ourselves (as when we first become parents, for example). The sequence begins from a stage of some insecurity in which we seek to feel safe in ourselves and our persons both physically and emotionally. Once we have established security, we next develop a drive to become distinct, to have tastes, styles, preferences, and values that we choose ourselves and that reflect the unique person we are becoming. Finally, as we continue to live and work within a framework of personal identity, our experiences and efforts lead us to become very good at some of the things we do, and then can we experience the feeling of personal excellence, and a sense of self-actualization or "mastery" in our lives and lifestyles. Needless to say, as consumers we will shift our interests according to our motivational focus (for example, from parenting products that make us feel secure, to those that reflect our particular tastes, to those that testify to our mastery of this life task).

The focus of our intrapsychic motivations at any given moment is often reflected in our interactions with the material and social worlds. When we strive for a sense of security, for example, we can be less willing to experiment with the unknown, whether it's a new task at work or a new friendship possibility. When focused on identity, we may be especially interested in doing things our own way and in developing social connections that reflect our sense of self. And as we begin to achieve a sense of mastery in life, we will become increasingly flexible in trying new things, and the opinions of others will begin to matter less and less. At this point, we have a chance of becoming self-confidence personified—Maslow's self-actualized individual.[3]

The Concept of the Self-Concept

Viewed through the lens of our intrapsychic motivations, our life's journey revolves around our ability to answer the question: "Who am I?" In that pursuit, we consciously and unconsciously set our sights first on discovering and then on building what psychology calls our self-concept.

That self-concept consists of a range of self-schemas that we have: the many facets of our personality, the many parts of our lifestyle, and the many roles in our social lives. Together, these make up our vision of who we truly are. In an intricate, fascinating dance, all of the psychological portions of us—including our self-esteem, self-knowledge, social self, ideal self, situational selves, past selves, and future selves—join together to form the picture of us we use to answer the question "Who am I?" Our self-concept represents the cornerstone of how we relate to the world around us. Robert Franken of the University of Calgary, a leading expert in the field of intrapsychic development, describes the conceptual, cognitive architecture of the self-concept as the foundation for all the emotional drives of motivated behavior:

> A great deal of research shows that the self-concept is, perhaps, *the basis for all motivated behavior* [my emphasis]. It gives rise to all of our possible selves, and these possible selves create the motivation for behavior.[4]

It would be nearly impossible to overstate the importance of understanding our consumers' self-concepts for our success in building relationships with them. The emotional drives that are fueled by how people want to think and feel about themselves are at the very heart of the forces we must persuade and sell to.

Whatever marketing strategies we employ and whatever motivations we target in our messages, we are always talking at one level to the consumers' concept of who they are and who they want to be and thus to the intrapsychic motives essential to the development of that self-concept. Thus, the discussions of security, identity, and mastery that follow in this section are critical areas of learning for the motivational marketer because they are always involved in consumers' vision of themselves.

Who am I?

As you might imagine, the study of one's self-concept has produced a robust body of literature in the field of psychology with plentiful dissertations on who we are, who we believe others think we are, and who we hope to be.

One of the most prolific and influential psychologists of the twentieth century, Carl Rogers, built on the work of Abraham Maslow to develop his ideas of the self-concept. According to Rogers, we need a positive self-concept to reach the highest level of our development as human beings, namely, the state of self-actualization.

Like Maslow, Rogers believed that exploring our inner landscapes is essential to becoming happy and fully "actualized," a goal we can attain only when our vision of our "ideal self," the person we'd like to be, is in sync with how we understand our current self.

According to Rogers, our self-concept is made up of three components:[5]

Self-worth or self-esteem: what we think and believe about our innate value to ourselves and to others, feelings largely developed in our childhood through our interactions with our parents.
Self-image: how we see and think about ourselves at any moment in time, including our body image and inner personality.
Ideal self: the person we'd like to be, the sum of our cognitively conscious goals and ambitions for ourselves. This version of ourselves also changes and adapts constantly: who we wanted to be in childhood isn't likely to be the ideal self we imagine in adulthood.

Let's look at each of these in turn.

Self-Esteem

Keeping in mind that we are the ultimate social species, it makes sense that how we think others view us might have a great deal of influence on how we value ourselves. As we perceive generally positive or negative responses from our interactions with others, our self-esteem grows or diminishes in response. These negative or positive *internal* perceptions of self, relative to our idealized vision of who we want to be, benefits or harms our self-esteem accordingly.

Some aspects of self-esteem are transient and changing, based solely on the events that occur around us and the feelings these evoke at the time. I might see myself as funny on any particular day according to the laughs I get from others on that day. Or I may see myself as fashionable, according to the compliments I receive about my wardrobe. These transitory elements of our self-concept are highly changeable; on days when "the world" doesn't interpret me as particularly funny or stylish, these positive elements in my self-esteem may diminish. Among children and teenagers, the variability in the experience of self can be painful; how attractive or popular we think we are (and we care tremendously about this in our teens) can change by the hour and can quickly plummet from outstanding to dismal in the course of a week or even a day.

Other elements of our self-concept gradually solidify and become internalized and more permanent over time. These become things we continue to believe about ourselves even when there's evidence to the contrary. This is known as the perseverance effect and it causes us to hold on to certain visions of ourselves despite the conflicting evidence of events surrounding us. That is, I can value myself as a compassionate or well-spoken or intelligent person even if I sometimes act in the opposite ways and am uncaring or incoherent or short-sighted. The reverse can also be true, in which case I might see myself as permanently clumsy or unintelligent, despite all evidence to the contrary.

A healthy, internalized sense of self-esteem grows out of the practice of self-reflection, self-analysis, and self-acceptance. For example, I may esteem myself to be responsible depending on how much I know commitments matter to me and on my track record in keeping them, and this positive self-esteem element would not then be disrupted by a single lapse in my responsibilities.

When we develop stable, internalized feelings of self-esteem, it helps us build toward such winner's strategies as optimism, independence from what others think about us, and decreased desire to be like someone else. By contrast, low self-esteem leads to negative cycles of low confidence, pessimism, constant worry about what others think about us, and a persistent desire to be like someone else whom we perceive to be "better" than we are. In these ways, our level of self-esteem becomes a self-fulfilling prophesy of our life experiences.

Self-Image

The next component of our self-concept, our self-image, is in some sense the object of our self-esteem. And like a host of other intrapsychic phenomena, our self-image doesn't always necessarily reflect objective reality. People with anorexia, bulimia, or other body dysmorphic conditions, for example, see a very different image when they look in the mirror than the more objective one we see when we look at them.

Our self-image is the composite of our self-perceptions as they relate to three defining attributes: traits, competencies, and values.

Traits

Traits are the fairly consistent patterns of reactions and behaviors we see ourselves expressing in response to stimuli from the world around us. As an element of self-image, they're like personal shorthand for describing the repeated patterns in our behavior. Our personality traits can be shaped by the ideal self we strive to become; they are a central focus of identity motivation, which drives us to define ourselves in ways that are emotionally fulfilling.

Competencies

This second defining element of self-image consists of the perceptions of skills, abilities, talents, and knowledge we possess. These can range from very specific skills, such as operating a Zamboni machine, to more general competencies, such as presentation skills or a strong work ethic. Our perceptions of our abilities—such as "I'm a good tennis player" or "I'm very articulate"—become the focus of the emotional drives of the mastery motive, which seeks to embrace and develop a sense of excellence in relation to our peers and which can support the feeling that we are realizing our potential, actualizing our inherent talents or abilities.

Values

The third major defining element of our self-image is our conviction about what matters most to us. Our values transcend specific situations and remain relatively constant throughout our adult lives.

Values can be a reflection of our political, social, or aesthetic beliefs about the kinds of situations and behaviors we feel are desirable or undesirable. They arise most potently from ethical, moral, or religious beliefs about what is right and wrong in an absolute sense. In a fashion that Freud once characterized as an "internalized parent," intellectual value structures can exert influence on our intrapsychic emotional motivations and can make us want to be or behave in ways that we think others would approve of.[6]

Ideal Self

Our ideal self, the final component of our self-concept, is the vision of how we wish we were or how we'd like someday to be. The ideal self is developed, as you'd expect, from an amalgam of influences, including positive and negative experiences we've had in our lives, expectations we perceive others have for us (and most powerfully our parents' expectations for us in childhood), and traits, competencies, and values we've admired in others who function as our role models.

As we engage in motivational marketing, we should bear in mind that consumers' intrapsychic motivations will constantly create an appetite for products or services that enhance their self-image and thus increase their self-esteem. This includes products that conform to our personal traits and preferences, products that stand for our personal values, and products that offer the opportunity to move closer to our ideal sense of ourselves, for example, as a parent or handyman, lawyer or surgeon.

Who Do You Think I Am?

"No man is an island unto himself" wrote the fifteenth-century metaphysical poet John Donne.[7] This early expression of human beings' fundamentally social condition is an apt characterization of our "outward reaching" sense of self. The influence of the opinions of others (or in the case of intrapsychic motives, what we *think* those opinions are) and our estimation of how we compare to others has a great deal to do with how we answer the question of who we are. Our answers to that question, placed against the template of "who I want to be," generate the emotional energies of intrapsychic motivations.

We all belong to reference groups that help to meet our need for a framework to ground our self-impressions, an external *reference point* to define "who I am" against "who I am not." Without reference groups, it would be difficult to keep clear about who we really are. How can we know we're intelligent, for example, without a yardstick of some sort to orient ourselves by? Intelligent *compared* to whom? Or intelligent *according* to whom?

The yardsticks of our reference groups have a great deal to do with how we see ourselves as we move about in the world. For instance, if I make $51,000 a year, I have different ideas of who I am according to the reference groups I belong to. If I live in a small rural town on the lower rungs of our socioeconomic ladder, I may have a picture of myself as wealthy, successful, secure, attractive to others, and so on. But if I live in a large metropolitan area where average incomes are much higher, I might see myself as struggling, less successful, insecure, overburdened, downtrodden, and so on. Depending on the reference points I use, I may thus go out in to the world with confidence, optimism, and self-assurance, or trepidation, pessimism, and self-doubt. And that is a game-changing difference.

As we identify our reference groups, we monitor our performance constantly to ensure that we meet the standards given by those groups, and we're highly motivated to do things that will increase our sense of self-esteem in the terms of those groups. Among members of my high school class, for example, I'm in relatively good physical condition. Among the folks I know who've completed the Boston Marathon, however, I still have a long way to go.

Marketing to Intrapsychic Motivations

When they are intrapsychically motivated, consumers are interested first and foremost in how a product or service will help them *feel about themselves*. You may have a new convenience food for dinner that gets a job done well and makes the family happy, but to fulfill consumer's' intrapsychic motivations, you must emphasize *a sense of mastery in the face of the dinner challenge*. These kinds of positive contributions to consumers' self-perception can often lead to a positive transformation in the external realities of their lives. Many studies show that our feelings about ourselves strongly predict the outcomes we actually experience. To paraphrase Henry Ford, whether one thinks they'll be successful or thinks they will not, they're right in either case.

It can be challenging to create visual imagery for your messages that speak to the intrapsychic benefits. It's relatively simple to portray the rewards of palpable instrumental results, for example, or to convey visible interpersonal outcomes. But when we aim to satisfy the strivings of intrapsychic consumers, the proof points and payoffs are largely internal and not visible to the naked eye.

As these examples demonstrate, in general, when marketing to consumers' intrapsychic motives, it's important to remember:

- What matters are feelings not facts; it may be important to show product outcomes to set up the intrapsychic message, but the important intrapsychic takeaway for consumers is *how they feel*, and that's what should be clearly telegraphed in your message.
- The point of view for intrapsychic messaging visuals should be *through the eyes* of the user as much as is practical.
- The voice used for message delivery is typically more effective when it is the voice of the user in first-person narrative. The classic voice-over delivery works against drawing intrapsychically motivated consumers into the story and diminishes their potential empathy with the portrait of the benefits.

Creatives who want to reach consumers intrapsychic motivations would be wise to create situations that make it very easy for consumers to imagine how they would feel about themselves in those situations. Visuals created from a clear user point of view can help create this kind of empathy. A reliable standby is a shot of a consumer reflecting on product benefits after the fact and clearly looking satisfied.

It's equally important to note that, even as the task of marketing to consumers' intrapsychic motives presents challenges, the payoff for carrying this off successfully is great. When consumers are motivated by intrapsychic goals of security, identity, and mastery, they appreciate messages that explicitly speak to their tastes and styles; they respond to promises that align with their values and priorities, and they jump at products that present ways to enhance their sense of self. Consumers driven by these motivations don't want to figure out whether your product will work; they need to decide whether it will *work for them*. They aren't worrying about what anyone else is doing; they need to decide for themselves. And despite our hard-earned grip on the realities of the material world, despite our evolved social nature, no product is more powerfully appealing than one that "takes care of Number 1."

Just Between "Us"

It's also important to recognize that the relationship we build with consumers via marketing to their intrapsychic motives is uniquely personal. Intrapsychic motivations move us to seek out products that understand and recognize the best in us, products that welcome and embrace our innermost selves.

That's why your brand's relationship with intrapsychically motivated consumers is singularly personal; your product or service can directly validate a consumer without any intervening events or opinions. When this happens, you help satisfy consumers' desire for internal harmony, including that drive toward a feeling of confidence and self-esteem that underpins all of what we do.

That's partly why long, secure, loyal brand relationships are a hallmark of consumers recruited by way of intrapsychic fulfillment. Once on a path of internalized fulfillment, intrapsychically motivated consumers create enduring relationships with brands that share their innermost goals. When they find this connection, consumers can incorporate a brand identity to make it a part of who they are. At this point, their brand choice becomes automatic: they do not look elsewhere; they do not quibble over price; they buy the brand that "gets them"—they buy the brand that "is them."

Conversely, brands trying to make inroads into such a secure relationship are well advised to steer clear of market segments with predominantly intrapsychic motivational connections to their brand. Once a current brand has developed the kind of solid relationship just described, it will be difficult to penetrate the brand affinity bond. When a brand has become an extension of who consumers believe themselves to be, brand switching happens only in the most exceptional of circumstances.

What do Consumers with Intrapsychic Motives Value Most?

Consumers driven by intrapsychic motives want most of all to feel that they are understood, supported, and encouraged. They desire to feel that their tastes, styles, and values are understood and accepted and that their particular skills and abilities are recognized and appreciated. Here are some ideas for communication strategies that will help marketers meet these goals:

- messages that celebrate independence and individuality
- messages that applaud the goal of continuous self-improvement
- "customized" messaging and images that align with targeted tastes and styles of consumers
- values statements consumers respect and respond to
- representation of products and brand as "good company" on the consumer's journey to find, know, and love themselves
- commitment to authenticity, not seeming to try and please "all of the people all of the time"
- acknowledgment of the value of freedom from what others think
- delivery of unique, quirky messages that match your target group's sense of individuality.

Intrapsychic Messaging that Works

The most successful ads to target intrapsychically motivated consumers provide a sense that the company, brand, or product really *sees* the consumer and understands the consumer's hopes, values, and priorities. When operating in the intrapsychic realm, consumers are on a mission of self-discovery, and they're most motivated by products that help them reach that goal. Take a look at these examples and you'll see what I mean:

Bayer: "Your Heart Attack Arrives in Two Days"

There is a long tradition of personal monitoring, and alarm systems that are advertised as relieving consumers of their sources of worry and anxiety. This is exemplified by the ubiquitous LifeCall monitoring device dating from the late 1980s, which reached out to seniors living alone who called out: "I've fallen and can't get up!" That slogan became a catchphrase in the late eighties, but its undercurrent—the very real fear of being surprised when alone and helpless—represents an archetype of security-based marketing.

Bayer aspirin's latest campaign does a particularly good job of understanding the fear of unpredictable emergencies and delivers what consumers want to hear: a solution based on safety, reliability, and the endorsement of respected authorities, in this case, medical professionals.

"Laura's Heart Attack Note"

This opens on a woman in early middle age on a lovely, sunny day in her beautiful home. She opens the mail to find an engraved announcement: "Your heart attack arrives in 2 days." At that point, viewers are forced to consider that if it could happen to this woman, it could also happen to them. The device of the note and its random, offhand arrival drives home the anxiety of the unknown: I could have a heart attack at any time on any day.

Bayer immediately steps in to offers a solution, endorsed by experts: "Laura's heart attack didn't come with a warning. Today her doctor has her on a Bayer aspirin regimen to reduce the chance of another one."

Bayer does several things right in this campaign: it takes a seemingly risk-free life scenario and overlays the risk of heart attack on this scenario, effectively arousing insecurity about a threat that can't be perceived (such as heart disease). It drives home the lack of warning for a heart patient with the metaphor of a "note" that gives (desired but inaccessible) warning. It then offers the (now worried and dismayed) consumer an alternative—the "insurance" of a daily Bayer aspirin regimen.

Bayer not only offers a welcome solution to a problem, but it also positions the brand as a kind of hero in the situation portrayed. Although generic aspirin is identical to Bayer's aspirin, it's likely that Bayer will be associated with the emotionally salient memory of this message.

Harley-Davidson: "Live By It"

For consumers motivated by seeking identity, the pitch-perfect message is often one where consumers, viewing themselves as original, one-of-a-kind individuals, are shown how a particular product will let them embrace the ways they are *different* from the masses. Harley-Davidson does a fantastic job of celebrating the renegade aspirations of its customers and aficionados while also presenting the romance and sensory thrill of a motorcycle ride.

In its "Live by It" spot, Harley offers a machismo sonnet to the shared passions of its drivers. This wonderful clip begins by introducing and celebrating the thrill of the ride. We're first treated to the site of a beautiful dawn on the horizon of an awe-inspiring mountain vista. The road marks slip past a lone driver, who smiles as he so clearly enjoys the real ride he's on—the outdoors and the freedom to see it without doors. As the scene builds, more riders join in the journey, which winds through more breathtaking scenery to the obvious delight of the riders.

Throughout, Harley's photography focuses on clear displays of individuality. A bride rides on the back of a bike in her veil, with the words "Just Married" perched on the "sissy bar" for those who follow to see. Other photography zooms in to celebrate other signals of subtle defiance of mainstream norms: nose rings, tattoos, dogs on board. All set against the background of the obviously liberated feeling of the wind in the hair of the bikers.

The voice-over narration for this ad tells us and the nameless "them" who conform to social rules exactly what Harley drivers are made of. You'll notice that Harley begins and ends each line of the manifesto with the word "we" in homage to the rebels who join together on the road. The result is a resonant ode to the renegade American spirit, I offer it whole.[8]

> We believe in going our own way, no matter which way the rest of the world is going.
> We believe in bucking the system that is built to smash individuals like bugs on a windshield.
> Some of us believe in the man upstairs, all of us believe in sticking it to the man down here.
> We believe in the sky, and we don't believe in the sunroof.
> We believe in freedom.
> We believe in dust, tumble weeds, buffalo, mountain ranges, and riding off into the sunset.
> We believe in saddlebags, and we believe that cowboys had it right.
> We believe in refusing to knuckle under to anyone.
> We believe in wearing black because it doesn't show any dirt or weakness.
> We believe the world is going soft, and we're not going along with it.
> We believe in motorcycle rallies that last a week.
> We believe in roadside attractions, gas station hot dogs, and finding out what's over the next hill.
> We believe in rumbling engines, pistons the size of garbage cans, fuel tanks designed in 1936, freight-train-sized head lights, chrome, and custom paint.
> We believe in flames and skulls.
> We believe life is what you make it, and we make it one hell of a ride.

We believe the machine you sit on can tell the world exactly where you stand.

We don't care what everyone else believes.

Amen.

After that last "Amen," do you have any doubt about the unique, distinctive values and priorities of Harley riders? I don't either.

Gatorade: "23 versus 39"

For a literal interpretation of the mastery motive and the drive that mastery-oriented consumers respond best to, it's hard to imagine a better example than Gatorade's "23 versus 39" 30-second spot. As the spot opens, we see 39-year-old Michael Jordan, arguably the best player in the history of basketball, practicing alone in a dimly lit, empty gym. He is a recognizable figure, a powerful athlete, and we prepare to see another demonstration of Jordan's prowess in the action that follows.

But suddenly Jordan looks up, and we realize—as he does—that another player is about to join him on the court. Through some complex wizardry that's still talked about, the 23-year-old Jordan (dressed in appropriate uniform and shoes of that past) dares his older self to a pickup game. A one-on-one ensues, and we are treated to a vision of mastery in action. "Older Michael" and "younger Michael" battle fiercely for control of the game and bragging rights. During the entire game, the versions of Jordan cajole and trash-talk each other. The younger Michael goads the older one with "Let's see what you can do now." And the older version returns fire: "You reach, I teach. The lesson just started." Such mastery can clearly be draining because the two Jordans pause to replenish with Gatorade. Gatorade, we're led to believe, helps current Michael be his best, as it's always helped him be his best in the past. At the end of the spot, a third thirsty contender arrives on the court: college-aged Jordan, looking impossibly fit and athletic in his Tar Heels uniform. Break out more Gatorade. The impression we're left with is an epigram for the mastery-oriented consumer: life is about competing against yourself, always learning, always striving, and always evolving. That's the mastery motive in a nutshell, and Gatorade ties itself firmly to this dynamic.

Let us now turn to the individual motives in the Intrapsychic column of the Matrix.

Takeaways

1. Our intrapsychic motives are the developmental and emotional "launching pad" for everything we do and feel. Regardless of the motivation that dominates a specific urge to purchase, every product we purchase is in some way an expression of and a reflection upon the consumer's sense of self.

2. For some consumers, and for all consumers on some occasions, the most important consideration in product selection and product satisfaction is how the product makes them feel about themselves. In these situations, products and messages should target intrapsychic motivations by looking for ways to enhance consumers' self-image and to celebrate their lifestyle choices.

3. Long, stable relationships can develop between consumers and brands when consumers choose a brand based on its ability to fulfill their needs for feeling a certain way about themselves. Such products can literally become part of a consumer's identity.

4. A big part of our self-image centers on how we view ourselves in relationship to others, especially our "reference groups." Linking a product to a compelling reference group can be an effective way of gaining the interest of consumers who identify with and desire status in this reference group.

5. The more mature we become, the more we become satisfied with our sense of self, and the more we expect others (including brands) to recognize our skills and abilities and our personal feelings of mastery.

This page intentionally left blank

CHAPTER 4

The Security Motive

The security motive is the most fundamental and universal of all of the domains in the Forbes Matrix. And there are two very good reasons why.

The first and most obvious reason is the simple life-and-death importance of security for all of us. We are hardwired physically and conditioned socially to seek out people and situations offering us security. We are driven toward those goals both by nature and by nurture, and so is every animal that shares our planet.

Security motivation is, at its core, the urgent drive to stay alive. Without first ensuring that we are safe, it's difficult if not impossible to think about anything else. We begin our lives completely vulnerable and dependent, incapable of meeting our most basic needs. To propel us toward safety and security, our very first, strongest urge is to attach, physically at first and then emotionally, to the sources of security in our environment.

Striving for security can sometimes take the positive aspirational form of motivation, as when we set aside money to protect us from future financial insecurity. But more often the security motive operates when we feel hesitant, anxious, or fearful or when we anticipate that we might feel this way in the near future. This predisposition to avoid negative feelings and outcomes sets the security motive apart from the other motives in the matrix. Fulfillment of the security motivation is usually felt in the form of freedom or relief we get by *moving away* from negatives in our lives as opposed to the satisfaction or delight we might feel when we *reach toward* the more positive outcomes around which the remaining eight motivations revolve. In psychological terms, marketing to security needs thus typically means making a promise of negative reinforcement by inviting consumers to experience the relief of being free from worries about the unpleasant results that would have awaited them had they not acted to dispel them.

A second way the security motive differs from others in the matrix is that it serves as a gateway function for all of the other motives. Our need to fulfill our longing for security is so powerful and important that we must address these foundational security strivings before we can even begin to move toward our higher-order motives.

This vision of the security motive aligns well with Maslow's model of motivation. Security lies at the base of Maslow's pyramid of self-actualization (see chapter 15 for a review of Maslow's theories), where it works alongside our purely metabolic needs (for food and water, for example) without which we will perish. As Maslow characterizes it,[1] security is a "deficiency need," that must be satisfied before we can move forward to love, to dream, and to feel.

It's important to remember that the security motive is not limited to dire circumstances that threaten biological survival. It is in play whenever a lack of personal experience or personal knowledge leaves us uncertain about our immediate or long-term future, or when we lack a sense of optimism about what the future holds. Whether it involves buying the next-generation computer or getting a stain out of clothing, gaining security gives us a sense of control and a feeling of inner peace and trust: a very comfortable conviction that everything really will be okay. In this way, the security motive helps us feel balanced and grounded.

The security motivation also operates when we strive to build a predictable world where dangers are minimized, change is rare, and perceived unfairness and inconsistency are held at bay. Security needs drive us to search out familiarity and to keep the unfamiliar a rare exception. Security needs can *also* drive us to make choices that might be deemed negative, such as staying in a job, relationship, or situation because it is familiar to us even though we are unhappy with it. Security needs can cause us to not take up new options, such as making a new investment, trying a new vacation destination, exploring a new hobby, all because the idea of doing so gives us the sense that "this may not be safe."

While everyone experiences insecurity from time to time, we can identify security-driven individuals who experience this motivation more powerfully and more frequently than most. People who have in general a higher need for security will be more deeply affected by any type of sudden change, including unforeseen events or changes at work or at home that feel like a threat to lifestyle or livelihood. These people will have a fearful vigilance that can lead them all too easily to become overly cautious, indecisive, "frozen," and, in extreme cases, even unable to function.

Instinctual Roots

The ability to recognize danger and the arousal of "flight, fight, or freeze" reactions to increase our chances of survival are primal capabilities seemingly present in our genome. Whether we're aware of it or not, we are all constantly on alert, constantly scanning for danger, constantly assessing threat levels. It's an evolutionary imperative as well as an evolutionary gift. In many ways, fear is good. Fear is necessary. Fear keeps us alive. All of us alive today are the descendants of those who were best at recognizing and responding to fear.

The Forces of Civilization

We're all afraid of something. No, actually we're all afraid of many things. A century ago, William James, considered the father of modern psychology, argued that modern life (his modern life, around the turn of the twentieth century) protects us almost completely from the common life-and-death threats we would have faced just a generation or two earlier (his example is our freedom from grizzly bear attacks.) James argued that in civilized life "it has at last become possible for large numbers of people to pass from the cradle to the grave without ever having had a pang of genuine fear."[2] What James didn't address in his work is the degree of anxiety and fear we engender among ourselves even in our most "civilized" circumstances. See the sidebar on our "Insecure Nation."

Indeed, it seems to many of us that fear is more prevalent nowadays than it has been in the recent past, perhaps even more prevalent than it was in James's time. While physical dangers have certainly declined in civilized society, the very nature of society can itself be anxiety-inducing. Environmental pollution, global warming, political unrest, and personal and societal economic disruption are just some of the "grizzly bears" we confront in our modern society.

Insecure Nation

Anxiety disorders are the most common mental illness in the United States, affecting 40 million adults 18 and older (18 percent of the US population), according to a study reported by the National Institutes of Mental Health.[3]

According to the National Institutes of Mental Health, America is the most anxious country in the world;[4] it is more anxious than Colombia, more anxious than Bangladesh. And seemingly much more anxious than in the early times of civilized society James spoke of. We have plenty of evidence of great strides toward physical safety in our world. Our streets are safer, our cars more crash-resistant, our food supply more dependable, and our medical care far more effective in treating our illnesses and injuries. But even as our lifespans grow longer, healthier, and more comfortable, we live in an unprecedented era of insecurity and fear. According to the 2002 World Mental Health Survey, people in developing countries are five times *less likely* to show clinically significant anxiety levels than people in the United States[5] despite having a less secure grasp on what Maslow would have called the basic necessities of life, namely, food and shelter. And guess what—when folks from developing countries immigrate to the United States, they quickly become just as anxious as we are! What does that tell us? Anxiety is not all about genetics, and not all about physical dangers.

Our capacity for feeling insecure has kept pace with the progress of our civilization. Our needs for security even when fulfilled at the physiological level now flourish in a range of situations in our social and psychological lives where we feel just as afraid as we would be while running from a dangerous animal in the woods. Our anxieties have become more abstract and plentiful but are no less painful.

German psychoanalyst Eric Fromm told us that we should strive not so much to feel secure as to be able to tolerate insecurity.[6] And I believe he was exactly right.

Sources of Insecurity

Researchers and clinicians in the field of psychology study all kinds of fear and anxiety, from phobias of things like spiders or snakes to fear of closed or open spaces to posttraumatic stress disorder caused by terrifying external events to general anxiety disorders. Sifting through the modern discussion of anxiety, we uncover four themes in the causes of our fears that all relate to how we live in the modern world.

Legitimate, Objective, Quantifiable Fears

The first reason we feel more anxiety and insecurity today is that we really do live in an era of endemic and strange new dangers and fears. You don't need me to tell you about them, but seeing some of these stressors listed here in one place is illuminating: terrorist bombings, AMBER alerts, product recalls, contaminated food, color-coded terror alert levels, school shootings, computer hacking, identity theft, credit card hackers, retirement uncertainties, rising medical bills, and home foreclosures—the list could go on and on, and as you see these "civilized threats" can enhance a general need for more security in our lives. But beyond all of these obvious and concrete reasons to feel insecurity, the literature suggests three other reasons for our increasing insecurity that are more abstract and psychological: the dissolution of kinship and community, the growing "global access to fear" that results from our omnipresent and nearly omniscient media, and the need for a "game face" in public life, which diminishes our ability to express and control our fears.

The Dissolution of Kinship and Community

In the modern hypermobile, hyperchangeable social structure, we no longer live in the close-knit, familial communities we evolved to depend on. For most of human history, human beings lived together in small, close-knit groups sharing everything: caring for children together, hunting, foraging, and eating together. In those days, we nursed our sick together, mourned our dead together, and experienced all of life's milestones together. Until very recently, our social structure all but guaranteed that we were *always* surrounded by people who could help, people we had known all of our lives. And they were always there. In fact, in the late eighteenth or early nineteenth centuries most of us didn't venture much farther than 20 miles beyond our birthplace. But in our current age, social changes have left much more room for feelings of interpersonal insecurity and fewer supports to cope with them.

The gradual dissolution of the connection between intimacy and propinquity in our social lives was driven in large part by the intensification of commerce. The agricultural and Industrial revolutions allowed and indeed required us to interact with a great many people we didn't know, strangers whose character we couldn't reliably judge and whose behavior was accordingly unpredictable. Our more recent technological revolution has created a highly connected world with previously unimaginable opportunities to interact with cultures and societies that are not only unfamiliar but are actually changing right before our eyes. Contrast the situation of the ancestral village with the ways our lives unfold today, and it's easy to see what's behind some of our pervasive angst. Keeping in mind that our instincts and our brains evolved to live in the "before" picture of our social environment, our "after" picture of life today is built around completely different rules and support systems. Today, we migrate all over the world, often to work in large cities where we know no one. Once we're in those cities, we most often live in insular apartments and homes, with much less sense of community than people even one generation before us felt. Add to that the fact that we spend less time engaging with people face-to-face and more time interacting with various screens and the virtual social worlds in our homes, pockets, and purses. Social scientists generally agree that on-screen connections are not even contenders when it comes to ways of feeling connected and supported. We might thus reasonably ask where we are to turn in today's stressful situations. Will we find a sense of security from our Facebook wall? There are dozens if not hundreds of studies that conclude that human contact and feelings of kinship dramatically alleviate anxiety and that if we have fewer people to depend on, we will inevitably become more anxious. Other cultures with lower standards of living, higher mortality rates, frequent hunger, less access to health care offset by strong connections to familiars and kindred are far less anxious than we are.

Streaming Fear

There's little debate that we live in a dangerous world, but that is not actually new. We've encountered dangerous times before, as the builders of bomb shelters of the mid-twentieth century can attest. But one key difference today is that we not only know about the dangers that threaten us personally, we are also inundated with anxiety-producing news complete with visually stimulating and disturbing images. The long-standing newspaperman's maxim that "if it bleeds, it leads" is now manifest 24/365. And coverage now spans the globe in living color.

Given our never-ending news cycles, our constant state of connection, and ubiquitous access to bad news, there is nowhere we can turn to escape our fears. A recent study showed that violence in films has tripled since the 1950s. Violence also increases apace in our television programming, where the FCC sees fit only to regulate sex and language. Our brains developed as exquisitely calibrated "computers" finely tuned to detecting dangers and threats. With today's constant access to vicarious danger, our natural reactions inevitably build up a toxic degree of anxiety and insecurity. And this problem is only compounded when many of the dangerous threats we face are unseeable or unknown. How do we protect ourselves, our family and friends, and our children from random shooters, terror networks, and rampaging, quickly mutating, untreatable viruses? Our modern state of ambient insecurity is no mystery. In the face of all these sources for insecurity, the desire of consumers to seek out products that make their lives a little more predictable is not hard to understand. And marketing products in terms of their abilities to increase predictability and reduce insecurity seems like a viable strategy indeed.

The "Game Face"

A third contributing factor to our anxiety level arises from our public social norms regarding the expression of emotions. As we spend most of the day among strangers or casual acquaintances, we feel constrained from admitting our negative feelings, our insecurities or sadness, and so we put on our "game face." In the context of relatively superficial interactions in the public social arena we deem it inappropriate to talk about our off days. Asked how we are feeling, we are supposed to answer "fine," regardless of how we really feel. As a society, we don't allow normal sadness or insecurities to emerge from behind our public masks. Instead, we strive to be confident, healthy, and happy every day. When we feel a little insecure, we mask it, either with bright smiles and "fake it 'til you make it" strategies or, more and more frequently, with pharmaceutical products that promise to relieve us of our anxiety or with distractions of unhealthy coping strategies like compulsive shopping, exercising, dieting, and so on to help refocus the fear. Without a meaningful outlet, with no chance for the reassurance that comes from sharing them, our fears can persist and grow unabated.

Social Media Insecurity: A Brand New Fear

In the year 2014, the *Oxford English Dictionary* added a new word for a brand-new social phenomenon of the connected age: FOMO.[7] This acronym stands for "Fear of Missing Out" and it is a real and recognized side effect of our newly connected world. Social scientists define it as a pervasive, gnawing apprehension that others are having wonderful, rewarding experiences filled with fulfilling, indispensable things, without us.

FOMO is characterized by a compulsive need to monitor what others are doing via social media. It's driven by the insecurity that we might miss an opportunity for social interaction, a novel experience, a new connection. Another part of the picture is that we often view others' lives as significantly better than ours. The lives of our Facebook friends and LinkedIn contacts, many of whom we've never met in person, seem full of great vacations, picturesque weddings, wonderful parties, and workplace triumphs—important victories and milestones that are sadly lacking when we examine our own lives in comparison.

In the face of seeming evidence of others' social superiority, we come to fear that we simply do not, cannot, and never will measure up. Our ability to recognize and judge where we and others stood in our social structures was critical to our survival. Our vicarious sense of "missing out" in our virtual social world, of not knowing where (or if) we belong, causes our ancient brains to worry that there will not be enough social "good stuff" to go around. That activates a primitive fear that we are being dangerously deprived of something we need *to survive*. That's why FOMO is so associated with negative emotions, especially insecurity and social anxiety. And that's why marketers can succeed handily by assuring their customers that using this product or that service will help them "keep up" in today's fast-paced world.

Average age for the onset of anxiety disorders in the United States is 11, according to the National Institutes of Mental Health.[8]

Marketing to Security Needs

With all of the ambient insecurity in our emotional world, marketing that focuses on a promise of something consumers won't have to worry about or on the promise of removing something they do worry about can be very compelling. In the context of all of our sources of anxiety, a promise of security in our lives, even if only in the laundry room, can be a very appealing marketing message.

Brands that promise consumers relief from insecurity have the opportunity to forge a very strong bond with consumers who are distinctively security-oriented, a bond that can last years if not decades. These consumers long for safe, predictable relationships with products that can help them dispel fears. Once you're accepted in this kind of consumer relationship, you have an opportunity to become part of your consumers' sense of identity

Windows of Insecurity

Big stressful life events are pivotal moments to market to consumers on the basis of their security motives. New college graduates, newly married couples, first-time home buyers, and first-time parents, for example, are all in the midst of ground-shifting changes in their lives. With these changes comes uncertainty, and with uncertainty comes insecurity. At these moments, consumers are likely to be open to products whose message focuses at least in part on security. Marketers of everything from first-time credit cards to first home mortgages to Pampers will benefit from recognizing the powerful insecurities of their audiences and from speaking to the emotional relief their products offer.

Fear and Economic Downturns

Tough economic times may feel like the worst time to be a marketer, but somewhat paradoxically, they actually can be the best time to build brands. An important emotional side effect of a downturn in the economy is the insecurity it often evokes; consumers fear that they will be not capable of fulfilling their needs and meeting their family's needs or that there won't be "enough" to go around. In the context of these fears, a very special relationship can develop between brands and consumers. Providing reliable value to consumers who are experiencing insecurity can make a brand feel almost heroic" to buyers. The literature on building brand relationships suggests that connections made during times of crisis are stronger than those made in times of prosperity.[9] Aggressively marketing the familiarity and reliability of your well-known brand in times of economic hardship may seem economically risky, but the potential payoff is great. Following the US stock market crash of 1987, for example, Nike tripled its marketing spend and emerged from the recession with profits nine times higher than it had going in. Taco Bell and Pizza Hut also took advantage of that recession, promoting themselves heavily. This strategy paid off in increases of their market share, earned largely at the expense of McDonald's, which had not increased its communications to consumers during the recession. See the sidebar on this page for another great example of marketing success in hard times.

Hard Times, Reassurance, and Good Company: How P & G Built Its Brand during Great Depression[10]

P & G (and other brands that managed to thrive in the Great Depression) actually bucked a trend by increasing marketing spend during crisis years to keep its products before the public eye. A cornerstone product, Oxydol detergent, offered tangible security and empowerment-based promises to housewives when ads invited them to use the detergent to wash clothes "25–40% faster" while getting them "4–5 shades whiter than other soaps."

P & G launched another invention and so started a new era when it created radio programming to keep women company while they performed these household tasks. These first serials—soap operas—set in motion a way of life for the American public that endures to this day.

Security and Brand Affinity

It's important for marketers to remember that every well-known brand is engaged in security marketing, even if it is not explicitly trying to accomplish that goal. Brand affinity—the emotional face of brand equity—has been increasingly implicated as a driver of brand loyalty. Brand affinity is the emotional attachment that grows over time, the non-rational glue that connects consumers to the brand in ways that go beyond rational brand equity. And the security that comes from the confidence and predictability of using a familiar brand can form an important part of brand affinity

Ever since the time of those early logos and cattle "brands," product brands have helped buyers feel secure, reassuring them that they were making the right decisions. In fact, the very earliest advertising messages often centered on reassurance: "We're John's sons' soap. You know us, and you trust us to clean better/cost less/smell great." What we're really selling in name-brand marketing messages like these is a lot more than just the product or its primary benefits. We are also marketing peace of mind, reassurance, and ultimately the fulfillment of a striving for security.

Conversely, every new purchase of every shiny new widget carries within it the (latent) fear that it will not do what it promises, and therefore it is necessary when marketing such products to build a base of credibility that allows consumers to feel at least somewhat secure in the face of the unfamiliar. Consumers will quickly abandon brands that fail to provide the security of predictable performance. Their trust is precious and fragile, hard to gain and easy to lose. Decades of incrementally acquired brand equity can be eroded over the course of a few months of bad brand management. As Warren Buffett reminds us, "It takes 20 years to build a reputation and five minutes to ruin it."[11]

Marketing to Insecurity

Another approach to marketing that taps security motivations is one that works to magnify or even create feelings of insecurity. Marketing messages that stimulate anxious responses can validate the consumers' unmet need for security and then go beyond that feeling to offer solutions. Since the beginning of time, craftsmen and manufacturers have first posed problems and then offered their unique and singularly effective solutions for them. And many of those problem statements begin with a negative emotional reference to the problem. Go online and watch the first advertisements for Wisk laundry detergent and see if the chant of "ring around the collar" doesn't sound like the jeering of a crowd around the insecure listener with less-than-perfect laundry skills.

Fear of the Unknown

Nexium, an OTC pharmaceutical for the relief of heartburn and acid reflux, sets up the problem of acid reflux for its consumers in a way that heightens insecurities:

"Don't let acid reflux eat at you!"
And then offers them the perfect solution to this threat.
"Next time, ask your doctor about Nexium."

Consumers are all too easily susceptible to fears about serious diseases that may lurk behind their symptoms. The phrasing "eat at you" in this ad aims to reframe the experience of heartburn, heightening the fear of the consequences, and associating it to acid reflux disease rather than an isolated incident. Now, we have a greatly enhanced desire to seek security by asking our doctor about treatment.

Beyond providing a platform for the "solution" statement that relieves the insecurity ("Wisk around the collar beats ring around the collar every time"), evoking anxiety in a marketing strategy can also drive consumers to action. People are creatures of habits, and we all learn to tolerate ambient levels of insecurity in our modern lives. If we want to change a certain behavior of consumers, we must rouse them to action, and when the feelings of discomfort and insecurity we evoke become uncomfortable enough, those consumers will become motivated enough to make a change and try a new product.

At the same time, it is important to remember that while creating some degree of anxiety with a marketing strategy may actually be good for business, there is a fine line that must be adhered to: consumers who feel very little anxiety may not be uncomfortable enough to seek a change from their status quo, but consumers overwhelmed by fear and anxiety can become immobilized, unable to search for options for change.

Given all this, is there an optimum range of consumer anxiety that can help you market some products? I think so.

Calculating Insecurity: The Extended Parallel Process Model (EPPM)

When we explore the potential effectiveness of fear-based advertising, we can look to a model to evaluate how effective it could be. This measurement mechanism, EPPM, first proposed by Kim Witte,[12] examines how a calculation of perceived threats, their perceived severity, and consumers' perceived efficacy can predict behavior change, including purchase interest and actual purchase behavior. Basically, EPPM examines how fear-based messaging works, and how it succeeds. The model has three components:

First, consumers look at a *perceived threat* and try to gauge the likelihood of the threat actually happening to them. They ask: "Could this hurt me? Is it likely to?"

If they answer yes to those questions, customers next look at the *perceived severity* of the threat. "How badly might this hurt me? Is this a big deal?" If and when the perceived threat and its perceived severity is alarming enough to warrant action, consumers then finally explore their own ability to do something to avoid or lessen the impact of the threat. This ability, their *perceived efficacy* in the face of a likely threat, is the linchpin for action, behavior change, and purchase. If the threat is far beyond their ability to handle it, consumers will become overwhelmed, perhaps even hopeless, and they will be less inclined to act and more inclined to hide. On the other hand, if the threat is likely, significant, and within their capability to mitigate, consumers' longing for security will be activated, perhaps prompting them to a purchase.

Building Security into Your Brand

The very essence of affinity for a well-known brand always rests in part predictable outcomes from the brand, delivered reliably, time after time. Brand managers who are working to fortify the security-fueled foundation of affinity and loyalty should also include the following strategies and tactics.

Be trustworthy. Live up to the promises you make to your consumers because you'll only get one chance to make them. Carefully cultivate their expectations and deliver what you say you will in the manner that works best for your consumers at the time you've promised. Trust plays an even more crucial role in the online purchasing process, where customers may experience insecurity and worry about many stages of the process: products not delivered, faulty products, payment fraud, impossible or nonexistent return procedures, misuse of personal data, and so on.

Build a relationship. Show consumers you can be a "trusted advisor" to turn to for assistance and advice. Amazon does an exemplary job of fostering

relationships with consumers by helping them make decisions through recommendations of items based on past purchases, user reviews, ratings, and
suggested complementary purchases. Allstate Insurance has built its business
over the years by consistently reassuring consumers that they are in good
hands if they have a relationship with Allstate.

Reduce risk. Let your customers know they have "nothing to lose" in
doing business with you. Diffuse their doubts with guarantees, money-back
returns, and assurances that you'll get it right or it's free. Offer secured, easy
exchanges and returns, fast delivery, and all with "No strings attached."
Show consumers how they are doing "the right thing, the smart thing, and
the safe thing." Consider brand testimonials from experts, but use them only
if they're independent authorities not employed by you.

Be a consistent presence. Take care to develop and commit to a personality
and a voice for your brand, and make sure every point of customer contact
reinforces it. When your customers seek you out online, make sure they recognize you as they would an old friend by the content, architecture, and art
of the site. The same holds true for packaging, display, point of purchase,
and all advertising: print, TV, banner ads, and so on. Be consistent (and by
the way, delivering the reassurance of consistency doesn't mean you can't be
exciting at the same time).

Be honest, even/especially if it hurts. Security-motivated consumers prefer to
hear that something has gone awry than to feel they've been duped. If something happens with their order or even with the character of the brand,
acknowledge it and offer immediate resolution. Target did a lot of work to this
end in the wake of the security breach (see the sidebar for their response).

Back from the Brink

Target shifted into crisis-management mode when it reached out to the
110 million customers—about one-third of the adult population of the
United States—whose credit security was breached in December 2013.

Gregg Steinhafel, Target's chairman, president, and CEO, shared
this open letter with guests in newspapers across the country.

"Dear Target Guests,

As you have probably heard, Target learned in mid-December that
criminals forced their way into our systems, gaining access to guest

credit and debit card information. As a part of the ongoing forensic investigation, it was determined last week that certain guest information, including names, mailing addresses, phone numbers, or email addresses, was also taken.

Our top priority is taking care of you and helping you feel confident about shopping at Target, and it is our responsibility to protect your information when you shop with us.

We didn't live up to that responsibility, and I am truly sorry.... You expect more from us and deserve better.

We want to earn back your trust and confidence and ensure you that we deliver the Target experience you know and love.

Sincerely,

Gregg Steinhafel

Chairman, president, and CEO, Target

Unfortunately, the public consensus about Target's security breach remained unfavorable, despite this yeoman's effort by their CEO. Still, I don't think we can fault the sincere and reassuring overture of the letter; it appears that some of our larger fears cannot be dispelled by statements of good intention, however well crafted.

Make good use of your "earned media." This includes not only customer recommendations but also reviews, yelps, etc. Make it easy for consumers to feel the security of belonging to a community, by sharing their own and reading others' experiences with your products or services online.

Keeping in mind that all of us feel the drive for security from time to time, let's take a more in-depth look at the kind of consumer who will be most responsive to security marketing.

Consumer Portrait: The Longing for Security

Ryan likes to view his world as a well-planned, carefully unfolding voyage. He knows what he's got, he knows what he needs, and he knows where he's going. He is happiest when his life moves forward as he expects it to, and he does everything in his power to keep the people and events of his life predictabe. He's tries to operate in fail-safe contexts in a circle of people he already knows.

Continuity and tradition are very important to Ryan; they're the sign posts he uses to guide his life. He likes to celebrate birthdays with the same people at the same place (and even with the same cake), year after year. He may still use a number of the brands that he grew up with, just because he likes familarity. Ryan also likes to keep the other elements in his life routine. He has two or three reliable restaurants he and his wife go to where they can count on the food being good, the service being pretty good, and the prices being excellent. He doesn't like to experiment with new restaurants or movie theaters with his family or friends, and he hates surprises.

Ryan's drive toward safety and security is directly reinforced by many of the products he owns. He has hired a home alarm company and has a dog, just in case. He belongs to a gym he uses religiously, the recommended three times a week. He does his own financial planning, and had IRAs and college funds set up before his children were born.

Because he dreads the unforeseen, Ryan carefully builds defenses against it. He and his wife are covered by several insurance policies: life insurance, health insurance, car insurance, and dental insurance. Ryan drives a Honda Civic—it gets great mileage and has good crash protection—and his wife, Maria, drives their Volvo equipped with the top-rated child car seats. Ryan and Maria made these selections based on plenty of research into the cars' safety, durablity, price, gas milegage, and resale value. To make sure he can always count on them, Ryan maintains his cars meticulously, changing the oil, rotating the tires, and performing all recommended service and mainte-nance checks exactly as specified. The feeling of knowing what needs to be done and then doing it with care and precision is very satisfying to him. As a marketer, you won't have to worry that Ryan will barge ahead and use your product without first reading the instructions

Ryan's default mode when faced with new trends is skepticism. Not only does he not "fall for" the latest thing, he's always amazed when others do. He's not about to pay $4 for a head of kale to green up his smoothie nor is he will-ing to pay exhorbitant prices to drink anything fermented from mushrooms.

When Ryan shops, he is very likely to stick to a list or to stay focused on the item(s) has has come to buy. He is typically not a great prospect for any new product unless it is accompanied by some serious scientific data or very credible endorsements. Still, Ryan is a great member of your brand franchise once you have won him; he is very loyal and very unlikely to switch brands or to try a new one simply because it's on sale or marketed prominently.

Recruit Ryan to your franchise if your product will make his life safer or more secure, and if you can offer him a long track record of reliable performance. Sell Ryan your new product only if you have carefully garnered consumer testimonials and certified product reviews.

Security-Oriented Product and Brand Promises

We all have a basic need to feel safe and secure, so we all can relate to this motivation. Marketing to consumers who identify strongly with the need for security involves promising or implying that your product will deliver freedom from the negatives your consumers will experience without it. Naturally, the choice of a specific negative reinforcement promise depends on the negative experience from which your consumers seek relief. In most cases, this includes negatives that are normally associated with a lifestyle niche (For example, "you won't need to worry about tough laundry stains" or "never again will you have to deal with freezer burn in your stored food"). Alternatively, your promise could focus on negative outcomes consumers might experience using a competitor's product ("Now you can accomplish this task without the [mess/smell/guesswork] of [your competitor's product]").

Because of the unique negative reinforcement orientation of the security motive, you can also consider emphasizing consumers' uncertainties or fears and then present your product as the hero that helps neutralize or avoid these fears. But be careful—remember that visuals or messages that are too strong not only distract from the product, but they could also be a turnoff and cause consumers to avoid your message altogether.

Consumers who are seeking security will also be attracted by messages that focus on objective, empirical proof that product reviews or other recommendations can provide.

Promising a Negative Reinforcement

Because security-oriented consumers are typically seeking to *move away* from fears and frustrations more often than they are moving toward hopes and aspirations for more security, messages that focus on the absence of a negative may be effective:

- Don't let "this" happen to you (or yours).
- No-risk guarantees/love it or full refund/free shipping, free returns.

- Buy this product, and you won't need to worry about wasting money on something inferior.
- Your data (identity, savings, health, home, kids, tires, cell service, etc.) are not safe. Use this product to protect them.
- Unscrupulous companies are trying to take advantage of you. Stick with who you know and trust.
- Make the safest choice.
- Use this product to be less socially unacceptable: fat, poor, wrinkled, etc.

Legacy Positioning and Record of Performance

Security-oriented consumers are also drawn to brands with a history of performance; they seek to be convinced that the product will do what it promises. Therefore, messages such as the following may also work well:

- We haven't changed our formula since....
- Safety has always been our number-one priority.
- We have a lifetime commitment to you.
- This product never fails.
- We've solved the problems, so you don't have to worry.
- No guesswork required.
- Your vision (retirement fund, family's health, etc.) is too precious to trust to just anybody.
- Turn to the company you've known and trusted for years.

Case Studies

Air Fresheners

Using air fresheners in their homes allowed the female respondents in our client's study to move away from their deep-seated fear that others would notice smells in the home and perceive those homes to be "dirty" or "disgusting." Through our research, we discovered that this security-based fear harkened back to the cleanliness standards set by the mothers or grandmothers of the women in the study. Respondents often considered their mothers and grandmothers the ultimate authority on their own success, not only in terms of cleanliness of the house, but also regarding "how to" be a successful housekeeper, wife, and mother.

Interestingly, insecurity around the adequacy of one's homemaking was not limited to age, education, or income in this study. Sitting judges and six-figure executives were as uneasy as full-time homemakers about the condition—particularly the cleanliness—of their homes. They all sought confirmation that they were doing a "good job" taking care of their homes and their families, and most were ready and willing to investigate and to accept products that helped them get there.

Another surprise in this study was women's ambivalence with regard to the "convenience products" they sometimes used to keep their homes clean. While many openly acknowledged that they put in far more hours working outside the home than did their mothers or grandmothers, they still experienced lingering feelings of guilt about taking "shortcuts" in homemaking tasks.

Our client's marketers were able to understand and address these emotional issues through marketing efforts they developed to address the desires the women voiced for approval and confirmation that they were doing a good job.

Infant Formula

Manufacturers of a national infant formula brand wanted to learn how best to communicate their product's benefits to new mothers, who were the most important targets in their market (the conviction was that feeding decisions once made were less likely to change with a second or third child.) The study revealed that a need for security was a dominant theme in the emotional orientation of new parents. As is often the case with complex and important tasks, those who are new at the task feel a strong emotional fear that they might not do it "right"—in the case of infant feeding, they even fear that they might do something harmful to their babies.

Levels of need for security generally rise with the relative importance of the task being performed. And as you might imagine, the care and feeding of newborns among first-time mothers was about as high in importance as a life task could get. First-time mothers needed reassurance that their decision to feed their babies formula was not going to be "bad" for the baby and that they were not being "bad mothers" in making this decision. And because the "gold standard" for feeding infants was widely considered to be breast milk, messages reassuring new mothers about the similarities between formula and breast milk seemed in order.

Experienced mothers, by contrast, had far more confidence in themselves as mothers; their basic sense of security in the mothering role allowed them to comfortably consider other options in infant nutrition as those needs arose. These findings both highlighted the challenges of attracting new mothers to formula and showed why marketing to mothers of second or later children should be different and less focused on security than marketing to first-time mothers.

OTC Pharma

Over-the-counter drugs that aim to alleviate or cure illnesses often need to appeal to consumers whose product searches are driven by strong security motivation. Underlying the experience of suffering from any illness is an emotional vein of fear of getting sicker rather than better. In this way, selecting and taking medication can be as much a story about how consumers can avoid becoming sicker as it is about how they can get relief from the condition they already have.

Our conversations with consumers on behalf of an OTC drug maker suggested that in many cases the insecurity that dominates emotional discomfort during an illness could be traced to childhood. The feeling we have (no matter what our age) that only our parents inherently "know" what to do in the face of an illness was apparent in the emotional underpinnings of product choices for a majority of respondents. And of course, buried in some of our childhood memories is the fairly common admonition that if we didn't do what we were told, we'd end up getting worse. And then where would we be?

It seemed that having an illness made the average consumer feel vulnerable, perhaps even childlike. Armed with this knowledge, our client felt confident going to market with a strategy that focused on the possibilities for a negative outcome if consumers did not take a drug as soon as possible and in full compliance with the directions for its use.

Takeaways

1. The drive toward security is an instinctive one; it is the most basic of all the motivations.
2. The longing for security is the gateway motive to every other human motivation. We must feel secure before we can work toward any other goals.

3. Unlike with all other motives, the fulfillment of the security motivation very often takes the form of "negative reinforcement," of freeing consumers from ideas or situations that make them worried or frightened.

4. Security-oriented consumers long for safe, predictable relationships with products and brands that put their worries to rest.

5. Marketing to security needs accordingly most often takes the form of reassurance that "bad things" won't happen.

6. Messages should focus on a sense of control that defends consumers against uncertainty and fear.

7. Consumers in the midst of transformative life changes are also highly motivated to seek security through the products and brands they choose as they work to combat the inherent insecurity that uncertainty and change bring with them. Becoming a parent for the first time is a classic example of such a life change.

8. Tough economic times can be a great opportunity to build product and brand loyalty through delivery of relief from life's insecurities. Consumer benefits delivered in times of crisis are more indelible than those delivered in times of prosperity.

9. Every product or brand is involved in security marketing to some degree as brands seek to build and maintain a relationship of trust with their consumers, a relationship that is based on peace of mind, freedom from worry, and unassailable credibility.

This page intentionally left blank

CHAPTER 5

The Identity Motive

Margaret Mead, the renowned American cultural anthropologist, used to tell her students that they should always remember that they were absolutely unique—just like everyone else. This observation by Mead is a favorite of mine, since it carries the promise of the paradoxical journey we *all* undertake: The path to finding ourselves.

As we travel the path on this long (actually never-ending) journey, we are propelled by the motivation to discover and to create a unique identity that is ours alone. When we begin to differentiate ourselves from others, we put in motion our desire to see ourselves—and our desire for the world to see us—as each a unique individual, with unique preferences, styles, traits, and abilities. It is an individual quest, but it's also a familiar process every one of us undertakes, by and large in the same way and in the same time frame.

Along the path of this journey, we are marked and changed by a host of powerful actions and emotions, and they become part of our journey as well. Our personal identities are shaped by the turns we've taken at each fork in life's road and, of course, by all the paths not taken. Throughout the journey we remain in flux, as we take in new ideas and preferences and let others go. As our external circumstances change, our identities change as well: the birth of a child, the death of a parent, new loyalties taken on and others surrendered. At every turning point in our lives a new "self" evolves.

Who am I?

This question is one of the core existential issues that demarcate the journey toward meaning and purpose in our lives. Within us all lies a deep yearning to know and to be known, both to ourselves and to those around us.

As we establish awareness and understanding of "who we are," we come to feel at home in our own skin, knowing—and, hopefully, loving—who we are, where we've been, how we've gotten there, and where we think we're headed next. Consciousness of our own uniqueness lets us know and appreciate what we offer that no one else can, and lets us celebrate our wonderful differences. "Know thyself" said Socrates, and that's an excellent summary of the quest for identity.

As we move through life, we develop and express our various and evolving "selves" through the consumer goods we use and display. It's no secret that the products we choose publicly telegraph our identity (or at least the part of it that we're willing to show to the world). The things we buy, use, wear, drive, or otherwise "consume" are important social cues, signals about who we are. In the business of marketing, understanding the identity of one's customers and prospects has heightened utility because the drive to express personal identity explains a lot about purchase decisions: If we "are what we eat," we correspondingly "buy what we are" (or at least what we want to be).

Finding Ourselves

We begin the process of discovering and defining ourselves as infants, as we work at discerning what is "me" and what is "not me." Nursing babies view every element of that activity, including their mother's arms and breasts, as part of themselves. At this stage, they are at the center of their known universe, both alpha and omega. Beyond infancy, we remain "egocentric" for a great many years, and in some respects and contexts, we stay that way forever.

As we progress in our journey toward ourselves, we become aware first that we are separate beings, but we continue to have magical beliefs about our abilities and powers. For example, Jean Piaget, the noted student of thinking in early childhood, observed that into middle childhood children still think the moon and the sun "follow" them as they walk. In these early years, our concepts of ourselves, like our concepts of everything else, are concrete and built upon observable facts. Preschoolers, for example, may say when they describe themselves: "I have blue eyes," "I run really fast," or "I'm the tallest kid in my class." In every case, our sense of self hardly extends at all beyond what we are physically and what we do behaviorally.

Throughout childhood, the markers of identity are often determined for us by others, chiefly by our parents, but also by teachers, coaches, and members of our extended family. Identity development throughout this period proceeds as self-expression takes place across changing situations, changing roles, relationships, and responsibilities. But our pursuit of the full sense of Socrates's dictum awaits the intellectual developments that mark (or perhaps actually propel) the onset of adolescence.

Adolescence and Psychosocial identity

In an often jarring transition, we then begin to move into the emotionally chaotic and transformative stage of puberty when everything we thought we knew about ourselves comes into question. In this stage of adolescence— the term comes from the Latin word *adolescere*, which means "to ripen" or "to grow up"—the chief focus of our intellectual emotional and social lives is the establishment of a personal identity that is uniquely ours, a particularity that is mapped across needs and wants, tastes and preferences, habits, beliefs, and values.

Constructing an identity in the full sense of the word is a complex undertaking for which there is no blueprint. It's akin to walking the high wire without a net; there's a great deal at stake, and the consequences of a misstep are very high. The challenges of identity formation in adolescence lead the typical teenager through a labyrinth of "trials" where tastes and styles, values and allegiances pass through their lives like stations seen from a fast-moving express subway—each is there for a moment and gone the next. (This is what makes marketing to "teen fads" a dizzying challenge of timing.) We emerge from our adolescence with the paint beginning to dry on a core set of tastes, styles, and values that will stay with us throughout our lives.

Erik Erikson,[1] sometimes referred to as the "architect of identity," developed a theory of identity formation that is still influential to this day. Though he may be best remembered for coining the phrase "identity crisis," the Pulitzer prizewinner's contribution to psychology went much further than that.

Stages of Emotional Life

Erik Erikson contended that human development occurs in eight stages. He was one of the first theorists to suggest that development continued throughout our lives, rather than ending in childhood.

- Basic trust vs. basic mistrust: infancy through 1 year
- Autonomy vs. shame: early childhood until about 3 years old
- Purpose or initiative vs. guilt: between 3 and 6 years old
- Competence or industry vs. inferiority: school-age, 6–11 years
- Fidelity or identity vs. role confusion: adolescence, 12–18 years
- Intimacy vs. isolation: young adulthood, 18–35
- Generativity vs. stagnation: middle adulthood, 35–64
- Ego integrity vs. despair: 65 and older

Erikson laid the groundwork for much of our understanding of what it means to form a sense of identity. In his account of human psychological development (see side bar), he proposed that we move through a series of complex stages of psychological development, each presenting us with an intellectual and emotional "crisis" to be met and mastered. Erikson discussed how unresolved or incomplete passage though the crisis of one or more developmental stage can have important psychological consequences for us, ranging from a minor, gnawing sense of discomfort to more serious emotional maladjustment.

Eriksen locates the process of identity formation in two "identity crises" in his theory of developmental stages, and he places these crises in early and late adolescence. The first of these, which he calls "identity vs. role confusion," involves the challenge of developing a unique sense of self while at the same time fitting in or being accepted by others. The second phase of identity formation revolves around the crisis he calls "intimacy vs. isolation" and concerns an individual's ability to maintain his personal sense of self while developing an almost selfless sense of intimacy with loved ones, including eventually life mates.

Unlike Freud, Erikson argued that social and cultural forces work alongside psychosexual ones to make significant contributions to the formation of our identities. Also unlike Freud, but in agreement with Maslow, Erikson based his theories about the development of identity on his studies of healthy people rather than of neurotic or mentally ill patients.

The Look of Adolescence through the Years

Every generation of teens seeks a new look to define its unique taste and style. Flappers, beatniks, and hippies were just three of the more distinctive styles in the twentieth century.

Essentially, as we interact with the world at the beginning of adolescence, we suddenly look, sound, and feel markedly different than we ever have before. See box text and images for looks adopted by adolescents in the last century.

We experiment with different tastes and values. We discover who we "really are" by trying on different roles in various settings and also by experimenting with various group identifications that can define where we fit in. We may feel at times like strangers—certainly to our parents but often even to ourselves. A new level of self-awareness begins to emerge as we distill our personal, social, and cultural identities from the experiments of adolescence. We achieve—we hope—a state of being true to one's self, complete with an understanding of who we are and who we want to be, and a sense of who we can—and *cannot*—be or become.

Peer groups play an enormous role in the path to identity formation during this period. While the social groups to which we belong are an influence on us over the course of our lives, in adolescence those peer groups have more impact than at any other times. Because peer group identification and acceptance play such an important role in identity formation during adolescence, we are likely during this period to modify our speech, dress, behavior, choices, and activities in potentially radical ways to become more similar to the peers with whom we seek to identify. Caught in the murky time when our bodies are mostly grown but our emotions are not, we may experiment with rebellion against parental values and lifestyles. Some of the choices we may make to signal solidarity with peer groups can be harmful or dangerous (using tobacco, alcohol, and illicit drugs or engaging in sexual and even violent behavior, to name a few).

Acutely judgmental, we pass through a period of nearly relentless self-analysis as we navigate the treacherous waters between fitting in and standing out. This delicate balance between identity and identification, between being unique and being accepted by our social groups may be an acutely felt challenge of adolescence. However, it will in some form be with us for the rest of our lives.

The Social, Reflected Self

Another important contribution to our understanding of the idea of the self comes from George Herbert Mead, who presented the self and the mind in terms of a social process. Mead distinguished between the "me" and the "I" in our sense of self; the "me" is created as we perceive and take in the collective attitudes of others toward us, and the "I" is the internal sense of self we create in part in response to the others in our social world.

During adolescence we invest a great deal of energy in creating the presentational "self" or "me" we want others to see. We try on different personae (an appropriate term, from the Latin word for "mask"), and as we do so, a delicate dance develops between our subjective identity and our reflected social identities. We refine our view of ourselves based on that external feedback, and that new, refined self is again reflected back to us socially. We move in and out of group affiliations for the rest of our lives although never again with the same poignancy or sense of urgency. No other passage in life's journey carries with it the huge swings from exquisite pleasure of acceptance and intense pain of isolation or rejection. (All this while fighting acne; no wonder it's such an exhausting time.) By the time adolescence subsides, we have established an enduring sense of "me" and "I" that we can count on to be there for us even as new thoughts, events, and people move in and out of our lives and serve to further refine and define who we are.

Needless to say, the marketer who can fulfill consumers' identity motivations by acknowledging and speaking to their hard-won identity by "understanding" their "unique and different" lifestyles and product needs, may gain significant advantage in the marketplace versus A "one size fits all" approach. And when marketing to adolescents, this gesture of identity acknowledgment becomes not just an opportunioty but a necessity.

The Building Blocks of Identity

Our identity—our uniqueness, our individuality, and the way we express these qualities—is often captured with the label of "personality." Personality traits are concepts designed to summarize and describe our ways of being in the world, our styles of action, how we express our attitudes, how we act upon our values. Traits can function as predictive mechanisms; for example, we can predict that an outgoing person will probably have a good time at a party, even if the crowd consists mostly of strangers. As such, personality traits are very important for marketers to study in that they can predict what we buy and where we buy it, our political affiliations, and even the pets we choose.

Personality is an enormous field of study in psychology and is beyond the scope of our discussion here. Our interest in identity formation and the identity motive is primarily focused on the motivating drive to live one's life as an expression of a unique individual personality, whatever that might be. But our interest in marketing generally and the power of personality in predicting *where* best to market a product (and sometimes also how to present it) suggest that we must cover personality theory at least in overview.

What we call personality is actually a compilation of character traits and behavioral patterns that remain relatively consistent over time. Understanding an individual's personality can help predict his or her behavior. This predictability is important: it lets other people know what to expect from us and creates a level of comfort and confidence that we will behave in a predictable way as we react to people, situations, tasks, and challenges.

Big Five

Roughly forty years ago, scientists at the National Institute of Mental Health identified a core list of five personality features that appear to be stable over the life span and are adequate for describing most of the major differences in personality. Since that time, research has also shown that about half of the differences between individuals on these five dimensions can be linked to heredity. These concepts are commonly referred to as the Big Five personality traits.[2] Here's a condensed version:

- *Openness to experience*: (inventive/curious vs. consistent/cautious). Involving the relative *presence or absence* of: emotion, adventure, unusual ideas, curiosity, appreciation for art, and variety of experience; preference for novelty, imagination, independence versus preference for consistency, prudence, and caution.
- *Conscientiousness*: (efficient/organized vs. easygoing/careless). Being organized and dependable, planful rather than spontaneous, efficient rather than easygoing.
- *Extraversion*: (outgoing/energetic vs. solitary/reserved). Energetic, assertive, sociable, and talkative versus independent, self-sufficient, and reserved.
- *Agreeableness*: (friendly/compassionate vs. analytical/detached). Compassionate, cooperative, trusting, helpful, as opposed to objective, dispassionate, and withholding.
- *Neuroticism*: (sensitive/nervous vs. secure/confident). Sensitive, emotional, insecure, labile, and impulsive versus stable, confident, and secure.

Combinations of these five dimensions create the multitude of individual personalities we encounter and experience. In each case and with each person, we may also encounter varying levels of the drive to *express our personalities*, to be the way we want to be, act the way we naturally would, and express the personal taste and style and values that are ours alone. These wide differences in the personality of consumers are important for marketers to understand because they generate wide differences in how consumers process marketing messages; this in turn shapes how marketers should communicate with consumers. Consumers who have an openness to experience are obviously great candidates for innovative and new products, being "novelty junkies" as they are. Conscientious consumers will want to hear how your products are carefully made, or will help them have conscientious lifestyles. The extraverted consumer is far more likely to want to listen to your marketing story if its about people playing together. Agreeable consumners may need less convincing overall, while neurotic customers will feel you understand them if you market to their identities as security driven (!)

For a more holistic sense of the identity motive, let's look at a portrait of one consumer, a person who is particularly concerned with her identity and with having marketers recognize her identity.

Consumer Portrait: The Drive for Identity

Karen likes to see the world almost as a stage that offers her endless possibilities to discover and express who she is. She reflexively resists being a conformist; in fact, resisting arbitrary social norms *is* the norm for her. Karen wants to look, act, and feel as though she is making her own rules.

Karen built her independent photography business by creating wedding portraits that outdid the staged, hyperformal style of the typical wedding portfolio. She has expanded her business by continuing to add her own perspective on new ways to imagine how photographs should look and by being especially sensitive to the particular tastes and styles of her clients regarding the important issue of wedding photos.

The birth of her first child brought enormous changes to Karen's personal identity. She was now a member of the very large group called "mothers," with the shared interests and needs of that group. Though she had less time to seek unique products, Karen nonetheless put her own stamp on mothering. She used online sources extensively; though she still prefers artisanal products, she will take the ones she can find in her local grocery.

As a consumer, Karen is drawn to products that are especially well-suited to her personal tastes and style. She is drawn to products that project a sense of personality, that have a commitment to uniqueness in styling. She also enjoys products that can be customized to fit even better with her needs and her values. She also prefers to do business with retailers and service organizations projecting a commitment to understanding their customers and whose offerings reflect that they "get" her. As a marketer, you can recruit Karen to buy your products by being committed to understand and respond to the needs and wants that define who she is as a person and by telling her that in your marketing communications.

Varieties of Consumer Identity Statements

Individuals can fulfill their identity motivation partly through the things they buy. The products we bring into in our lives can confirm and support how we see ourselves. They can set us apart from some people and connect us more closely with others. The products we choose can announce who we are and let others see what matters to us.

There are several paths consumers can take to express their identity through the products they choose. They can avoid similarity by not purchasing or wearing things they see on others. They may wish to express an identity that includes being *like* certain groups of others (identification), or they can also conform to nonconformity, as when they choose products that are embraced by a group of consumers who collectively see themselves as "non-conformist."

Consumer Need for Uniqueness (CNFU)

Consumers exhibit varying degrees of the need to feel unique, to define themselves primarily in contrast to others by focusing on how different and unique they are. One scale to measure this desire is called the Consumer Need for Uniqueness or CNFU.[3]

At one extreme on the CNFU scale are people who desire to be "just like everybody else"; at the other extreme, there are people who want to be as different and distinct from others as it is possible to be. Students of the CNFU have discussed how it may be that expressing a desire for uniqueness through one's posessions and mode of dress if a far safer way than expressing it through behavior—where deviance in the social group poses far greater risk of ostracism.[4] Typically, people seeking strongly to feel recognized in their individuality respond well to identity marketing

Brand Identification

One category of groups to which almost all of us belong—sometimes without realizing it—is that of brand user groups. I have friends who wear Rolex, Timex, Swatch, or no watches at all. They're about as different from one another as those brands. I know people who wear jeans from Carhartt, from Gap, and from Levis, and again, some of the more differentiating qualities of these brand images are ones that also describe those people. My friends who still hang on to their inner hippie persona continue to sport Birkenstocks.

Perhaps no material possession is more widely recognized as a projection of personality than the automobile. Ranging from performance focus to image focus, from counterculture to understated wealth, from pragmatic to environmentally concerned, owning a car like a BMW, Lexus, VW Beetle, Honda, or Prius can be a significant statement of the owner's identity. And marketers of these brands are highly aware of the cars' identity badge value, and they often begin their advertising with an allusion to a value system that describes who the car is for. Dodge invites drivers to "grab life by the horns"; BMW offers the "ultimate driving machine"; Jaguar tells us that it embodies "the art of performance," and Porsche tells us that "there is no substitute."

"Cult" Products: Building an In-Group

At the extreme end of identity-focused marketing are products that offer opportunities for exclusive in-group" self-definition to consumers who adopt them. Such "cult" brands can offer users the double benefit of providing both a unique identity *and* a sense of exclusivity, in a rather fascinating example of being unique together.

Cult brands bring together folks who are happy to belong to a band of outsiders and who in the process form a band of insiders with exclusive knowledge about the superiority of their product. Apple is an example of a brand that has established cult status among its users by contrasting them to the outsider group of IBM format users. Recent Apple ads actually personify these two user groups in an interaction that makes it all too clear that Apple users are "cool"—innovative, creative, laid back—while IBM users are clueless—not even aware of the disadvantages of their product choice.

In some cases, the loyal fans of cult products adopt their own style of dress, language, and even literal badges or symbols of membership. Harley Davidson does a great job of inspiring this level of allegiance. Beyond the utility of those motorcycles, Harley offers an enticing group identity the company's customers are proud to embrace (recall the Harley anthem that we presented in introducing Intrapsychic motives). And interestingly, this brand appears to succeed at building brand identification across different groups, from aging, affluent baby boomers to young motorcycle riders seeking to upgrade to a "serious" motorcycle. In both cases, the "young, tough outlaw" image drives the brand appeal, and for both groups the image is much more an aspiration than a reality. Harley again does a great job at offering that promise of distinction in its tagline: "We're all created equal. After that, it's up to you."

Because cult products are so emotionally appealing, they don't usually need to compete on price. They're not commodities; they're irreplaceable. And they are perfect just the way they are.

Today's "Parrot Head" fans of Jimmy Buffet form a kind of community and spend plenty of money (estimates of Buffet's yearly income: $100 million) to travel the country to be a part of that unique and highly bonding experience, just as "Deadheads" in my day (and, okay, some are still doing it today!) traveled the circuits with their favorite band.

Today's highly connected culture offers endless opportunities to create small cult brands and to reach and develop an audience for them. Consumers tune in to satellite radio stations devoted to their niche point of view and focused on their iconic content and brands. Mail advertising can target consumers using nine-digit zip codes classified by the typical attitudes and lifestyles of people who live in them. And e-mail advertising can target consumers individually based on traits revealed by their online browsing histories.

Consumers of cult products are usually very loyal. Because their product actually defines them in some way, there really are no competitors to lure believers away. Just try to get an avowed Apple user to consider other PC options, and you'll see what I mean.

Ironically, consumers who have chosen a brand for its uniqueness may actually be lost to the brand if it becomes successful. By the time most of us get around to adding kale and chia to our smoothies, identity-driven consumers formerly in the "kale cult" are already off to the next new thing. And they're not telling anybody what that is. I once worked on a project where the client was trying to understand how teens defined "cool" and learned that an important part of something being really cool was that "most people don't know what it is." A new cult band would instantly lose its cachet if (shudder) one's father came home with a T-shirt featuring the band's name.

Marketing to Everyone's Identity Motive

Identity motivation doesn't only operate among consumers who are in search of brands that will help enhance or define their identities. People of all types will appreciate a company that seems concerned about understanding and meeting their particular needs—thereby *recognizing and validating* their identities by giving them just what they want in the way they want and when and where they want. Most all consumers like to feel as if understanding and meeting their needs and wants is important to the companies with which they do business.

In this light, marketers of any brands are well advised to practice the kinds of corporate behaviors that will appeal to their consumers identity motivations simply as a matter of good business. This approach will build positive emotional connections just as effectively with consumers who are, for example, most in search of a sense of mastery or who primarily seek a sense of achievement.

Basic guidelines for marketing to consumers focused on identity include the following:

Do your homework: Understanding your consumers' wants and needs, including identifying distinctive subgroups, is always a good idea.

Choose your channels: You say something to consumers without even trying to when you reach them in their specialty publications or on their niche media channels.

Solicit input: When the makers of Doritos reach out to users to create a new flavor, they get a lot of mileage from signaling that they care about who the customers are and what they want.

Make a statement: Signal shared values to consumers who care about some particular activity, for example, choose to sponsor the Olympic Games or the X Games or the Special Olympics or perhaps the Westminster Kennel Club Dog Show.

Identity-Based Marketing Principles

This involves the following principles:

Understanding. Basic marketing to consumers focused on identity motivation involves the promise that you understand "your" consumers better than anyone else. Communication should align with target consumers' language as much as possible (though be careful of inexpert attempts to be "hip," which will fail). Talking to consumers in a consistently developed voice makes a distinctive impression.

Specificity. A corollary of understanding your consumer is that you can conform very precisely to their specific needs and wants—that you can offer them just what they want or need, when and where they want it, in a way that speaks to who they are and what they value.

Customization. Marketing to the identity motive succeeds well with products that offer high levels of customization and with products that come in a wide range of alternative versions. Many new products today are offered to consumers in a "design your own" format that accomdates a range of taste and style choices. Established brands such as Nike have also come to provide a high level of customization. Retailers like Amazon.com and eBay succed in part because they do a great job of enabling their customers shop and compare endlessly—until they find just the product they are looking for.

Brand Identification Marketing

Not all brands have the outsider/insider edginess, the devoted fan base, or the niche category positioning to have cult status. But many do share qualities that make it possible for them to engage in marketing based on brand identification. Think of any product where attachment is more than a matter of judgment, and you are likely to be looking at a brand encouraging the emotional bonds of consumer identification. Good examples here are Tide (who switches detergents?), Crest (its either "your toothpaste or it's not"), and Hellman's (isn't it the only real mayonnaise?). To build a program that encourages and strengthens brand identification, a few ground rules are worth bearing in mind:

Have a distinctive image. A brand identity that consumers can really connect with needs to be clear and well-defined. Envision this identity as if it were a person—a person with his or her own values that define who he or she is. Let your brand stand for its ingredient provenance, its production quality, its distinctive taste, or its unattainable performance, and you will invite consumers to connect your identity with theirs.

Take a stance of exclusivity. Identity-driven brands become the only brand their users see. Coke drinkers don't even turn their heads to see the Pepsi display, Grape Nuts eaters aren't in the market for another cereal to eat, and Boar's Head meats don't have to compete on price or variety among their core user group. Assume your users might walk away empty-handed if your brand isn't available.

Reward loyalty and commitment. Acknowledge your consumers' loyalty and offer rewards for it. I recently received an "appreciation pack" from the maker of my car brand offering me a range of small gifts I could choose "for being a part of our family for over 10 years," and I will reflect fondly on that brand every time I use one of the little gifts.

Encourage advocates willing to "spread the gospel." The most valuable members of a brand franchise are the "evangelists" who spread the word about a brand with the credibility and influence of personal acquaintanceship. Brands can encourage these customers to "tell a friend" and even offer rewards for those who go that extra mile to expand the circle of brand identification.

Recognizing Life Stage Identity Opportunities

We all continue to refine our identity as we move through our lives and react to new life situations. We enter new professions; we get married or divorced; we have children; we have newly emptied nests; we move to new cities or new neighborhoods with completely different character. And with these changes in circumstance comechanges in many of the ways in which we express our identities: our clothing choices, our food selections, our music and reading preferences, our work styles, and our play styles. Marketers may successfully turn to identity-focused messages when they offer products to people who are at any of these majorchanges in their identity: newly graduated, first home buyer, newly married, new parent, new golfer—the list goes on.

Most Effective Identity Marketing Messages

Successful marketing to consumers seeking to express their personal tastes and styles can be grounded in a celebration of difference:

- Who cares what everybody else thinks/wears/uses/drives?
- You're not a cookie. You don't need a cookie-cutter approach.
- No lemmings allowed.
- Never follow.
- Why be normal when you can be spectacular?
- This is not your mother's/father's...
- You broke the mold, and now so have we.

Identity marketing can also succeed by focusing on the idea that *the brand understands the consumer's uniqueness:*

- It takes one to know one/ we're different, just like you.
- We get you—you should get us.
- For people who...(be specific but idiosyncratic: "eat cold pizza for breakfast").
- Experience the unexpected.

Finally, marketing to the identity motive can be structured around a product's *customizability:*

- Available any way you want it ("Have it your way").
- There are 1000 ways to make a table—and you can choose any one of them.
- You select the transmission, you select the seating, you choose a paint style...
- Most people can't even imagine this, but you can

Identity Case Studies

Beer

There are few iconic brand "badges" as strong, emotionally resonant, and symbolic as the beer brand we choose when we drink socially as adults. And beer marketing clearly emphasizes how drinking beer is about lifestyle, about priorities, and about connecting with the important people in our lives. The choice of a beer brand can help tell a story of who we are and what is important to us.

Although we might be peripherally be aware of its "special" ingredients or its manufacturing process, we really choose our beer brand based on its symbolic values, and we also interpret social signals about personality, attitudes, or lifestyles from other beer drinkers around us: down-to-earth Bud Drinkers, discriminating Heineken drinkers, or cutting-edge connoisseurs of microbrew brands.

As one study of ours showed, the appeal of a beer brand can depend less on a narrative about its taste or ingredients than on the appeal of its "heritage story," that is, on the tale about where it was created, and *why* it was made in a specific way (as opposed to *how* it was made).

For example, a client of ours had a new microbrew that was made with a very special brewing process. The company's marketers wanted to talk in detail about how special this process was and how much difference it made in the taste and drinking experience of the new beer. By the end of the research, the descriptions that emerged as most likely to attract new drinkers were those that referred in detail to the history and provenance of the special beer recipe and less to the actual details of the beer. The beer drinkers needed a legacy to connect with, a set of values and a style that they could identify with. They didn't need a brewing lesson.

Soda for Boomers

Our soft drink client was launching a new soft drink aimed at baby boomers, that huge generational cohort of people born between 1946 and 1964, now quite firmly entrenched in middle age (between 50 and 69). Our client made the understandable and logical assumption that boomers would be most interested in a new variety of cola that offered unique, age-appropriate health benefits.

But our research revealed that in trying to appeal to the aging cohort's health concerns, the manufacturer actually alienated the majority of Boomers who didn't want to be reminded that they were growing older. And our results showed that our client's brand name on a can represented a pleasant, iconic image from the teen years when a personal brand of soft drink was most often chosen. A quick return to the established brand identity platform for marketing these healthier sodas brought consumers back to the fold before it was too late.

Psoriasis

Nearly eight million Americans—more than 2 percent of the population—suffer from a kind of skin inflammation known as psoriasis. Researchers and doctors customarily define the severity of the condition in terms of how much of the body is affected. Our matrix analysis suggested another tack.

Our research revealed that what really matters to patients is the part of the body affected. Psoriasis on the hands or feet, for example, compromised patients' sense of mobility (feet) or dexterity (hands). These patients felt "trapped" and compromised and often felt like "failures."

The most emotionally impactful symptoms, however, were those that appeared on the face. Facial symptoms impacted not only how the sufferers believed others saw them, but also their own sense of personal identity.

Our research on the emotional experience of psoriasis transformed our client's communications platform from targeting a general sense of emotional distress to a highly targeted message that focused on treatment for the most psychologically sensitive areas of suffering: offering a renewed sense of empowerment for sufferers whose hands and feet were afflicted with the disease and a promise of regaining personal identity for those affilicted on the face.

Takeaways

1. The consumer goods we purchase are often key markers of our identity: we often buy what we are, and we often become what we buy.
2. When those pursuing the identity motive embrace a product or brand as a key component of their identities (who they are "down deep"), they can be unbelievably loyal and place far less importance on price.
4. Take great care in determining the "voice" of your product or brand. Those motivated by seeking identity relate to those expressions of your brand personality more than other groups.
5. Peer group marketing can be an effective variety of identity marketing among consumers who identify themselves with groups that are outside the mainstream.
6. Choose channels carefully when marketing to identity: your choice makes a statement about who you think they are based on where you think you'll find them.
7. When consumers are guided by the identity motive, they can have very strong opinions on what they want and how they want it, and they really want to be heard. Ask them. Thank them. Use them.
8. Iconic "rebel" evangelists can help you market your brand to those focused on the identity motive; they love to be associated with people, personalities, and ideas that stand out from the crowd.

CHAPTER 6

The Mastery Motive

The final motivational domain in the intrapsychic column is the mastery motive; it is focused on our desires to reach our full potential as individuals, to make the most of our talents, and to realize our skills and abilities to their fullest.

The drive toward mastery propels us toward the rewards of feeling strong and capable, skilled and talented. The pursuit of mastery can evokes in us the qualities of passion and persistence.

Mastery motivations make their appearance in areas of our lifestyle where we have successfully navigated the two intrapsychic stages that precede mastery: security and identity. Before we can aspire to be masterful in any particular area of our lives, we first need to be basically *secure* in that area so that we can develop a unique, distinctive *identity* that reflects our unique tastes, styles, and values. With that secure identity in place, we can work to discover and develop the qualities that mean the most to us, and to perfect the skills we excel at.

As an intrinsic force, the drive toward mastery is the capstone of our desire to feel good about who we are. The pursuit of mastery lifts us toward self-actualization, toward being someone who pursues excellence as its own reward, learns for the sake of learning, and does for the sake of doing. Feelings of mastery bring the satisfaction that comes from striving mightily to improve, the delight that comes from knowing we have done our very best, and the pride of knowing that our best is—by our own personal standards—excellent.

As a fundamentally internal journey, striving toward mastery is primarily about discovering what we're good at. It's about managing our sense of self as our capabilities and interests expand. Ultimately, striving for mastery is about finding, nurturing, and celebrating the best of what makes us "us."

Inner Journey

The Mastery motive calls us to set our sights on a vision of ourselves that embodies our hopes and dreams for who we would like to become, tempered by our perceptions and convictions of who we think we can realistically be. This vision of an idealized self can fuel us to go for it, stretching toward our vision with all of our mental, physical, and emotional resources. Fulfilling the mastery motive leads us to deliver the ultimate high five: the one we give ourselves.

Working toward mastery involves the sequence of getting good, getting better, and then becoming as good as we can be. While there may be competition involved in the journey to mastery, our own evaluations are most important and are generally made against an *internal* set point. Mastery is about our own progress toward excellence. The world may or may not embrace our objectives or appreciate our performance. But when mastery is the aim, external endorsements are of lesser consequence.

Mastery versus Achievement

It's important at the outset of our discussion of mastery to distinguish it from the achievement motivation. An individual striving toward achievement can look superficially very much like one seeking mastery: both will have similar high performance goals and experience much the same joy in meeting them. The important distinction is that mastery—as an intrapsychic motive—focuses on *how the individual feels subjectively about themselves* while achievement is typically measured against external objective standards.

A job well done, for example, can fulfill mastery or achievement motives or both. When the pleasure in results is viewed by the individual attaining them as a reflection of the skills of the individual, then the mastery motivation is in play. When the pleasure is focused upon the quality of the results measured against an external standard of excellence, then the achievement motive is being fulfilled. A perfect example of this distinction drawn from the real world arose when Olympic officials a few years ago decided to ban a new swimsuit technology that allowed swimmers to swim faster. The judgment here was clearly that the sport should be about mastery of the sport by the Olympic athletes and not just about better times in the races. It's important to keep in mind that striving to fulfill the mastery motivation does not need to take place in isolation from other motivations—even achievement motivation. Students seeking mastery won't refuse a good grade or a public commendation; employees won't turn down a pay raise, bonus, or promotion nor would they reject a special parking place for "employee of the month." Athletes wouldn't refuse a medal, a record, or a championship ring. And politicians motivated by seeking mastery would probably enjoy a ticker tape parade as much as the next guy. Being motivated by seeking mastery just means that those external validations of success *aren't the reason* we engage in those activities in the first place. Those external payoffs are nice additions to accompany the real goal: getting better at something we love to do.

Development of the Mastery Motive

The drive toward mastery begins early in life, not long after we gain the distinctly human capacity to self-reflect. While we are infants, our mastery motives are undifferentiated from achievement and esteem motives, as we strive to "make things happen" in our world and also to gain positive feedback from those around us.

Our nascent sense of mastery is very much tied up with feelings control over our environment, the enjoyment of performing any particular behavior, and the pleasure in its outcome, accompanied by the feeling that "I made that happen." Through our initial experiments in making things happen, we acquire the first and most important element of the mastery motive: feelings of self-efficacy. We do something, get a result, do it again and watch for a better result, do it a different way and look for corresponding improvement, and so on.

Relatively early on, babies and toddlers experience great and obvious delight when they make things happen through their own efforts and concentration. For a vivid demonstration, watch the intensity and dedication babies bring to turning themselves over, beginning to crawl, balancing first, and soon, walking under their own power. Recognizing that actions produce outcomes and taking joy in making the outcomes happen, toddlers are unstoppable and persistent, regardless of the falls or "failures" they experience along the way. Watching themselves get there generates joy in the effort itself. That's the essence of fulfillment of the mastery motive.

All of this playful experimentation with our sense of agency propels us through toddlerhood until, at around kindergarten age, when we begin to develop a real capacity for self reflection. At that point, the possibility of a true sense of mastery emerges. Without any visible result, without anyone's approval, we finally become able to look at our own behavior and to give ourselves an "A for effort". This form of pleasure in ourselves quickly becomes self-perpetuating: the better we feel about the results of our actions in any one area, the greater our overall sense of self-efficacy. And then the harder we'll work at mastering the next thing. That upward spiral of internally felt success is what produces the mastery orientation in adulthood.

To really appreciate the power of our early drive toward mastery, take a look at the array of devices available to parents to childproof their homes. Millions of dollars are spent by parents trying to defend against the inexhaustible inventiveness and curiosity of children as they energetically set out to discover what's in light sockets, what household cleaners might taste like, and all the many wonderful objects, including pets, that could be flushed down a toilet.

Try and Try Again

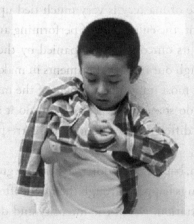

Educational researchers at the Urban Institute tell us how all that painful-looking trial and error in childhood fuels a developing sense of mastery:

"A healthy sense of mastery motivation grows in part through trying and failing at complex tasks. For toddlers, this may be getting into a shirt with head and arms in all the right holes. For elementary-school-age children, perhaps it's long division. At a certain point, we're actually helping our children more by letting them struggle into garments, or repeatedly redo their arithmetic, rather than swooping in to manage the roadblock for them."[1]

The years of middle childhood are jam-packed with a mixture of mastery and achievement motivations as children move through the elementary school years and all of the learning these involve. From adding to algebra, from foursquare to soccer, from chopsticks to Chopin, the years of middle childhood are filled with opportunities to master. Research on teaching methods suggests that delivering messages of approval by emphasizing the mastery displayed in a *task well done* rather than focusing primarily on the external achievement itself is the best way to build a healthy sense of self-efficacy in children, and it is the best way to fuel a continuing eager pursuit of learning.

As they enter adolescence, young people focus more and more on goals shaped by their own evolving interests and abilities and move away from striving for adult approval. The internal fulfillment of the mastery motive takes on a larger role in teens' feelings about their skills, abilities, and accomplishments. A great deal of research tells us that teens who have a solid positive sense of mastery are likely to navigate the stormy seas of adolescence more smoothly and with fewer painful effects than those who don't have that sense of mastery.

Mastery in our DNA

In the long evolutionary path we have traversed from primate origins to modern humanity, the drive for mastery and its manifestation as insatiable curiosity has arguably played a significant role. We are inherently tinkerers, experimenters, and explorers; we are innately curious and creative by nature. Our taste for the unknown and the novel is a central element in the evolutionary bonanza that bought our tickets out of the African savannah.

Our continuing drive to understand and master the new and unknown has propelled us all the way to modern vistas that embrace Earth's poles and the deepest ocean floors, from the center of the world to the reaches of deep space. Had our ancestors not been blessed, and perhaps sometimes a bit cursed, by the desire to learn more, go farther, and investigate options, chances are we would have been extinct a long time ago. Let's face it: We are not built for speed or physical domination: we're built to think, to figure things out, and to look for new solutions to old problems. That drive to explore and to master keeps us open to serendipity, new ideas, and trying new things just for the fun of getting good at them. Our drive for mastery is behind questions like: "What happens when I do it this way?" "What else can I get from this?" or "How far can I make it go?"

If you're thinking those questions sound a lot like the toddler questions we encounter in our childproofing quest, you're right. Questions like these and the drive to answer them keep us in some ways "eternally young." And, indeed, we are functionally younger and look younger longer than other members of the animal kingdom. This brings me to the subject of neoteny. In a nutshell, neoteny explains the extended juvenile period of development of humans and what we get as a result of it. In important ways, we humans stay childlike in our outlook and orientation throughout our life span. Our childlike motivational drive for mastery "just for the heck of it" is what really stacks the deck in our favor. That is, we hold on to the curiosity and playfulness of our childhood years, for all our lives if we're lucky.

Baby Face

Neoteny, or *juvenilization*, is the retention of childhood traits into adulthood. It's a double-edged sword for us: We humans remain physically smaller and weaker into adult years than our primate cousins, but our minds stay more active and engaged than those of adults of other less "neotonous" species.

The marketplace is full of products that tap into our innate drive to solve puzzles simply for the sake of it and to acquire skills simply for the pleasure of them even when they are useless in a real-world context. If we added together the time spent solving Sudoku problems or playing "Words with Friends" we might be shocked at the magnitude of our collective playfulness. We love to solve problems and create new solutions. And we always want to know more: what we're made of and what the universe is made of. Curiosity and a drive to understand and master the unknown are the driving forces behind scientific research and other disciplines of human study. Curiosity and a drive toward mastery are tremendous resources for the marketer who is seeking to sell a new way of doing things, or a new thing to do. They are a big part of the reason you're reading this book.

Scholarship on the Mastery Motivation

Abraham Maslow argued that self-actualized people (his subjects for a large part of his work) are motivated by the desire to grow and the striving toward mastery as well as by the rewarding outcomes of personal growth and fulfillment of our potential as humans.

Robert White focused on motivations toward mastery and adaptation in his seminal article "Motivation Reconsidered: The Concept of Competence."[2] He introduced his theory of *effectance motivation*, which he defined as a "tendency to explore and influence the environment." White argued that the "master reinforcer" of higher human activities is *personal competence.*

> Only one who devotes himself to a cause with his whole strength and soul can be a true master. Mastery demands all of a person.
>
> —Albert Einstein[3]

White believed that competence motives are never fully satisfied; instead, they drive us to constantly improve ourselves and always reach for higher and more significant goals.

Susan Harter, a psychologist from Colorado working with elementary school students, developed a "mastery scale" to measure the strength of children's motivations toward mastery in classroom performance.[4] The four items on her scale are:

- Learning motivated by intrinsic drives toward curiosity (versus trying to please a teacher or to get a good grade)
- Having internal criteria for meeting tasks successfully (versus relying on external criteria like grades or praise to evaluate success)
- Feeling satisfaction from doing good work (versus from getting praise or receiving a good grade)
- Having a preference for challenging work (versus a preference for easy work)

In Harter's four dimensions we can see the faces of the Mastery motive, which drives us toward work that is interesting, challenging, personally satisfying, *and* provides an opportunity to meet personal standards of excellence.

Understanding these roots of the mastery motivation will prove helpful to the marketer who wishes to target products to this consumer motive. In particular, the work summarized here tells us one way we can harvest the energies of consumers' mastery motives is with products that

- can be enjoyed alone without a need for others involvement or appreciation,
- offer levels of complexity to be sequentially explored and mastered, and
- deliver results that are inherently rewarding.

The Mastery Orientation

All of us are activated by a pursuit of mastery at some points in our lives and lifestyles; among us are exceptionally motivated by the pursuit of mastery. When motivated by the pursuit of mastery, people cherish the feelings they get when they work hard getting better at something, and they are likely to view failures as simply opportunities to succeed by trying again and trying harder. They thrive on challenge and experience personal improvement, no matter how small, as an emotional high. When they are mastery-oriented, people typically have a very strong sense of "perceived competence" and "perceived control" when it comes to taking on challenges. They have faith in themselves, and that faith, known as "self-efficacy" in psychological terms, grows with each success. They are not looking to get lucky en route to solving a task or meeting a challenge; they expect that persistence, together with talent, will get them to their goals.

As the position of this motive at the bottom of the intrapsychic column would suggest, the mastery-orientation taps a well-developed internal reward system. Unlike situations where people are driven by high instrumental or interpersonal goals, when we are driven by the mastery motive, we value our own opinion most. At these times we know and love the sense that we're doing a good job.

Generally, when people are striving for mastery they are determined and tenacious. They succeed because they will do whatever it takes to reach a goal. Once a personal goal has been identified, those striving for mastery go for it wholeheartedly. They are capable of working very hard and with a dedication few other motivations can generate. And they can sustain this "fire in the belly" for years. Persistence, stamina, and long-range thinking are tremendous assets aroused by the mastery motivation.

When we are at work in pursuit of the sense of mastery, we can often have a laser-like focus on the task at hand. In this way, the inner drive toward mastery has a lot to do with the experience of flow, a level of engagement from the instrumental column we'll learn more about in chapter 9.

One very integral quality of those seeking mastery is what we in the field of psychology call "failure tolerance." People pursuing mastery have a much easier time accepting failure en route to ultimate fulfillment.

Since people striving for mastery feel that the circumstances of their efforts are under their control, failure becomes just another data point, a stepping-stone toward eventual success. In this way, those focused on mastery are supportive and encouraging with themselves, *especially* if they fall short of their goals. They view their missteps as natural and necessary parts of their learning curve and respond to them with redoubled efforts and redoubled persistence, not with resignation or surrender. They firmly believe that the way to get better is to continue to try.

One place where we find a high frequency of mastery orientation is in the world of sports. Professional and aspiring athletes typically spend endless hours in practice to jump further, run faster, hit harder than in their previous efforts. And while these exceptional measures may also result in a winning score or a trophy, tangible rewards are not the only things motivating most of these athletes. The experience of creating personal excellence is the goal that keeps athletes pushing their limits.

I have missed more than 9,000 shots in my career. I have lost almost 300 games. On 26 occasions I have been entrusted to take the game winning shot, and I missed. I have failed over and over and over again in my life. And that is why I succeed.

—Michael Jordan[5]

Likewise, professional musicians are often driven by the mastery motivation. Here again, we find endless hours of practice, repeating difficult passages of music until they sound just right. In his work on exceptional performance, *Outliers*, Malcolm Gladwell[6] tells us that it takes roughly *10,000 hours of practice*, which is roughly equal to a decade of practicing three hours every day, before a person can become truly exceptional at any complicated task.

The Mastery Motive at Work

We've come a long way in thinking about workplace motivation since the early studies on employee or worker motivations were conducted by Jeremy Bentham, when a "carrot or stick" view of motivation distinguished workers who respond best to tangible rewards, the carrots, such as money or power from those who responded best to avoiding negative consequences, the sticks, of demotions or job loss.

Modern day students of workplace motivation in the developed world have since recognized the motivating power of opportunities for mastery. They understand that many of us in the workplace have a thirst for novelty and challenge and will work best in inherently challenging jobs, where success is its own reward. They understand that workers are likely to fail at a job that requires performing repetitive and unchanging tasks, with the result that rote tasks in today's world of work are increasingly given over to automation or outsourced to workforces still functioning under the sway of the carrot and the stick. First-world organizations are now less hierarchal, and workers are given more room to define their own challenges, devise their own strategies, and succeed on their own terms. Studies show that employees are more often motivated by being given autonomy and by the opportunity to use and enhance their skills, strengths, and habits of mind. Not surprisingly, studies also show that intrinsically motivated workers are more creative, quicker to process information, more determined, and more persistent in the face of difficulty. For those of us marketing products Business to Business, remembering the power of worker autonomy and the prevalence of the mastery drive in the workplace may prove helpful in shaping how we design and sell our products

Consumer Portrait: Striving for Mastery

Mark lives almost all of his lifestyle under the sway of the mastery motive. He works hard at everything he does and holds himself to his own high standards regardless of whether he's at home, at work, or at play. He studied engineering in college and fell in love with the endless levels of complexity that engineering problems (always recast as "opportunities" by Mark) can present. As a professional, he views his projects as a perfect combination of problem solving and personal growth. With each new undertaking, Mark feels the invigoration of embarking on something unknown and exciting, bringing with it the chance to internalize new skills and hone his older ones.

From his earliest memories, Mark has loved the idea of setting a challenging goal and then going for it with all his might. He remembers fondly the maple tree in his parents' backyard as a childhood episode in the pursuit of mastery. As a young boy, Mark repeatedly and unsuccessfully tried to reach the lowest branches of the tree until he used a kitchen chair to bring them into reach. Over time he could scale the branch at a single jump. From there, he progressed higher and higher up the tree. When he could reliably reach the top branches, he began to time himself on how fast he could get from the porch door to the treetop. When he became as strong, nimble, and fast as he could get at that, he took to jumping from the treetop to the roof of the nearby garage. His mother put an end to that objective, which was just as well: it was time for Mark to find a new task to master.

Mark's shopping habits reflect his dedicated striving for mastery. He is interested in products and services that help him do what he wants to do to better than he currently does it. He is also very particular about who he buys from and avoids commodity producers because he prefers companies that have conceived and created their products at high levels of excellence. His Bose speakers do that. So does his Dyson vacuum cleaner.

Mark is not interested in the new version of anything just because it's new. It's important to him that the benefits he sees in the products he's drawn to contain *meaningful* advances or improvements. He's interested in innovation that allows products to change for the better. His new Mercedes brings Mark pleasure not as a status symbol but as an embodiment of an excellently conceived, beautifully realized piece of engineering from a manufacturer that continuously innovates ahead of other car makers. This car maker has created technologies such as a complex and effective new avoidance system that automatically warns Mark if he drifts out of his lane and alerts him if it detects pedestrians or cyclists on the road.

When Mark sets out to buy a new product in a category with which he's less familiar, he is likely to check *Consumer Reports* to see how objective tests rate the various brands. He is not overly concerned with price where quality is concerned; he prefers to have fewer things of very high quality and is happy to delay a purchase if it costs more than he can afford at the time. Marketers can best reach Mark with high-quality products and breakthrough innovations and by appealing to the shared appetite to reach for the best. As a marketer, you can reach Mark with an excellent product or with a product that will help him excel.

Are You Right for Mastery Marketing?

While many of the nine core motives in the MindSight Matrix can be used to focus marketing strategies for a broad range of products, the mastery motive should be more selectively utilized. Consumers who are looking for mastery tend to select items that are *themselves* masterfully conceived and produced—products of the mastery motivation on the part of the maker. Thus, consumers who are shopping for meal ingredients shop for products with an eye toward masterful meal preparation, and will also want the *products themselves* to reflect mastery: to use the finest ingredients, to be prepared in the most careful manner, to be sourced from the most authentic provenance.

Therefore, before you consider targeting mastery-oriented consumers, decide if your product is suitable for mastery marketing. The following questions can help make that decision:

- Is your product uncompromising in quality?
- Is it recognized as among the best in its class? Does that recognition come from "the cognoscenti" in your product category?

- Does your product represent the acme in standards that are relevant to your product category: technology, durability, purity, aesthetic beauty, etc.?
- Did you assemble it from the very best ingredients, using the highest production standards?
- Do you package, preserve, protect, and ship it in ways that guarantee its wonderful qualities will arrive intact in the consumer's hands?
- If your product is a service, do you perform it more carefully, more thoroughly, more expertly, or with ingredients that fit the above descriptions?

If you can answer "yes" to a good many of those questions, and "does not apply" to most of the rest, then your product may well be a good candidate for mastery marketing.

Brand and Product Mastery Marketing

When consumers are motivated to master activities in their lives, they will buy and use products that help them reach their powerful inner goals. When you promise your product will help consumers fulfill a consumer's need for a sense of mastery, you acknowledge that you understand the standards they have for themselves and you demonstrate that you understand and value what's important to them.

In targeting the mastery motive, it's important to make a sound and persuasive argument that your products have been designed for with consumers' mastery motivations in mind. As a result, owning and using these products will make consumers smarter, faster, stronger, or better in some way. Communicating a sense that "only those at a certain level" can gain access or best use the product also reinforces mastery benefits.

Mastery-oriented consumers will also respond well to messages that acknowledge the distinctive value they place upon improvement, perseverance, confidence, and endurance. They'll be interested in products that hone, fine-tune, or perfect their performance in or experience of life: nutrition bars proven to be nutritionally optimal, television sets representing the latest and best technology, clothing made from the finest materials by the most expert craftsmen, food products for "the discriminating palate." The Bose brand is a good example of effective marketing for consumers motivated by the mastery motive. Bose relies upon "better research" as a basis for its promise of product excellence, and it delivers products that meet its promises: incredibly great sounding speakers that are distinctively small in size. The brand's campaign "Better Sound through Research" in its understated way hits the bull's eye for mastery marketing.

The quintessential appeal to the mastery motive is the United States Army's "Be all You can Be" recruiting slogan. It promises enlistees a long-term vision of becoming masterful at their personal skills and abilities and of pursuing their push toward the "self actualization" that is mastery.

Sample Marketing Messages to Mastery-oriented consumers

When consumers are motivated by a longing for mastery, they are particularly attracted to the opportunity to continually improve until they reach their best. Messages like the following offer or imply ways to reach those goals.

- Great things take time.
- If it were easy, everybody would do it.
- Unstoppable. Just like you.
- Trial and error: It's a beautiful thing.
- Time to raise you're the bar again.
- Because one size never really "fits all."
- Calibrated to highest performance. Yours.
- We'll help you be your personal best.
- We're redefining excellence, just as you are.
- Research-supported excellence, time-tested performance.

Case Studies in Mastery Marketing

Recruitment

Representatives of a branch of the US military were getting considerably less traction than they would have liked on recruitment messages they had created and were testing among eligible men and women in their late teens to early twenties. Our client expected the target audience would be most driven to enlist by the satisfaction and increased self-esteem the enlistees would experience from doing their duty, doing the right thing, or answering the call to serve.

While these esteem-focused benefits were certainly in play, our motivational analysis indicated a much stronger force in play, and a much more promising marketing direction for our client. Among the young men and women we studied, the opportunity to better themselves was by far the highest motivation for serving in the military.

Rather than seeking sociomoral satisfaction, people in this target group was really drawn by the opportunity to build their talents and skills through military service: to increase their personal sense of mastery. They were most interested in enlisting when messages focused on self-improvement and training, particularly when those factors could be carried over into their civilian lives after they'd served. They were deeply drawn to the idea of "making something of themselves" and believed that the technical and vocational skills military service would impart would be the best way for them to make that self-improvement happen.

On the heels of that insight, our clients revamped their message to highlight the self-improvement priorities of their target group. They received far better results in their next concept testing. As a result, they developed the advertising and communications material with the "better yourself" message that we are all familiar with.

Birdseed

Clients wanted to understand more about the reasons why people feed wild birds. A MindSight consumer segmentation study of heavy bird food users revealed two important motivational segments.

The first consumer segment was driven by motivation that the client had long recognized and understood—that of seeking to nurture the birds and care for them as if they were pets. These bird feeders experienced emotional satisfaction in choosing the appropriate mix of seed and providing them to their "family" of birds as the birds visited their bird feeder every day (a beautiful encapsulation of the nurturance motive in action). These birdseed buyers might even recognize the individual birds that stopped by for regular visits.

Our MindSight segmentation also uncovered a second, previously unidentified group of users who were both a big surprise and a big new opportunity for our clients. These users viewed bird feeders and the birds that visited them more as an element of home décor. The birdseed and the birds who consumed it offered this group the opportunity to increase their sense of mastery—over the process of making and keeping attractive homes, complete with picturesque bird feeders and beautiful song birds in attendance.

On the strength of this motivational analysis, we also helped our clients reconceptualize their product line. For the nurturing feeders, we suggested products that focused on good nutrition, complete with varying nutritional content according to season. For the mastery-oriented feeders, we recommended birdseed that would look good in the feeder, not make a mess on the patio, and attract beautiful and unusual birds.

Innovating in Golf

Perhaps no leisure activity in life poses more potential for frustration than the game of golf. That's partly why the golf industry goes to great lengths to develop equipment to improve the golfer's game. Interestingly, we found that the measure of promise for a new idea isn't only found in the possibility of a better score for the golfer.

It turns out that golf is highly inwardly focused. The sense of mastery that comes from feeling one has played extremely well is what really keeps most golfers coming back to the game, much more so than the feelings of achievement that come from getting a really great score (though nobody would claim that a great score is not also a part of a good game). If a new idea for golf equipment seemed as if it offered an improved "tool" to help the golfer develop expertise in the game, then enthusiasm for the idea ran high. But if new golf equipment seemed to "magically" improve the scores of golfers, this objective benefit of achieving a better score, was often dismissed as "not really playing the game" or was even viewed as "cheating."

Takeaways

1. When consumers operate with a mastery orientation, they find the greatest pleasure in doing their best and in continuously making their best even better.
2. Mastery-oriented individuals can have tremendous "failure tolerance" and be relentless in pursuing a goal, regardless of setbacks. In this mindset people view failure as just another step in their journey to excel.
3. Mastery-oriented people can also be very dedicated and tenacious. They possess a determination well beyond average.

4. When people have a strong mastery orientation, they are not strongly motivated by external recognition, such as high scores or praise. They seek their satisfaction from within.

5. Mastery-oriented consumers are most likely to be drawn to products that are of the highest quality and/or offer meaningful innovations—that is, they should be made by companies that are themselves masterful.

6. Mastery-oriented consumers will be particularly interested in owning or using products that recognize a high level of expertise they already have and that help them perform better still.

This page intentionally left blank

CHAPTER 7

Introducing the Instrumental Motivations

INSTRUMENTAL
The object world

Free, Powerful

EXPECTATIONS
For the future

EMPOWERMENT

Trapped, Frustrated

Involved, Absorbed

EXPERIENCES
In the moment

ENGAGEMENT

Passive, Indifferent

Victorious, Productive

OUTCOMES
From past behavior

ACHIEVEMENT

Defeated, Pointless

The vast material culture we humans have created is one of our most distinguishing characteristics of our species. It's born from our forward-thinking imagination and our inextinguishable curiosity and is carried aloft by our aptitude with the tools we make and use. While the ability to use rudimentary tools is now understood to be shared by some other primates (and a sea otter or two), the distance between using a stick to pry termites from a nest and using scalpels and balloons to transplant a beating human heart highlights the uniqueness of our human ability to create and shape our world.

From the time each of us embarks on our very first attempts to grasp a shining object in our crib, striving to make things happen is a central part of the human experience. As we grow older, we develop and pursue goals almost all of which have to do with how skilled we are at using or managing objects: from pencils to keyboards, baseballs and bats, kitchen utensils, garden tools, cars, and, of course, our many screens.

And so the instrumental category of motivations takes us beyond the self. We fulfill our instrumental strivings through events that happen in the material world, and the outcomes of these strivings are most often visible, and our fulfillment of instrumental motives depends on getting results from the objects around us, from things we do not completely control.

As with the other columns in the Matrix, within the category of instrumental motivations, we can map three distinct forms of fulfillment, with three corresponding instrumental motivations. The most elemental instrumental striving is for empowerment, for the *potential for* taking action in the face of a challenge ("I can do this"). On the foundation of empowerment is the motive of engagement, which is fulfilled as we experience *the process* of our actions positively in the moment, immersing ourselves in the pleasurable experience of taking action ("I am really doing this well and loving it"). The final instrumental motivation involves our striving to be happy with the *outcomes* of our actions. This motive of achievement is fulfilled through getting the desired results, reaching the best outcomes ("Wow, I made that happen!").

An Instrumental Species

That the Matrix devotes an entire column to instrumental motivations underscores how important they are to us and to the generations of scholars whose work we've built upon here. Our species' survival and our place at the top of the food chain have a lot to do with the ways we interact instrumentally with the world around us. Our ability to imagine and devise instruments or tools and to shape the world around us to our benefit was probably the primary factor that took us from our original rather lowly rung on the food chain all the way to the moon (see box below).

In fact, scientists point to a series of events early on in our evolutionary history that fundamentally changed who we are and what we can do. Our large frontal lobes give us the capacity to think hypothetically—to imagine and to have the foresight that imagination can deliver. Our bipedalism gave us free hands, and our opposable thumbs gave us the dexterity needed to make and use tools. The importance of that evolutionary "perfect storm" of our imagination, foresight, bipedalism, and dexterity is the underpinning of our success.

In our shadowy beginnings, when we lived under whatever shelter we could find and travelled constantly in search of more or better food (including scavenging leftovers from the meals of stronger, more effective predators), our day-to-day existence was on a par with that of other social, hierarchical primates. Together, we searched endlessly for food, and when we ran out of food in one place, together we moved to search for it in another.

At first, like some of our higher primate neighbors, we used crude tools—adaptations of rocks and branches—to increase our efficiency in killing or gathering food. These early tools weren't anything special and didn't provide many unique or game-changing advantages, and archeological evidence confirms that we found them where we were, used them in that environment, and then left them behind until we needed a similar tool in the next place. There just wasn't enough value in our early tools to warrant the effort of taking them with us. We had yet to work our magic on them.

In Search of Our First Technology

Part and parcel of our new ability to use tools, to feed, and to clothe ourselves, and part of our migration out of the savannah was the development of one of the other most important discoveries of humankind: fire.

The ability to make fire gave us a tremendous opportunity to influence and change our environment (in this way, fire making was one of our first real technologies). With fire, we could stay warm away from our caves and shelters, so we could go wherever the best food supply was, even as it migrated. We could also begin to control the length of our days and to make time for activities not directly related to our survival—including establishing a culture—after sunset. In this way, fire gave us a prototype for a "hearth and home": small bands of our ancestors could sit around the fire at night, communing with each other and telling the stories that became the roots of human culture everywhere.

With the advantages of fire, we had the time and opportunity to create more and better tools. From there, it was just a blink of an eye, in terms of evolution, until our instrumental strivings catapulted us to the moon.

Over time we used our big brains and our superior dexterity to develop truly transformative instrumental innovations. From rocks, we graduated to clubs. From clubs we moved on to spears and crude knives. These tools allowed us to kill and butcher larger animals than we would have been able to kill otherwise since we lacked the speed, the power, and the teeth needed to bring them down on our own.

Our ability to imagine tools before they existed and to create, use, store, and protect them resulted in nothing less than—pardon the drama—world domination. Together with our butchering tools, crude ivory needles appeared, allowing us to cobble together clothes and shelters that helped us adapt to a greater range of climate conditions and environments. With protection against the cold, small bands of early humans migrated away from the African plains to the woodlands of what is now Asia and southern Europe.

Because we had hunting tools suited to the job, we didn't have to confront the problem of feeding ourselves solely on dormant and snow-covered plants in our new home. Now we could hunt. And once a population can control its food sources, it can exist anywhere.

Out of this World

The NASA program boasts some 1,800 spin-offs that have made their way into our everyday lives. The sneakers you run in today are direct descendants of the boots astronauts used to walk on the moon.

A few of the other most common instrumental inventions for which we have the space program to thank:

- Cordless tools
- Water filters
- Smoke detectors
- Computer mouse
- Invisible braces
- Scratch-free lenses
- Ear thermometers

Marketing to the Instrumental Motives

From our vantage point at the top of the food chain, we continue to experience the drives to feel capable of tackling the challenges of our lives, to make the process enjoyable, and, finally, to achieve the very best results from our actions.

As we work toward creating compelling messages, connections, and relationships with consumers motivated by instrumental strivings, it's important to remember that whatever the ultimate emotional needs are that a product may fulfill, the process of *shopping for that product* will always be driven by instrumental motivations. Consumers of all stripes want to shop efficiently and enjoyably for products and services. They want to feel they get the very best results from the purchases they ultimately make. In the brick-and-mortar marketplace, this means beautifully designed stores, well-organized shelves, and knowledgeable, available store personnel who can offer assistance to consumers who need it. Shoppers' instrumental motivation to "get the job done" will drive them out of retail settings where they feel that their time is being wasted or where they feel that they are prevented somehow from getting the best result (as in the case of an overeager sales person trying to upsell them).

Meanwhile, the interactive virtual marketplace—where a good deal of shopping takes place nowadays—creates both new opportunities and new challenges for satisfying shoppers' instrumental motives. We need to instill confidence in consumers and empower them the instant they make contact. Confusing websites or complicated products that are difficult to understand can make online consumers feel they won't be able to get the job done—and so we lose them. Similarly, arduous site navigation, ugly pages, and seemingly "hidden" information will make the shopping process unpleasant to instrumental strivers; if consumers do not feel the pleasure of engagement in their shopping environment, they will go elsewhere. Finally, being able to compare products and prices will give consumers the basis for confidence in the achievement of an outcome from their shopping efforts and will encourage them to come back and shop again.

Consumer 2.0

The demands of fulfilling consumers instrumental motivations have steadily increased as we enter the age of consumer-driven marketing, where information and innovation flow both ways (as opposed to the unidirectional messages that characterized marketing in the past). Information technology gives consumers more power than ever to fulfill their instrumental motivations in the marketplace. This pushes marketers to communicate with our empowered consumers in a new way that is built on collaboration as opposed to directives, on invitations rather than command performances, on conversations instead of pitches. We now can, and must, learn from and include our consumers in all phases of our business, from product development to placement, communications, and even our sourcing and supply chain decisions.

Meanwhile, if your product or service is designed in any way to "get stuff done" in the material world, then your marketing should focus directly on benefits that fulfill the instrumental motives. Your advertising should talk about how your products can help make consumers empowered, engaged, and high-achieving. Consumers for products with instrumental benefits will respond to messages that make them the heroes in their own lives.

Let me show you what I mean: At the forefront of this new era of the empowered consumer are some very powerful campaigns launched by very powerful brands to target confident, empowered consumers. Here are a few that do that job particularly well.

Nike

Nike's "Just Do It" campaigns have been celebrating individual achievement for 25 years now. And one look at Nike's campaign portfolio shows why: It's always the athletes, never the shoes, who have the starring roles.

No Nike campaign captures the nobility and the spirit of athleticism, determination, guts, and glory—and makes promises for fulfilling instrumental motivation—like the 2008 "Courage" campaign. If you've seen it, odds are you still remember it. But if you haven't had the pleasure, here's how it unfolds. There are no spoken words in the spot at all (only the musical score). Instead, the ad is bookended by two written phrases. The first sets up the scene in so many words: "Everything you need is already inside." Then Nike treats us to a display of what really is inside: inside world-class athletes like Michael Jordon, John McEnroe, Maria Sharapova, Mary Lou Retton (and many more), and of what really is inside all of us ordinary people who have courage, determination, and grace (and thus are clearly extraordinary in Nike's point of view).

Those vignettes come at us in rapid-fire cuts, accompanied by chanted lyrics "I've got soul but I'm not a soldier" over and over. Nike goes on to show us what "soul" really looks like, what courage and dedication and single-mindedness look like and what it means to never give up, no matter what.

The first images are of difficulties: a gymnast falls in the midst of her vault, runners double over in pain; John McEnroe sits on the court in disbelief. The images transition to triumphs: sprinters merge into graceful gazelles; hurdlers become powerful cheetahs as they charge toward their finish lines. A baby takes her first steps in her yard and an astronaut takes his first steps on the moon. All these images appear as Nike's rallying cry of "Just Do It" calls for our best efforts and assures us that we really can do anything if we have the right frame of mind.

Everything in this commercial tells us that we really do have "everything we need inside" and that all we need to do is "just do it." It positions Nike as our ally, a brand that celebrates every beautiful thing we're capable of. And just for the record, in all that empowerment, engagement, and achievement, Nike never mentions—nor does the ad ever show—the shoes.

Dove

Dove soap created one of the first and best examples of a new generation of ads that make positive promises of empowerment, telling women that they can be beautiful and indeed that they already *are* beautiful. With its "Real Beauty" campaign, now a decade old and still going strong, Dove calls for women to celebrate beauty as it exists in the "real world," not in the contrived, outdated, or airbrushed versions of femininity that are all too common in beauty product advertising.

In a particularly profound commercial, the 2013 spot called "Real Beauty Sketches," Dove asked women to describe themselves to a forensic sketch artist who drew them according to those descriptions (the artist never sees any of the women). Next, Dove asks acquaintances of those women to describe the same woman the artist just drew. Another forensic sketch is created, based on those brief eyewitness reports.

Dove got some pretty amazing results: the sketches drawn from the women's self-descriptions were invariably "fatter," "sadder," and more focused on "flaws." The bystander's version, in stark contrast, focused on the beauty of the women: the sparkling blue eyes, the high cheekbones, and so on. When Dove places the two sketches side by side, it offers women a great reality check. By the end of the spot, Dove makes the powerful assertion that "you are more beautiful than you think." In this message they empower women to practice self-care without resorting to the painful prodding of negative motivation.

And like Nike, Dove got this message across without mentioning—or even showing—the product. It's clearly a message that's taken hold: a press release from Unilever reported that "Real Beauty Sketches" was the most watched video ad of all time.[1]

Barack Obama: Yes We Can

Whatever your politics, there's no doubt that Barack Obama's 2008 presidential campaign represented a powerfully effective marketing strategy. Coming at a moment of serious national discouragement, the three words of hope and optimism—"Yes, we can"—issued a call to arms to the can-do spirit of the country.

The Obama campaign set several records with that advertisement and went on raise more than $500 million in donations from online contributors alone, primarily from small individual contributors—people just like your customers—who felt empowered enough by the message to become a part of it.

To continue or extend your reach among consumers looking to feel empowered, engaged, and excited about achieving something important, here are a few additional approaches to keep in mind.

Messaging Tactics for Instrumental Strivers
Don't Waste Consumers' Time

Today's empowered consumers know how to do the research to confirm your claims. They can complete this research in minutes if not seconds and post their results for the entire world to see with a single click of a mouse.

So don't waste these consumers' time with obfuscations or even small fabrications. They can spot disingenuous exaggerations and superficial flatteries from miles away. Meanwhile, needing to fact check your advertising claims slows down their instrumental charge to get the shopping job done. Let your customers know you value their time and won't waste it.

Let Your Consumers Make a Difference

Make it easy for consumers to let you know how they feel with online polls and other feedback instruments. Gather their feedback and act on it—and let them know they really do have power with your company and can influence your business practices. Crowdsource your business ideas wherever possible and advertise the fact that you do. Anheuser-Busch's Budweiser is the best-selling beer in America. When the company decided to align with emerging trends for less widely distributed, craft beers, it got input from its customers before developing this product. This project had over 25,000 collaborators and became the basis for a lager named Black Crown, which began from the time of its launch to make a substantial contribution to the AB beer business.

Characteristics of Consumers with Instrumental Motivations

As we move forward to learn more about ways to understand and appeal to consumers operating with instrumental motivations bear in mind the traits they all share:

- They seek knowledge and they know where and how to get it.
- They share what they learn. Information is power, and consumers driven by instrumental motivation are driven by the desire for empowerment. Peer-to-peer marketing is a major way instrumental consumers gain knowledge.
- In an instrumentally motivated frame of mind, consumers will call out and punish companies that waste their valuable time with obfuscation, exaggeration or fabrication.
- Instrumental motivation leads us to feel capable and powerful, and to want to get things done.
- Whether instrumental motivation drives the desire for your product or whether it only influences the process of shopping for your product, you can build consumer loyalty by helping customers get what they really want in the way they really want it.

With your updated vision of how instrumental motivations shape consumers' behaviors you can create marketing messages that are likely to get consumers out of their seats, charged with the enthusiasm of getting things done, eager to engage in the process, and confident of being successful.

We'll begin that process by meeting consumers motivated by the initial instrumental motivation, namely, the desire to feel empowered.

Takeaways

1. Our ability to imagine and invent—which generates our culture of instruments—or tools—is a defining characteristic of our humanity. We are *driven* to be creative and to look for ways to solve the problems we encounter in our world.

2. Unlike intrapsychic motivations, instrumental motivations find their fulfillment outside the self in the material world, where outcomes are generally visible, often quantifiable, and frequently out of the control of the actor.

3. Shopping—for any product, anytime—is always driven by instrumental motivations. Shoppers seek to get the job done well and attach feelings of satisfaction to their ability to reach their goals efficiently and effectively.

4. Instrumental striving will drive shoppers to seek out answers, comparisons, and statistics regarding the brands they choose.

5. Instrumental drives will lead shoppers to be offended if you waste their time and they will spread the word about this through their networks.

6. Instrumental striving in today's world leads consumers to want a two-way relationship with the products, brands, manufacturers, and retailers they choose so they can have an impact and make a difference. Consumer feedback within those relationships is likely to be well-researched and valuable.

7. You sell most effectively to instrumentally oriented consumers by helping them understand exactly what your product will help them do. Provide details—help them learn how your product works, and the results it can deliver.

CHAPTER 8

The Empowerment Motive

Have you ever heard a pep talk so motivating that it leaves you energized and pumping your fists (literally or figuratively) and saying (or thinking) "yes, I can!" or perhaps "bring it on!"? Have you ever held your breath at the start of a brand-new project or situation and felt the exhilaration—including the butterflies in the stomach and elevated heartbeat—of stepping in to the unknown? Have you ever walked into a new opportunity, a challenging work assignment, an advanced class, a job interview and smiled to yourself, thinking "I'm totally up for this"?

If you've answered yes to any of these questions, you've experienced the tremendous rush of fulfilling the empowerment motive. It's one of our strongest and most elemental drives.

At its most basic level, striving for empowerment involves wanting to feel capable and competent in the face of the unknown and to gain the basic sense that we can successfully take action toward a result we desire. When we achieve the emotional experience of empowerment, we affirm to ourselves that "I can do this." Strong feelings of personal empowerment can equip us handle the ups and downs of life gracefully and with a growing degree of ease. When we're faced with new challenges, a feeling of empowerment emboldens us and makes us confident, thus increasing the likelihood that we will succeed in meeting those challenges.

We all experience the desire for empowerment every day. It's not possible to move through life without encountering challenges, just as it's not possible to face even everyday life challenges without a core sense of empowerment, an underlying belief that "I can do this."

Scientists have recently uncovered a genetic factor in our innate curiosity and our love of novelty.[1] This genetic tendency is very likely linked to the human desire for empowerment. Our inquisitive nature inevitably leads us into new situations featuring challenges we've not faced before. Our natural response is to rise to the occasion of this novelty because we love to figure things out, and we love to affect the way things happen around us. In other words, we love to feel empowered.

As the gateway motivation for the instrumental motivations, the drive toward empowerment is fundamental to our experience as humans. Like the other gateway motives—security in the intrapsychic domain, and belonging in the interpersonal domain—the drive for empowerment begins to be expressed very early in childhood and may be, in part, instinctive.

That's because humans are among the most dependent of animals in infancy and childhood. In the beginning, we can't hold up our own head, feed ourselves, or move about under our own power. Given our degree of helplessness, it's imperative that we strive mightily toward meeting our first core instrumental goals—like staying warm and getting fed. And that's why striving for empowerment is hardwired into our psyches.

Development of the Empowerment Motive

We can chart the milestones in our development of increasing prowess in completing increasingly more complex interactions with the tools and objects that populate our instrumental world.

For example, as children, we develop the skill to move an object from hand to hand at around six months. From there, we graduate to stacking objects, then on to feeding ourselves, coloring, and then, soon, dressing ourselves, and eventually we reach one of our first pinnacles of instrumental achievement: we can tie our own shoes.

At each milestone, we can see and feel the overarching desire to feel competent, to feel capable, and to feel empowered. To see the empowerment motivation in action, just observe a toddler at play, struggling at a task, red-faced and huffing and puffing with effort, as she continually rebuffs all offers of help, insisting "I can do it myself!" And eventually, of course, the toddler is right because being highly motivated to feel empowered puts us on a path that leads to instrumental success.

A Theory of Progressive Empowerment

The work of Jean Piaget delineates several stages in our growth toward understanding and mastering our world. The sequence of events begins with the infant who is confused about where his or her body stops and the world begins. The infant moves through the discovery of how actions and outcomes are related, develops the rudiments of a sense of empowerment, and finally learns to think hypothetically, a distinctly human capacity of imagining alternative possibilities for the future and generating and weighing alternative plans of action for those possible futures.

From these early childhood adventures and on through the course of our lives, opportunities to seek empowerment are almost limitless, from the mundane—painting our kitchen, driving a car with stick shift, trying a new route in search of a shortcut—to the sublime—hiking the Appalachian trail, piloting a sail boat, ice-skating backward, cooking a new dish with ingredients we have never used, or playing the guitar. And our drive to increase our sense of empowerment is a self-propelling process: we try, we learn, we get better, and then we try again. Our drive to feel empowered moves with us through life as we rack up significant life achievements. That's because no matter how competent we become, no matter how skilled, there is always room to experiment, to expand beyond our previous limits. In this way, empowerment motivations play a significant role in our lives right up to the end. And any decision to expand our horizons—to take a chance and try new things—requires that, just like our toddler selves, that little engine, and our hero Rosie (see box below), we first have a sense that we *can* do it ourselves.

As it is foundational, our drive for empowerment underlies each of the more complex motives in the instrumental column. Just as fulfillment of the security motivations form a foundation for pursuing a sense of identity and then building a sense of personal mastery in the intrapsychic domain, so the drive toward empowerment underlies our other instrumental motives to engage and to achieve. And while any of the instrumental motives can be a focus of striving at any moment in a consumer's life, it is not unusual to see the three instrumental motivations playing out in sequence in a single life event. We've all experienced this motivational evolution in our lives. We first strive to make ourselves feel *empowered* to achieve a simple goal ("I want to be ready to host a party"); then we seek to become *engaged* in the process of pursuing this goal ("I love the different looks I can get just by rearranging the living room furniture") until, finally, we revel in our sense of *achievement* when we've successfully completed the task ("Everyone raved about my party; I did a really great job!"). Striving for empowerment frequently happens when the other motives are also in play. We need to feel empowered, for example, to approach a stranger at a business meeting and make a connection, thereby fulfilling our drive for belonging, the gateway motive in the interpersonal domain.

An early and effective icon of female empowerment, Rosie the Riveter symbolized the can-do attitude of millions of American women who entered the workforce at the start of World War II. They took over for enlisted men serving overseas, and participation of females in the US workforce increased from 27 percent to 37 percent between 1940 and 1945. By the end of the war in 1945, about one in four married women worked outside the home, a paradigm shift that ushered in our modern workforce. Norma Rae, Mary Richards, and the girls in *Nine to Five* are just a few examples of empowered women in workforce following Rosie's lead.

As with all of the motives in the matrix, our desire for empowerment includes both aspirations for positive empowerment as well as a desire to move away from the disempowerment of life's setbacks and frustrations. This "negative reinforcement" keeps us moving toward feelings of power and away from powerlessness, toward self-confidence and away from self-doubt, toward victory and away from defeat.

As part of our motivations regarding actions in the material world, our commitment to seek empowerment is not really truly fulfilled until we *actually try* the activity or action we have become empowered to undertake. That first step in our journey needs to happen, at least in part, in the real world. We experience our sense of empowerment most fully when we are confidently attempting a task we previously were unsure we could successfully complete.

Our perception that we ourselves, rather than external forces or other people, are in charge of what we choose to do, and our conviction that we are more likely to succeed than to fail in what we attempt, are extremely fulfilling emotional states that motivate and spur us on throughout most of our daily activities.

Often, our desire to feel empowered first arises because we aspire–to do, to go, and to be—in ways and directions different from before. In those times, that first feeling of empowerment, when attained, becomes a sort of catalyst helping us to discover our potential and then to do the variety of things that make life comfortable, enjoyable, and meaningful.

Albert Bandura, the prominent psychologist who has written on the topic of empowerment, proposes that a person's attitudes, abilities, and cognitive skills comprise what is known as the "self-system." This system plays a major role in how we perceive situations and how we behave in response to different situations. Empowerment—what Bandura terms "self-efficacy"—plays an essential part in this self-system. According to Bandura, self-efficacy is "the belief in one's capabilities to organize and execute the courses of action required to manage prospective situations."[2] At a certain stage of personal development, the fortunate among us begin to experience an enduring sense of self-efficacy or empowerment, a delicious feeling that we are up for whatever challenge is at hand. This sense self results from a successful track record of our actions in the past. Successes begin to reinforce each other and to strengthen our feeling of being empowered. Over time, this can lead us to feel generally capable and competent. When that happens, we sense that we have a more permanent foothold in our personal world and exert at least some degree of control over the events that unfold.

Still, even for those of us predisposed to feel empowered, our feelings of confidence can vary widely by situation For example, I may feel very empowered and capable in my ability to synthesize complex ideas and theories in psychology and to present them to others in a way that makes sense overall. But I may (indeed I do) feel less capable or empowered to complete a downhill ski run. In similar fashion, I feel quite empowered to talk with business leaders and executives about the psychological dynamics of their markets, but I feel dramatically less so in discussing the finer points of wine cultivation in European microclimates. Our feelings of empowerment can indeed be partly a function of our general predispositions to feel capable; they also vary, however, as a function of our prior experience with a situation and as a function of our sense of *mastery* regarding the skills demanded by a particular situation.

And so it goes for all of us: we have areas where we feel very empowered and capable (and masterful), and we have other, perhaps new and unfamiliar, areas where we are far from being experts. When those new areas appear to us as something we'd like to do or learn, we first need to feel empowered to set about gaining the confidence that leads to taking the first step on that journey and then all the next steps that follow. As this account suggests, the process of empowerment is dynamic and recursive. Once we feel empowered, we take action, and then we assess our impact and refine our efforts until we feel newly empowered and take action again. Each small success we achieve along the way creates another building block we can use to create a stable and lasting sense of personal empowerment or self-efficacy.

Feelings of empowerment affect every area of human endeavor. All of us have goals we want to accomplish. Empowerment comes from our belief that we have (or can have) what it takes to achieve them. Meanwhile, the beliefs a person holds regarding his or her power to affect situations strongly influences *the power that person actually has* to face challenges competently. Feelings of empowerment actually shape the way we see the world, including our understanding of what is possible and what is not. (See box below.) Moreover, our feelings of empowerment affect the way the world sees us and the expectations others have about what we can and cannot do. It's important to keep in mind, however, that motivational empowerment isn't about any particular skill; rather, it's about our belief in ourselves that we have (or can get) what it takes to accomplish a goal. For example, if I've never gone rock climbing but believe in my athletic abilities and my abilities to learn by observing and doing, I'll put more effort into my lessons, and this will then make me more likely to succeed. That success will soon carry over into other areas of my life. When we understand the ramifications of our own power and influence and accept responsibility for the circumstances in our lives, we feel less at the mercy of chance. While that acknowledgment of our own responsibility and our role as the prime mover in our own lives may not always be easy, it's far more empowering than the feeling of helplessness that accompanies a notion that everything in our lives just happens to us. Even with generally high self-efficacy, we might still occasionally make a mess, but when it's our mess, we're more likely to feel that we can limit the damage and that we can learn from our mistake and improve next time.

On the other hand, if I don't have an inherent sense of confidence in my athletic abilities or my ability to learn, I will likely not put much effort into my lessons, if indeed I ever take any or make the climb at all. It's easy to see how feeding or starving my sense of empowerment quickly becomes a self-perpetuating cycle, imbuing me with the more general traits of self-efficacy or self-doubt.

The Power of Empowerment

Our confidence that we can successfully complete the tasks before us is the single most reliable predictor of success in health and wellness programs, including quitting smoking, working on a fitness or exercise regimen, dieting, dental hygiene, and seat belt use. We need to have faith in our ability to succeed in order to gain the determination necessary to hang in there for the long haul.

People with high self-efficacy generally believe that they are in control of their own lives and that their own actions and decisions shape their world. In contrast, people with low self-efficacy see their lives as outside of their control and themselves as victims of circumstance. People with high self-efficacy believe they make their own fate; in contrast, those of us with low self-efficacy believe that we are at the mercy of the unknown forces conspiring to become our destiny.

Bandura, who has done extensive research on the effects and characteristics of self-efficacy, recently published several studies that give us an idea of how our view of ourselves and our abilities colors everything we do. In general, Bandura suggests that people with high self-efficacy attribute their successes to internal factors such as ability and effort.[3] On the other hand, people with low self-efficacy attribute their successes to outside influences, but they feel that their failures are the result of their own internal failings, lack of ability, or lack of effort. As we'd expect, these two approaches to life lead to different results. Because they generally believe in their own abilities, people with high self-efficacy tend to be more resilient in the face of failure, more willing to take risks and embrace change, and able to generate more effective task strategies for reaching their goals. On the other hand, people with low self-efficacy experience their world quite differently. They tend to avoid challenging tasks, give up more easily when they encounter obstacles, set lower goals for themselves, and often feel hopeless and helpless.

Two quite different pictures, as I'm sure you'd agree. So how do we—and how do our consumers—build up a sense of empowerment, a feeling of self-efficacy?

Bandura mentions several ways we can develop feelings of empowerment or self-efficacy. Chief among them are the following:

- *Past Experience*: The most common and effective route for establishing or increasing our feelings of self-efficacy is to have successfully met other, similar goals. When we have a fairly consistent track record of success, our faith in our abilities becomes stronger and we lay the groundwork for a heightened sense of self-efficacy:

  "I made a great lasagna last time; I know I can make a good one now too."

This means that as marketers we can help increase the empowerment benefits of our products by emphasizing how they make consumers more likely to succeed at an undertaking. For example, we can do the following:

- ○ Make usage *"fail safe"*.
- ○ Divide use into *small steps* to create multiple small successes for the user along the way.

- *Social modeling*: Another effective means of building a strong sense of self-efficacy is to witness other people who are similar to us in skill level and abilities (no Olympic athletes, please) successfully complete a task.

"I just saw my brother ski down that black diamond trail. If he can do it, I probably can, too."

This means that as marketers we can build a sense of empowerment in our consumers by *leveraging social media* where "real people" can talk about their positive experiences with our products.

- *Social persuasion*: When it comes to bolstering our belief in ourselves, the encouragement of others we trust goes a long way.

"My kids think I'm ready to run a triathlon. If they think I've got what it takes, maybe I should give it a try."

As marketers, we can leverage *user testimonials* as a means to deliver success messages from trustworthy public figures.

We may deepen our appreciation of empowerment motivation by examining the profile of an individual who is focused on feeling empowered in her life.

Consumer Portrait: The Longing to Feel Empowered

Allison likes to view her life as an ever-expanding opportunity to learn and do new things. She seeks out challenges, new problems to solve in life, and gains a lot of satisfaction from growing as a person and proving herself equal to the next task. She is happiest when she discovers new activities or new ways to do "old" activities.

Though she's a successful and very effective teacher today, that wasn't always the case. Allison looks back with pride as she charts her progression from her first days as a shaky student teacher to her comfort in leading her own classroom today. Allison learned her profession in small stages, eagerly progressing from doing paperwork as a student teacher to brief interactions with her students in reading labs and math workshops and eventually to her first experience at taking the lead in the classroom.

Even as an established teacher, Allison continues to push the boundaries, researching alternative teaching methods, building new lesson plans, and presenting materials to her fellow teachers. Now, after almost 10 years as a teacher, Allison is applying for a job as assistant principal.

Allison and her husband live in a fixer-upper, and she is excited about her home renovation projects. She's determined that she and her husband will do as much of the work as possible by themselves, and she is always on the lookout for DIY projects. She started small—painting the living room—but she now feels confident enough to tackle more complicated tasks: refinishing her cabinets, installing new fixtures in the bathrooms, and staining the deck.

Not surprisingly, Allison and her husband lean toward adventure travel in their spare time. Most recently, they visited the spectacular waterfalls that follow a rainy winter season in Yosemite National Park. They're also willing to try new things in the new places they visit. Segway rides and snorkeling are two of their recent successful experiments. However, in future they'll give adventures that involve burros a miss.

In her habits as a consumer overall, Allison always has an eye out for products that can help her expand her abilities: new gourmet dishes or unusual ingredients or new how-to books about container gardening or tax preparation. She is the kind of consumer who is likely to be attracted to a new product in part simply because it is new, provided that the novelty is meaningful and interesting. Allison knows how to do the research required to identify the best products for her needs and wants, and she knows how to navigate customer service loops to resolve issues with her purchases when these arise. She has no qualms in returning items that don't deliver or that simply disappoint. Allison also makes good use of the growing information resources of the web to learn about her problems and uncover the best ways to solve them. The best way to recruit Allison to your brand is to make all the relevant information about your product advantages available to her, and invite her to "decide for herself."

Empowerment-Oriented Product and Brand Promises

Marketing to the desire to feel empowered is probably the most appropriate if your product can promise to help consumers grow in, or gain more control over, important aspects of their lives by doing things they previously couldn't do or by taking on responsibilities they'd normally be afraid of. Products that promise expanded capabilities along the lines of "you can do it" speak very successfully to the empowerment motive.

Products aimed at life stages or life events that bring significant changes for consumers—such as a new house, a new baby, or a new city—can also easily be marketed to consumers who generally seek empowerment in life. The empowerment motivation has heightened relevance as consumers want to be assured that they're capable of tackling the new tasks these kinds of major life changes bring into their lives.

Even products that don't inherently deliver empowerment for consumers can sometimes be effectively marketed to empowerment-oriented consumers by positioning the *purchase process* and the *ongoing brand commitment* as forces of consumer empowerment. Putting product information critical to the purchase decision in the consumer's hands can empower the shopper, allowing customization of complex products will deliver a sense of empowerment, offering a customer service relationship that empowers them to achieve and maintain optimum satisfaction with the product—all these will attract consumers who are seeking empowerment.

Empowerment as Permission to Consume

A special case of empowerment messaging can be a useful marketing strategy when the product to be sold might tend to be viewed by consumers as "forbidden." Products of this type can include quick-service restaurants (which can signify bad nutrition choices and laziness), expensive cosmetics (which can be seen as vain and self-indulgent), and sweet and salty snacks of all kinds. These kinds of "taboo" products need to provide consumers with a "permission structure"—a perspective on the product that makes it acceptable to buy and use. One message of empowerment in a marketing situation like this might consists of telling the consumer "you deserve this." This type of Empowerment message encourages consumers to suspend otherwise harsh value systems and go ahead and enjoy a small indulgence that might be considered a "guilty" pleasure. Another strategy to empower consumers to purchase a "taboo" product is to focus on elements of the product that may not be taboo. For example, as a marketer, you could mention the fiber in a salty snack product or talk about the good cause that some of your profits will support.

Sample Marketing Messages: Empowerment

People longing to feel empowered are drawn to messages that offer them the opportunity to stretch their limits *while* encouraging and supporting them in their efforts:

- You're a first-string player. You need first-string products/tools/methods/role models.
- You've got what it takes!
- It's time to be way better than "good enough."
- It gets easier as you get better.
- You can do this, we can help you.
- There has to be a better way....
- You'll never know unless you try.
- This product will get you further, take you higher.
- You'll be getting better every day.

By focusing on "permission," marketers can empower consumers to use potentially impermissible indulgences (like confection or spa treatments):

- It's okay to indulge yourself.
- You deserve this.
- Go Ahead—life is short!
- Life moves on. Move on with it!
- You've come a long way.
- Finally, its time...

Empowerment Case Studies

Power Tools for Women

One of our clients wanted to explore the notion of marketing specially designed power tools for women. Since this was a new target for potentially new equipment, the company's marketing people came to us early on for help in understanding the subconscious motivations that might drive women to opt for power tools designed uniquely for them.

The information that emerged from our motivational research made one thing perfectly clear: women were not interested in tools that had less power than those available for the general, mostly male, tool user. They were not looking for "girlie" versions of tools that had been modified to do less. Instead, the female market was very interested in tools that were "heavy-duty" and equal to the tasks any handyperson might encounter.

What got women most interested were tools that had been modified to fit the size and proportions of a woman's hand. The final result of our work with that client was a line of tools that a woman could use as if it were an extension of her own hand—accompanied by a marketing message that strongly emphasized how these tools empowered the woman using them to "take care of things on her own."

Permissible Cookies

As we know, food, and "reward" food in particular, is a highly emotional product category. For example, we consume sweets because they taste great, and make us feel great. But with the growing focus on healthy living in our culture, and the uproar over levels of obesity, scarcely anyone can consume sweet snacks without at least a small sense of guilt regarding their "negative" nutrition.

One of our clients had developed a delicious, almost irresistible, new cookie. But the company knew that was only half the battle and that it still needed a way to market this new product in a marketplace where the pleasure of sweet snacks had become a bit "forbidden."

The research my colleagues and I did for this client uncovered a hidden opportunity in cookie labeling and marketing. Our client learned that if the label and marketing messages prominently mentioned some of the "nutritional/healthy" ingredients in the cookie, consumers felt that this gave them some degree of "permission" to enjoy the product. These positive nutritional ingredients had the effect of empowering consumers by giving them a rationale of "It has this, but it also has that" so they could focus on "healthy" reasons for eating those cookies and feeling good about that choice.

Our results formed the cornerstone of this client's product packaging and marketing platforms. The company has been very successful with those cookies, which are still found in the cookie aisles of most grocery stores today.

Home Improvement Stores

One of our clients in the home improvement retail business was looking for a way to give customers the very best shopping experience in the company's stores. Key to doing that, of course, was first understanding what did and didn't work for customers when they were shopping in the stores as they were currently operated.

We conducted motivational research to understand the emotional needs of consumers who were shopping in our client's stores, and this analysis revealed unexpected opportunities for customer fulfillment. It turns out that even as they came to the store to buy the tools or the materials, a lot of these DIY enthusiasts were secretly worried about their ability to do a good job. In the context of this self-doubt and uncertainty, customers most needed to feel capable of planning and beginning their home improvement projects. They needed to be empowered to undertake the task.

With this insight, our client developed staff training and supporting materials to help customers outline and launch their projects from the start, envisioning the necessary steps, tools, and materials with confidence.

Takeaways

1. Empowerment is a gateway motive for all of the instrumental motivations. We hesitate to take action regarding a life task until we have some sense that we can succeed, that we are empowered.

2. The drive toward empowerment leads consumers to seek out new and different challenges in their lives. Your product will sell well to these consumers in an empowerment mind-set if it *helps them succeed* at a new or challenging task.

3. Consumers with greater pull toward empowerment love to develop new skills and to improve their range of skills over time. They search for products that will help them on their way.

4. *Novelty that surprises* is in general a pull for consumers seeking empowerment. "Gamify" your product to give consumers new skills to practice, new problems to solve, and new complexities to unravel.

5. Consumers increase their desire to feel empowered when they enter new or unfamiliar life circumstances. Empowerment marketing messages during those times (e.g., new child, new residence, new job) can be particularly effective.

CHAPTER 9

The Engagement Motive

Beginnings and endings form the punctuation marks in our lives. Most of us record and recall our life's journey as a sequence of these punctuation marks (*before* I moved to LA; *when* I finished grad school; *right after* we got married). But the bulk of our lives happen in the hours and days we spend between the beginnings and the endings. As John Lennon once observed, "Life is what happens when you're making other plans." In the nineteenth century Henry Thoreau, a famous lover of the world around him, advised us to live in the present, to find eternity in every moment.[1]

Living a fully engaged life, getting the most out of every moment, is another one of our core motivations in life. In the world of work, for instance, we all want an engaging job where we can use our talents, a job where we can enjoy the challenges and the process of our work, a job where we can lose ourselves in the details. We complain and feel discouraged when our work *doesn't* provide this opportunity. If the disconnection becomes serious enough, we look for other work.

If we are fortunate enough to work in an occupation that fully engages our interest and utilizes our talents, we may even occasionally experience a feeling of getting lost in what we're doing; in those moments time slips by unnoticed while we are completely engrossed in what's before us. This opportunity to be fully engaged in the moment, to lose track of time in our absorption, is the *sine qua non* of a great day at work. And it's the height of fulfillment of our engagement motivations.

In our free time, we also look for activities that will cause us to feel involved in the moment. The activity may be a high-energy one, or it may take place

> Vincent van Gogh is widely quoted on his engagement in his art:
>
> *"The emotions are sometimes so strong that I work without knowing it. The strokes come like speech."*

in a hammock. In every case, what we seek is that opportunity to be absorbed completely in the activity. Anything short of this can become the feeling of boredom, the almost palpable discomfort of needing something more.

The formula for engagement is pretty much the same regardless of whether the activity is an endeavor calling for high or low energy. First, engagement requires a certain amount of stimulation, which could mean sensory or intellectual stimulation that will rouse and hold our interest. Second, engagement requires an enjoyable way of processing or responding to this novelty. Third, engagement requires a task where it is necessary to pay close attention.

The relatively new discipline of positive psychology has taken a long look at what motivates us to feel fully engaged in our lives and has begun to understand a kind of psychological "sweet spot" for optimal engagement. At work, it turns out that if a task is too easy or unchallenging, we're likely to become bored and restless; on the other hand, if it is too difficult or even impossible, we'll soon be frustrated. Those distinctions hold for play as well; we find a certain amount of ongoing novelty and unpredictability to be stimulating and entertaining. Too little novelty causes us to quickly disengage, and too much novelty makes us feel overwhelmed and needing to shift to something that feels more attuned to our experience and skills.

At work and at play, then, being engaged requires hitting an optimum level of novelty to combat our risk of boredom without ratcheting up the stimulation to a point where it overwhelms us. Right in the middle, in what we might call the Goldilocks zone," are activities that provide just enough novelty to be arousing but not so much that it overwhelms us.

Happily Engaged

Mihaly Csikszentmihalyi, founding codirector of the Quality of Life Research Center, is the preeminent scholar on the topic of engagement. In his research, Dr. Csikszentmihalyi explores when and under which conditions the greatest amount of fully engaged happiness occurs.

Although we may harbor notions that we are happiest doing nothing, relaxing on the hammock, reading the Sunday paper, or binge watching our favorite shows, Dr. Csikszentmihalyi's work has led him to conclude that the happiest times in our lives are not "passive, receptive, or relaxing."[2] Instead, our best, happiest moments occur when our body or mind is challenged and when some effort is required to respond to this challenge. As a review article of Csikszentmihalyi's work in the *New York Times* succinctly put it, "The way to happiness lies not in mindless hedonism, but in mindful challenge."[3]

In the present era of positive psychology, clinical thinking and practice is broadening its focus to explore ways to improve the life experiences of people who already feel fairly happy. This focus among today's scholars of happiness somewhat echoes the precepts of Abraham Maslow. Maslow saw self-actualization as a supreme achievement of emotional fulfillment and satisfaction and not as something that "just happens" to us or that we're born with. Rather, self-actualization or full engagement in life is a result of the striving we undertake to be as happy as possible.

Getting "into the Zone": Mindfulness in Action

When our mind is wandering unattended, we are all too likely to think of our frustrations and disappointments and to dwell on them as if we were fascinated by the pain they evoke. Research confirms that fully engaging with the activity we are about in any particular moment of life, and nurturing the capacity to participate fully in life's moments, lets us avoid this free floating anxiety.

Obviously, this message about the value of the engagement motivation is not entirely "new news:" religious leaders have invited us for millennia to be present in each moment and to experience each moment fully. Whether or not it might be true that this mindfulness is linked to communion with a greater or a higher consciousness, we can safely say that being fully mindful is a great way to be happy in life.

> Terry Bradshaw, Hall of Fame quarterback, described the feeling:[4]
>
> *"All of a sudden, I felt a sense of total control of this game. A sudden calm came over me. I felt invincible. It was like a flash of light: I knew what I was doing. Looking out over that field I could see the picture so clearly."*

We've all had glimpses of this state of mind when we are completely capti-vated by what we're doing, oblivious to the day-to-day details that surround us, and unmoved by distracting sounds or sights. Another way to think about this state of full engagement is to note that it is the antithesis of boredom. It's also the opposite of the distractibility we call attention deficit. Engagement is instead full fascination and complete immersion in the moment at hand.

The State of Flow

Csikszentmihalyi calls the state of full engagement the experience of "flow." He created the concept of flow from his studies of artists who get so absorbed in their work that they often forget to eat or sleep. In his studies of excep-tional flow, Csikszentmihalyi tells us that it is a state in which people feel "swept up" in the unfolding of something larger than themselves. Though Csikszentmihalyi sees flow as a state most often found in artists, musicians, and athletes, I think a great many of us also have this experience and seek avidly to replicate it. Those of us who experience the state of flow character-ize it as an almost magical experience. Indeed, some of the words they use to describe it echo terms from the magician's trade: being enthralled, enchanted, spellbound, captivated, transfixed, entranced—in other words, engaged.

And just like a magical state, the feeling of flow is difficult to maintain or manufacture. You can't ask for it, and you can't fake it. Flow "just happens"; it appears quickly and vanishes without a trace. "What happened?" we might ask if we've been lucky enough to "go there" in the first place. "Where did it go? How can I get it back?" Small wonder that this state is the target of one of our core motivations, and that consumers in the marketplace are often searching for products that might help them experience the state of flow.

The truth is that nobody fully understands why or how flow happens, what we can do to get more of it, or why it suddenly disappears. According to Csikszentmihalyi, the best thing we can do is stay out of its way when it "wants" to happen.

Being in the Zone

Dr. John Silva, a University of North Carolina sports psychologist, has stud-ied the experience of being in the zone as described by many athletes in different sports and at all different levels of these sports, from Little League through high school, college, professional sports, and the Olympics.

> You pull something that doesn't exist out of the air when you're stand-
> ing there in front of your audience. Nothing exists in that space until
> you go 1, 2, 3, 4 VOOM. You and the audience together create an
> entire world.
>
> —Bruce Springsteen[5]

Silva's research has produced a psychological profile of performers in the
zone of optimal performance and the experiences they have in that state,
including feelings of increased control and capability, a sense of time slow-
ing down, a sense of quiet, a feeling of complete awareness with no tension
attached, and a heightened sensory awareness that brings with it the ability to
anticipate, see, and react to circumstances much more clearly and effectively
than they ever have before.

Take a look at the words athletes and artists use to describe their state
of flow in the text boxes in this chapter. You'll see what it means to be so
engaged that you are transported to a new state of being.

High engagement to the point of experiencing flow can occur for anyone
if the right circumstances align. Think of the potter at her wheel, endlessly
turning, wetting, and shaping the clay until it becomes just what it should be.
Or the craftsman at his trade sanding and polishing his wood or stone until it
reaches its optimal state.

Meanwhile, a heightened state of engagement or an experience of flow
doesn't necessarily need to be fun. Surgeons, bomb squad members, or high-
rise construction workers are not necessarily jolly in the situations they're in,
but you can bet that their engagement in their tasks is total.

Development and the Engagement Motive

The capacity to be fully engaged in the moment seems to come with our
original equipment. Indeed, watching young children in a great many of
their activities means watching complete engagement. In early childhood,
life seems to consist of a nearly continuous sequence of engagement experiences: try interrupting a young child at play and you will often see how fully
he or she is engaged.

As children grow older, the ability to feel *disengaged* becomes more prevalent, and by early adolescence, the search for engagement—and feelings

of boredom and disengagement—become a real issue. Complaints of "I'm bored," or "There's nothing to do" frequently come from preteens and teenagers. And sometimes, what these teenagers engage in to relieve that boredom is not what their parents might have chosen.

As adults, most of us make some progress at identifying the pastimes and activities that will draw us in and let us be fully engaged. When our interests broaden and our skills and abilities increase, our potential to find engagement in life increases accordingly.

And still, many of us struggle with the distractions in our lives that prevent us from engaging in the moment. Others have a reduced capacity to be truly immersed in an activity or are generally susceptible to being bored. Part of the challenge in achieving engagement is first to identify activities that draw us in because of who we are distinctively as people, to find pastimes that fit naturally with our interests and tasks that align with our skills and abilities. The path to engagement is thus a very different journey for each of us.

The Autotelic Personality

In his extensive study of flow, Csikszentmihalyi has identified the character traits and habits of people who are motivated to engage fully in life. His efforts point to several shared qualities among them. Taken together, these attributes describe what is called an "autotelic personality."[6]

True to the Greek roots of the word (the Greek word "auto," or self, combines with "telos," or goal), the person with an autotelic personality is intrinsically motivated to seek her own goals, and the pursuit of these goals is an end unto itself. People with an autotelic personality engage in activities because the doing of the acts themselves is so deeply rewarding, and they tend to experience a great deal of joy and satisfaction in their lives overall. Let's take a look at the profile of an individual who is exceedingly focused on experiencing flow in his life.

Consumer Portrait: The Engagement Orientation

Ben views his world most of the time as an exciting, vibrant place where he can live his life to the fullest at every moment. "Carpe diem" has most certainly always been his motto. He is an energetic, exuberant person who eagerly embraces novelty and surprise. From the time he was a young boy, Ben tended to become deeply absorbed in whatever he's doing, from the

Rubik's cubes and skipping stones of his childhood to the photography and ice climbing that interest him now.

Ben's hobbies and his work activities have often blurred into one. He took his hobby of photography to work, for instance, and quickly became the go-to guy for site photography at his architecture firm. He tends to put his time and energy into pursuits that captivate him regardless of whether or not they result in a paycheck.

Ben's always looking for ways to experience life full throttle, and he's always happy to put his money into the things he loves. He may be a prospect for a sound system that makes truly beautiful music; he will be interested in an automobile if it drives like a dream. He loves travel and adventures in all sizes and is generally looking for things that offer him a change of pace or a change of scene—even if the change is only a sensory or emotional one. He's convinced that life is really about the experiences it offers.

When Ben shops for things, he looks around. This makes him a good prospect for new products, but he is perhaps harder to retain as a loyal customer unless your brand can continue to offer new news. Ben thinks a lot about how a product will work, how it will look and feel, how it will move. His tendency for seeking novelty may make him the first one to bring home a new breakfast cereal or a heat-to-serve entree from Thailand. Romancing the *experience* of using the product will be effective for Ben—tell him how the product will feel as it does its job in an amazing new way, how it will provide a sensory adventure as soon as he opens the box. Speak to Ben through his senses, and you will get his attention.

Engagement-Oriented Product and Brand Promises

Marketing messages to consumers who are striving to feel engaged should *focus on the product experience*. Products that promise to deliver their users an experience that's vibrant and compelling or that offer the prospect of making the users' overall experience of life more exciting will strongly appeal to engagement-oriented consumers.

Product messaging that romances the consumers experience with strong sensory imagery will likely arouse the engagement motive. Great visuals, compelling testimonials, and the overall celebration of the usage moment—in pictures and in prose—will capture the attention of those oriented toward engagement.

Marketers can speak to the engagement motivation in all of us by paying more attention to the experience of using their products. Roberto Verganti's book *Design Driven Innovation*,[7] for example, promises to add engagement value to a lot of the products we use in our everyday lives. For example, one our clients, working to create a company-wide design-driven innovation process has started to reexamine the packages for the company's line of home care products. The goal is to see if the company could change the packaging to aid in delivering powerful emotional experiences to the products' users.

Most Effective Marketing Messages

People who long to feel engaged are looking for immersive experiences and for the products and brands that can provide them. Ideas that help deliver that promise most often make compelling reference to living the moment:

- See it! Feel it! Taste it!
- Picture yourself here.
- Feel the "rush"/Go for the total experience.
- Feel/feed your passion.
- Make the thrill stronger
- We design our products with your experiences in mind
- Life should always feel this way.
- Let us help you live in the zone.
- Don't miss a moment.

Engagement Case Studies

Chocolate

When it comes to food choices, there aren't many product categories that are more emotionally evocative than chocolate. Our client had developed a very robust market for its biggest product based on positioning it as a "reward." However, this message about chocolate had become submerged in a crowded conversation about "treat yourself," and the client was looking for something new to set it apart from the competition.

We performed a motivational analysis among our client's brand-loyal consumers to understand what really drove their love affair with chocolate. The results of that analysis spelled out the basis for their loyalty quite clearly.

It turns out that chocolate-loving consumers in this case were motivated by the feeling of being keenly engaged with the product: they wanted to "lose themselves" a little when they indulged in their chocolate. Our clients developed a strategy that "romanced" the small sensory details that went into the chocolate-eating experience. They invited these consumers to revel in the sensations of chocolate, to "feel it slowly melt on your tongue," and they extended the sensory experience into the emotional sensations of the chocolate's "little rush." As you can imagine, this focus on the immersive experience of chocolate did a good job of reflecting the enjoyment of the eating experience and generating excitement toward the next time.

Tunnel Shopping

In a study of consumer in-store shopping patterns for a national convenience store chain, we uncovered a very prevalent style of customer behavior that we called "tunnel shopping." Tunnel shoppers displayed an exceptionally high level of engagement in their shopping. These customers were totally focused on completing a particular mission in their shopping excursion. They zeroed in on what they were looking for with almost laser-like focus and sought to get in and out of the store as quickly and efficiently as possible.

Not surprisingly, shoppers who were this highly engaged in their shopping mission were difficult to reach with traditional in-store marketing materials; they simply ignored or didn't notice these advertising tactics. They were literally in a perceptual "tunnel" when they shopped, not looking up or around to even encounter the marketing and merchandising materials for other products in the store.

Knowing that these shoppers had a powerful engagement motive for "paying attention to the task" in the store, we helped our client develop merchandising and cross-selling strategies that focused on "dropping into the tunnel" and "breaking the engagement trance" in order to make their products appear as "part of your task." For example, signage for salty snack promotions was placed on the doors of soft drink coolers, and conversely, coupons for soft drink promotions were attached to racks offering salty snacks.

Celebrating Travel

In a study of customer satisfaction for a global tour company, we learned that the most satisfied customers processed and remembered their touring experience at a very detailed, sensory level. Memories of these great trips were often brought to mind in the form of mental movies of specific exceptional events or as snapshots of memorable moments. Consistently, travelers told us that they remember their great trips most of all in terms of the little details within the bigger picture of their tour.

We worked with this company to envision a suite of pamphlets and interactive guides to emphasize the "small things and personal experiences" in each trip. These materials detailed opportunities for each guest to experience sensory engagement and pleasure in the moment on each day of the trip. For example, materials on travel to Turkey featured the sights and smells of the Grand Bazaar in Istanbul. First person experiential narratives were solicited from satisfied travelers; experienced guides provided stories of their most exceptional experiences; every attempt was made to "take customers there" and help them "experience the moment."

Takeaways

1. When consumers are seeking a sense of engagement, they will appreciate products primarily in terms of their experiential, sensory manifestations.
2. Reach out to these consumers with stunning visuals of your product or its results or use stunning sound tracks to turn people's heads
3. Consumers motivated to engage will also appreciate displays of joie de vivre. Make this your brand attitude, and they will come.
4. Capture engagement-seeking consumers by intriguing them—give them interesting points of view, and new perspectives to consider.
5. Whatever you are selling, sell it to engagement-oriented consumers with sensory romancing—communicate the user experience from a first-person point of view.
6. Consumers looking to feel engaged are motivated by products and services that help them live life to the fullest. Show images of users having this type of experience, and consumers will identify with them.
7. Stay fresh, evolve, experiment and engagement-oriented consumers will be your best friends.

CHAPTER 10

The Achievement Motive

Achievement is the most common and familiar of all the matrix motives. Being achievement-oriented is a common description on résumés, references, and job interviews. That's because, at the end of the day, we are all motivated to achieve—whether it's in taking our first steps, learning to make a gourmet meal, graduating from school, or any of the other myriad stepping stones in life that require concrete accomplishment.

The achievement motive appears early in childhood (whenever a child calls to an adult to say "Look what I can do!" or to a playmate: "Hey, can you do this?"), and strivings to achieve increase in scope as children grow and develop new goals and skills. Physical achievements soon evolve to include intellectual achievements as well. As adults, the motivation to achieve can often be part of the journey in striving for other motivations. In this way we can see achievement overlapping with all of the motivations identified in the Matrix (as we seek to achieve a feeling of security, a sense of identity, a degree of mastery, and so on). Incidental feelings of achievement can be experienced by working through a pile of laundry, for example, although the primary motivation in play there may be to *nurture* one's family. The achievement embodied in that pile of clean clothes may also support a different motive, perhaps a primary sense of personal *mastery* in tackling the task so effectively.

Often, we can see fulfillment of the achievement motive as a waypoint to fulfilling other motives. When we make statements such as "I want to lose weight to be more attractive" or "I want to own that car so I'll be perceived as successful," we are being explicit about how an achievement will then lead to other forms of fulfilment. To gain and keep a clear understanding of consumers' primary, underlying motivation behind any particular episode of behavior, however, it's important to attribute the motive of achievement only when other motivations do not appear to be in play. For example, when the desire is truly to lose weight or own a car with no implications for a subsequent sense of security ("I will look better") or esteem ("Look how successful I am"), we can then, and only then, assign an achievement motive to these behaviors. This chapter focuses on those times when we seek to achieve certain things in our lives simply for the sake of the achievement, when the need to achieve prevails as the dominant motive.

For our marketing messages to be as appealing as possible to people in an achievement-oriented frame of mind, we must clearly show how we help them meet their very specific goals or conquer their very specific challenges. People who are motivated to achieve don't live in the world of merely "performing well" or "being satisfied." They want a precise goal to reach: a 3:10 marathon, the most nutritious lunch for their kids, a well-attended party, a signed contract, no points on a mortgage, and so on. They are serious about results.

What We Know about Achievers

A great deal of today's thinking on the motivation to achieve comes to us through the work of David McClelland, an American psychologist noted for his work on needs theory. When he began his study of achievement, McClelland was interested in learning how managers, business leaders, supervisors, and human resources teams could better motivate employees to do their best work.

Though at first blush the tasks of learning what motivates people at work might seem similar, McClelland's work was a far cry from the earliest motivational studies of Jeremy Bentham in the Industrial Revolution (see chapter 15). Working conditions had changed dramatically since Bentham's time, and the jobs that required men, women, and children to stand and churn through the same rote tasks for 12–15 hours a day were, thankfully, no more. By contrast, the employees McClelland studied in the 1950s were important, highly valued contributors to the successes of their teams and their companies. They were seen as assets, valued as individuals, and given a fair degree of autonomy and responsibility in their positions.

When he began his study, McClelland[1] was interested in testing the hypothesis that understanding what really drives and emotionally feeds an employee, and contriving to deliver employees those rewarding experi-ences, would be a win-win for everyone involved: the company, the supervi-sor, and the employee. He reasoned that assigning roles, responsibilities, and tasks that played to each person's strengths would reap obvious and immedi-ate rewards: better and higher-quality work fueled by enthusiasm, dedica-tion, and ownership of the process, happier, more engaged employees who didn't need to be replaced very often.

In his book, McClelland identified three primary emotional drivers in the workers he studied: the need for affiliation (classified as "n-Affil"), the need for power ("n-Pow"), and the need for achievement ("n-Ach"). Although he believed that each of us are driven to varying degrees by all three motivations, McClelland focused on three types of workers with each type representing a primary motive and each bringing distinct personality traits, strengths, and weaknesses to their jobs.

Employees motivated by the desire for affiliation (n-Affil) tended to be team players who were happiest and most productive when they had close, supportive, friendly relationships with the people they worked with. Members of this group need to be liked and well-regarded and strive to feel connected to others. They long to have a mutually beneficial relationship characterized by great loyalty and support: they want a sense of what we might today refer to as "having each other's back." In the Forbes Matrix, n-Affil would fall within the motive of wanting to belong.

Employees motivated by the desire for power (n-Pow) were hard char-gers who valued and sought authority above all. They have a tremendous desire to be influential and to make an impact on the people and tasks they engage in. They're also attracted to other activities that increase their status or stature both in their professional and their private lives. In the Forbes Matrix, n-Pow would span the motivation categories of empowerment and esteem.

n-Ach in the Workplace

McClelland found that people who were high in "n-Ach"—those we seek to understand in this chapter—love to set firm, distinct goals and to move toward them with persistence, dedication, and energy. They find the lion's share of their pleasure and passion in life in setting their sights on and attain-ing difficult objectives they can strive for. They are focused on the outcome of their efforts and generally won't give up until they've achieved success. Then as now, achievement-oriented employees are invaluable team members who enthusiastically produce consistently high-quality results—and they do it all under their own steam. They require little or no supervision to maintain very strong levels of dedication and determination as they move toward their goals. Over time, people who are motivated to seek achievement make more effort, give up less frequently, and accomplish much more than do people who are driven by other motives. Multiple studies also show that companies grow faster and prosper more quickly when they have the support of achievement-oriented employees.

In part, this is because people motivated to achieve are persistent, even relentless, when they set their sights on a goal. They know, appreciate, and enjoy that it takes continuous effort to get to the top and stay there. They commit quickly and completely and know how to stay committed. They are also very motivated by having to mobilize their own abilities to advance: they love the feeling of striving toward something important to them.

McClelland and others note that people who are motivated to achieve share some additional characteristics; a list follows:

Focus on Accomplishment over Rewards. Accomplishing the goal or achievement itself matters more to high achievers than the extrinsic rewards of money, title, praise, or appreciation they might receive in return for their efforts. It's not that high achievers don't value recognition for the fruits of their labors they work so hard to produce—they certainly do, no less than other, less achievement-oriented workers would. But the money, title, praise or other reward they might receive is experienced more as an index of their performance, a demonstration of their success, rather than as a focus of satisfaction in its own right.

Someone highly motivated to achieve would not be content or happy, for example, in a job that offered higher pay or a more impressive title if this new job came without significant goals to strive for. Employees with this primary motivation are not in the game for the money or the accolades; they're in it to win it.

Internal Locus of Control/Belief in Themselves. Achievers typically also have what psychologists term a "high internal locus of control," which means that they believe, more completely than others might, that they are personally responsible for the outcomes of their efforts, and they wouldn't have it any other way.

For example, a person motivated by achievement might accept responsibility for doing well on a test by acknowledging that she studied hard or that she studied the right content or even that she got the right amount of sleep on the night before the test. A person *without* a high achievement motive receiving the same grade on the same test might explain the result by crediting the instructor for teaching skills, noting that the contents of the test luckily happened to overlap with what they studied. The strong internal locus of control in achievement-oriented people makes them more inclined to attribute success to their own efforts/skills, rather than to luck.

Moderate Risk-Propensity. To by truly motivated toward a goal, achievement-oriented individuals need to believe that success will require all of their skills, that success will be measured by standards that are almost, but not quite, unattainable. For the undertaking to be this difficult and challenging, it must typically also present a degree of uncertainty or risk. And thus willingness to take risks, enjoyment of risk even, is a quality of the achievement-oriented. It's important to be clear, though, that people who are motivated to achieve are not gamblers, far from it. They enjoy an element of risk that is a result—a side effect, if you will—of setting very difficult objectives.

A similar paradigm of risk taking is found in elite exercise programs that focus on overloading the muscles to become stronger. Exercisers aim to reach for, but stay just short of, a task so difficult it can't be completed without injury. These exercisers seek to challenge muscles to a point where their fitness is greatly increased, while stopping just short of causing damage. High achievers live in that zone.

Winner's Attitude. When people motivated to achieve are on a path that offers a high degree of difficulty and a measurable way to judge their results, they work longer, harder, with more dedication and a singleness of purpose not found in other groups.

They're also usually competitive and select fast-paced careers and pastimes that put them in the company of other high performers. And they are typically quite confident—a lifetime of successfully dealing with challenges has given them faith in their own abilities to perform well.

Winning as a Trait

Winners of the Scripps National Spelling Bee have studied literally thousands of hours to gain their skills, all while meeting the contest requirement of maintaining good grades. And all this effort is directed toward a contest where only one candidate can win.

This kind of dedication to winning appears to be a lasting trait. Here's a sampling: The 1969 winner is a Pulitzer Prize-winning journalist at the *San Francisco Chronicle*; the 1973 winner went to MIT and spent a decade at NASA's Jet Propulsion Lab; the 1998 winner started studying at Stanford at 16 and now teaches at UCSF Medical School. The 1992 winner graduated from Harvard Law School and now works for the ACLU.[2]

Clearly, a winning attitude can carry an individual through life.

Achievement Orientation and Propensity for Innovation

When they are achievement-oriented, people see difficult tasks as opportunities to succeed against the odds. They can be highly innovative in the face of challenges, trying and trying again in new ways rather than giving up, fine-tuning their efforts if necessary to meet the changing demands of a task. In general, achievement-oriented people spend time thinking about ways to do the job best, and most efficiently, paving the way to still more opportunity for further achievement.

Achieving First Flight

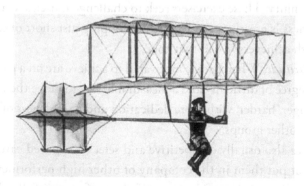

The Wright brothers made some 69 flights, each leading to improvements, and most also leading to crashes and complete destruction of the aircraft.

Orville and Wilbur finally took to the air on December 16, 1903, in Kitty Hawk, North Carolina (the site chosen for its favorable winds and soft, sandy spots to cushion the expected crashes that were part of each flight). The first "flight" lasted 4 seconds and covered 110 feet. Three days and four flights later, Wilbur stayed aloft for 59 seconds and covered a whopping 852 feet.

Viewing Challenges as Opportunities

Obstacles often stimulate people with high achievement goals to even greater efforts to achieve ever higher results. They tend to see setbacks as important learning opportunities. They study the things that didn't work and look for patterns and details that will offer them the chance to get a better outcome. Since they enjoy being in situations where they're challenged, achievement-oriented people can turn almost any task into an opportunity to achieve.

A Light Finally Went On

Thomas Edison reputedly made a thousand unsuccessful attempts at inventing the lightbulb. When a reporter asked how it felt to fail a thousand times, Edison replied, "I didn't fail a thousand times. The lightbulb was an invention that took one thousand and one steps."

Edison is an archetype of the achievement motivation, with over 1000 US patents to his name, and nearly 2500 worldwide (see figure 6.4 in chapter 6). Let's now turn to an in-depth look at another (hypothetical) individual with a strong achievement orientation.

Consumer Portrait: Striving to Achieve

Frank likes to view his world as an exhilarating series of contests, all of which he's playing to win. He is determined to make a mark in life. He's a "work hard, play hard" kind of person, a man who believes it's not about how you play the game, but about how often you win it. For as long as he can remember, Frank has loved having a goal in sight, a place to aim, and a reason— preferably a big one—to jump out of bed in the morning.

Frank is a successful entrepreneur leading a team of top-level business consultants who help identify, create, or expand promising businesses. Frank and his team help businesses on the cusp of success to draft business plans, form strategies, and develop marketing campaigns to help drive their success. His track record of business success is Frank's chief source of pride and joy. His analysis and foresight have given Frank the opportunity to get in on the ground floor on investment opportunities with a select few fledgling companies. As he suspected, those "gambles" (he'd call them smart picks) have paid off handsomely and allow Frank and his family to live very comfortably.

Although his firm is flourishing now, Frank and his family endured a few lean years in its early stages. But Frank didn't mind delaying gratification while waiting for the bigger payoff. He was confident that the results would come. That ideal of dedication and determination has been a part of who Frank is for his entire life.

When it comes to his shopping habits, Frank believes that in general "you get what you pay for," and he tends to evaluate products with a focus on performance and results: "What does it give me?" He is not a good target for socially responsible products, or environmentally friendly ones, if these product qualities are created at the expense of product performance. He loves product and performance specifications, and likes to know that the products he chooses are winners in their categories. He may not always do a lot of research before he buys; he tends to gravitate toward the most expensive products and services in the belief that the more expensive products are typically the better ones and with the conviction that he has earned the best. To sell to Frank, you should market with hard facts about your product's performance and its advantages over the competition.

Achievement-Oriented Products and Brand Promises

Marketing to the people who are driven by the achievement motive involves focusing on outcomes, promising or implying that the product will increase the likelihood that consumers will be able to accomplish their goals or conquer their challenges. The achievement promise has the maximum impact when it is a comparative one, such as when the product promise offers a *superior* result. Comparisons and superlatives are key to achievement marketing: "Thanks to this detergent, my family's clothes are the whitest of white." "This lawn care product makes my grass the greenest in the neighborhood." "This diet plan helps me lose the most weight." Your product message will have distinctive appeal to achievement-oriented consumers when it communicates a distinct and superior accomplishment that will be possible with the product.

Another approach to achievement marketing is fueled by staking a claim to "be the best" where cost is no object. Achievement-oriented consumers can relate to the idea of being so successful that they only deal with "winner" products in their lifestyles. "Drive only the best." "Reach for the most select ingredients." "Never accept second best."

Still another alternative tactic for achievement marketing involves promises that your product will help the consumer to overcome frustrations or irritations that can impede the drive to success. For example, achievement-oriented consumers will understand the joy that comes from finally getting rid of that crabgrass in the front lawn. Likewise, they know the pleasure they'll feel when they've finally devised a strategy to convince their daughter to keep her room clean. Clearly other motivations can also be satisfied by these outcomes, but the primary achievement hook in these kinds of messages is the actual, tangible result.

Sample Marketing Messages

Consumers motivated to achieve will respond best to messages that promise them a product that will help them reach explicit goals or one that helps them celebrate the success of reaching a goal. Ideas for messages that will work well in this manner include:

- Results speak louder than words.
- Our determination and your tenacity—a win every time.
- Winning isn't everything, it's the only thing.
- To the victors go the spoils. Introducing... the spoils.
- Make it happen.
- We keep on working so you can keep on winning.
- Lead the way—we're on your team.
- High performance is in our blood, too.
- Because you've earned it...
- Feel the pride of ownership.

Achievement Case Studies

Car Wax

A client asked us to conduct motivational research to help them make a choice among messaging strategies for the company's car wax products. After evaluating motivational alternatives (e.g., nurturance, "take the best care of your car," and mastery, "the wax car care experts choose," etc.), the client found consumers resonated most with advertising that focused on prolonged beauty shots of highly-waxed vintage cars that showcased the visual qualities of the wax job.

It turns out that the dedicated car enthusiasts who were the optimal target for this car wax got the most emotional satisfaction from appreciating the *results* of their efforts, the sense of achievement that comes with creating a lustrous shine on a beautiful car. These visual effects—the eye candy—were the most enticing and the most satisfying evidence of a job well done.

Rx Pharmaceutical

This case is an example of marketing by appealing to the achievement motivation of consumers who sought to escape the negative energies of feeling like a failure. Our clients in the pharmaceutical industry were launching a new drug for Type II diabetics. As a part of this launch, they wanted to understand what diabetics most want to change about the way they feel about themselves. This research was intended to guide a communications program that would be launched together with the new drug.

We discovered that what Type II diabetics responded to most was a promise that focused on *negative* achievement motivation. They felt acutely that they were "failures" in their own lives and longed to relieve this feeling. It turns out that this form of diabetes appears relatively late in life (compared to Type I diabetes that appears in adolescence) and it is strongly linked to diet and lifestyle choices. Thus, Type II diabetics typically feel that their disease and their suffering are, at least in part, "their own fault." An important negative result of this mind-set is that patients very commonly decided it was "no use" to try and stay on a medication regimen or to work to control their diet or exercise. They felt they were "doomed to fail."

To help Type II diabetics overcome the sense of failure in their lives and to give them the positive energy required to manage their condition and its treatment, it was first necessary to liberate them from the trap of repeatedly trying and failing to change their lifestyle entirely and all at once. The program our client developed breaks down the lifestyle changes recommended for Type II diabetics into small, achievable increments that could be presented as part of a journey along a "path to success" with many milestones of accomplishment along the way. This allowed patients who lacked the feeling of success in their lives to experience it in small bites rather having them attempt sweeping changes only to encounter failure time and again.

Personal Health

A large hospital wanted to mount a public service campaign to encourage adults over 40 to get colonoscopies. The hospital engaged us to help explore the emotional benefits of getting this procedure, which is widely avoided by patients of all ages.

Initial expectations for the outcome of this research were focused on motives of nurturance or esteem. The thinking was that an individual's motivation for having a colonoscopy might lie in the area of providing good self-care or of setting a good example for others, or it might be a combination of the two.

Instead, we were surprised to learn that a sense of achievement was the dominant feeling of fulfillment among individuals who had recently completed the procedure, and this was also the dominant form of aspiration among those who intended to get a colonoscopy soon. It seems that the general opinion about a colonoscopy is that after a certain age everyone "has to get one." Linking this activity to nurturance or personal care required individuals to think about the real prospect of getting colon cancer. And nobody wanted to do that.

Instead, almost everyone in our study responded with a resounding, "I know you've got to get one." The motivation required to push respondents into action involved positioning the procedure as a responsible "job" of being an adult. This job was an accepted "should" by virtually everyone.

The achievement motive, manifest in the message of "just get it done," was most effective in motivating these health care consumers to fulfill their very adult responsibility.

Takeaways

1. The motivation to achieve is the most familiar of all motives in the Matrix.

2. When they are achievement-oriented, consumers focus on the *outcome* of their efforts rather than on the inner satisfaction of being a success (the mastery motive) or the admiration or recognition of others (the esteem motive).

3. When consumers are motivated to achieve they are goal-oriented and capable of great—even relentless—determination. They have amazing singleness of purpose when they're striving to realize an important outcome.

4. Achievement-oriented individuals have a high "internal locus of control," which means that they believe they are responsible for the outcomes of their efforts (rather than luck, fate, or the actions of others).

5. Those driven by the achievement motive are capable of prolonged preparation, tolerant of slow incremental improvement, and capable of delayed gratification. They love a challenge and prefer goals that are possible but difficult to attain.

6. Consumers driven to achieve may gravitate to fast-paced careers and pastimes, and they often work or play with other high achievers at a very high level. They are very competitive and they want to win.

7. Consumers motivated to achieve are drawn to product innovations that are examples of high achievements.

8. Messages to consumers driven to achieve will have the greatest impact if they allow the opportunity to measure or quantify the outcome of the consumer's efforts with the product.

9. Achievement-oriented consumers are all about results; to reach them, the message about your product must highlight the latter's superior results.

CHAPTER 11

Introducing the Interpersonal Motivations

INTERPERSONAL
The social world

EXPECTATIONS	Accepted, Belonging
For the future	**BELONGING**
	Isolated, Lonely

EXPERIENCES	Sharing, Caring
In the moment	**NURTURANCE**
	Selfish, Unloved

OUTCOMES	Proud, Respected
From past behavior	**ESTEEM**
	Ashamed, Disgraced

homas Jefferson declared in 1776[1] that "the pursuit of happiness" would be both a founding tenet of our country and a long-standing mainstay of our culture. But the question remains: What reliably makes us happy? How do we flourish? Where do we start?

If we had asked these questions in any other era than the one we're lucky enough to be in now, we'd have had to be satisfied with philosophical theories and anecdotal evidence. Fortunately for us, though, the answers to these questions are now, for the first time, being explored scientifically.

The burgeoning discipline of positive psychology is now delivering research-supported details on what it takes to make and keep us happy.

> *As a professor, I don't like this, but the cerebral virtues—curiosity and love of learning—are less strongly tied to happiness than interpersonal virtues such as kindness, gratitude, and the capacity for love. (Martin Seligman, a pioneer of positive psychology)[2]*

The result of these efforts is a consensus across a wide range of studies. What are the chances that scholars, psychologists, and sociologists working independently across the country and around the globe would agree on their findings? And yet, in the most important respects, that's what they've done.

It seems that, no matter how they parse the data or view the results, the pioneering scholars of the new science of human happiness confirm that what we really need to be happy are close and constant connections with other people. In other words, a reliable basis for creating and maintaining our happiness lies in the fulfillment of our interpersonal motivations, those we're about to study in the next three chapters: the striving to build bonds of belonging, the urge to nurture—to give and receive affection—and the drive for the positive regard from others we call esteem. These three motivational forces make up the third column of the Forbes Matrix.

Does Happiness Matter?

If we are to be successful—and our Western culture insists that we should all strive for success—we are taught to keep our eyes on the ball and our noses to the grindstone (not the best positions to take in the scenery or to say "hi" to a passing friend). We learn to delay gratification, to rise earlier and work later to protect our positions and our paychecks. According to assumptions like these, material success and its trappings are what will make us (eventually, someday) happy.

But now it turns out that the inverse is closer to the truth: being happy is what helps us succeed.[3] Science now offers quantitative proof that beyond just giving us a nice feeling, happiness has real impact on our health and well-being. By contrast, the hectic pursuit of financial success has actually been found to hinder our ability to savor experiences, a key component of happiness.

The Real "Happy Place"

Nestled deep in a remote region of South Asia is a tiny country that appears to have a leg up on commitment to the really important things in life. In fact, you could say that the kingdom of Bhutan (population 750,000) is in the global news precisely *because* of its dedication to its own uplifting priorities.

Rather than measuring its gross national product (GNP) as most Western nations (including the United States) do, the government of Bhutan measures its performance according to the gross happiness product (GHP) of its people. The government, headed by a constitutional monarch, believes that the happiness of the Bhutanese people is a much more important measure of economic success than the products produced or imported or the money made by the collective efforts.

And data are pouring in telling us that what we really need to do to achieve this important state of happiness is to get busy building a large and loving network of family and friends. Researchers in positive psychology note that there are other factors that feed our happiness: a sense of purpose, an interest in the world around us, a sense of humor, and a habit of appreciating beauty when we come across it. But what makes us happy most of all are our interpersonal connections with others.

University of Illinois psychologist Edward Diener, one of the leading researchers on the subject of happiness (he's also known in some circles as "Dr. Happiness"), discovered that people who were the least depressed and the most happy had very strong ties to their families and friends. "It is important to work on social skills, close interpersonal ties, and social support in order to be happy" he says. Another University of Illinois Professor, Dan Gilbert, who authored *This Emotional Life*, and is also one of the founders of the positive psychology movement, puts it succinctly: "We can't be happy alone."[4]

Consider some of the evidence we now know to be true, all of it centering on the importance of building strong interpersonal connections:

- People with families and friends are happier than those without them.
- People with strong social networks have a longer life expectancy.
- Cardiovascular health is highest among people who have good social support.
- Married people are happier, live longer, are healthier, make more money, have sex more frequently, and enjoy it more.
- People with grandkids tend to be happier than those without.
- Just being around our best friends makes us calmer. Best friends also measurably decrease the levels we produce of cortisol, sometimes called the "stress hormone."
- Population groups who show the fewest signs of depression are those with the firmest ties to friends and family and—this part is important— the greatest commitment to spending time with them.

A Happy Time

For thousands of years, humans didn't really have the chance to enjoy much of a social life. Certainly these were social connections, between parents and children, and among members of the same small communities. But without tools or technologies to ease the burden of just staying alive, we had very little free time for socializing. Before the social revolutions we've discussed elsewhere in these pages, our hunter-gatherer ancestors lived a very precarious existence until death in their early twenties; most of their children died before the age of five. As Thomas Hobbes famously put it, life in the state of nature was nasty, brutish, and short.[5]

With the great leaps of the Agricultural and Industrial Revolutions, human beings experienced for the first time the option of improving their quality of life and of thinking explicitly about happiness. Abraham Maslow reflects these realities in the development of the human condition with his theory about the hierarchy of human needs. According to Maslow, only after we meet our needs for sustenance (food, water, sleep, and warmth) and our needs for safety are we able even to consider our interpersonal needs—the need to belong and connect with others, to nurture, and to gain social esteem.

What's in a Word?

Language, in all its richness and nuance, is part of the psychological bedrock of our social nature. Although many animals communicate and express their emotions in a "language" of their own, the ability to speak to one another with the subtlety and precision of words sets us apart from all other animal groups.

Language allows us to share experiences and to reach out to each other with a perception, an idea, an interest, a thought, or a feeling. It provides a way to create abstract social connections that go beyond the experience of the moment. "Friendship" is just such an abstract emotional idea that lets our connections last beyond the immediate time in which they occur.

The Interpersonal Motivations

All of the motives in the third, interpersonal column of the matrix are related to these important yearnings to create and enjoy life experiences in the social world. As in the other columns of the matrix, three distinct types of fulfillment from our social strivings can be identified. At the most fundamental level, the belonging motive fuels our efforts to reach out to and be a part of others, to have people in our circle with whom we share a constant, reliable, and reciprocal relationship.

Building upon this network of social connections, the nurturance motive drives us toward all those forms of social exchange that carry positive emotional energy. This energy comes in diverse forms and levels of intensity:

from romantic love to caring and caretaking to team spirit and cooperation with others in our neighborhoods and communities.

The third and final domain of interpersonal motives, the domain of social esteem, involves the drive to obtain positive social regard from the people in our social circles. This esteem results from how others come to view and evaluate us or, more accurately, from how we believe they view us based on our interactions with our social world. Here again the specific emotional forms that fulfillment of the esteem motive can take are numerous and range from general social respect and admiration to fame and celebrity.

Messaging Tactics for Interpersonal Strivers: The Sign Painter's Sign

An old adage tells us that the sign painter must be especially careful in creating his own sign since the advertisement for his shop is also a testament to the quality of his work. So it goes with marketing to people's interpersonal motivation. Marketing is about relationships: establishing them, nurturing them, and protecting them. Every bit of marketing and messaging we create is in some respects an interpersonal overture and stems from a desire to reach out and connect, to build relationships with our consumers and prospects. Therefore, every marketing message, regardless of what its core motivational strategy is must conform to the forces of interpersonal motivation. And this means that every marketing message needs to succeed in establishing a connection with the consumer (belonging). It has to offer to provide something that the consumer needs or wants (nurturance), and it needs to do all this with an attitude of respect for the consumer (esteem). Marketing is never just about marketers "building" or consumers "buying" products or brands; instead, marketing is always a first step toward a mutually rewarding relationship that, everybody hopes, can stand the test of time.

And, when we reach out to consumers who are focused in their lives on fulfillment of interpersonal motivations, the test of our relationship building skill is an even more critical one. When we as marketers seek to attract consumers looking for ways to enhance their sense of belonging, we need to make it very easy for them to feel connected. When we reach out to consumers looking to nurture themselves or their friends and family, we need to do so in a way that is in itself caring and nurturing. And when we seek to market products that help consumers gain the esteem of their fellows, we need to project the esteem in which they are held by us and by our brand.

In short, when we market to consumers who are seeking interpersonal benefits from a product or service, we must adopt an interpersonally interested and skilled posture that invites them to join us. If we appear indifferent or disinterested in our marketing messages, we can't expect consumers to turn to us in search for interpersonal benefits. For those seeking to fulfill their interpersonal motives, our gestures of connection function as the "sign painter's sign" for our brand, and our interpersonal blindness or tone deafness will have adverse effects on our marketing success. Toward this end, a list of some basic tenets of marketing to consumers' interpersonal motives follows here.

Tell the Truth

Marketing is one of the human activities that the average person often suspects of being deceptive and false. Remember, consumers have learned about *caveat emptor*, "buyer beware," and so they come to the marketplace in a constant state of vigilance against the dishonest salesman or the counterfeit product. The more honesty and transparency you as marketer can convey through your business practices and your marketing communications, the more your interpersonally motivated consumers will reward you with their loyalty and advocacy.

Be Trustworthy

A critical element in any social relationship is the ability to trust the other person to fulfill the commitments and promises made. And so it is in the world of marketing. Be sure to align your marketing promises with the ability of your product to deliver. Take care to alert consumers to changes in your company or product, whether they are good or bad. Help your customers feel they can trust your company and your products to follow through on promises; they in turn will respond with an enduring emotional attachment. The emotional bonding that can occur when this distrust and fear of deception are completely dispelled, when the customer can relax with a sense of trust, can be powerful enough to overcome market threats of cost and competition.

Be Explicit about Your Values

For interpersonally oriented consumers, an important part of feeling good about a brand includes appreciating the values that drive the company making the brand. Demonstrate that you value the same things your customer values. Make it clear that your products don't negatively impact the things your customers care about. Interpersonally motivated consumers will walk away if they discover that your employees are not treated well. And they will vilify and boycott companies if they think those companies do not uphold ethical and moral standards in their business practices.

Really Connect

Finally, if you succeed in making consumers feel they're in a relationship with you, you need to reciprocate. Here are a few ideas:

Have the best customer service team anywhere. More than any other group, interpersonally motivated consumers value the quality of their actual interpersonal interactions with brands, especially through your customer service team. Don't rush, be friendly and supportive, address customers by name, and follow up on your conversation. Ask them how you did and if there's anything you can do to improve. Speak to them as friends.

Reach Out. Provide special deals to "the family." Offer a look "behind the scenes" in your business process. Build a well-run affinity program. Help your consumers develop a strong sense of community.

Express Gratitude. Your customers are doing you a service by choosing your brand over the scores of alternatives they have in the marketplace. Do what your mother told you to do: always explicitly say or demonstrate your appreciation to these critical players on your team. Create loyalty programs to reward their support.

Characteristics of Consumers with Interpersonal Motivations

When you market products that seek to deliver interpersonal benefits, bear in mind some of the traits that consumers share when they are interpersonally minded:

- They want to feel connected, cared for, and respected.
- They seek to make connections, not just to complete transactions.

- They care about how you feel about them, not just what you make for them.
- Whether interpersonal motivation drives the desire for your product or whether it just influences the experience of being in a relationship with your brand, you can build consumer loyalty by helping your customers feel that you care.

Do a good job of marketing to your interpersonally motivated consumers, and you will be handsomely rewarded for your efforts. These consumers can be incredibly loyal; they are "in the family" after all. They can also be outstanding ambassadors and cheerleaders for your brand.

Interpersonally oriented consumers want to feel that the brands they use are valued, trusted friends who have their best interests at heart. They want to know we embrace and share their priorities and that we won't waver in those convictions. They want to believe that we value what they value, love what they love, and can demonstrate being this simpatico with them by means of products and marketing messages "with a soul."

Interpersonally motivated consumers insist that we see them not as challenges to be "won" or "conquered" but as someone, a unique someone, we want to bring into our family. They're not waiting for us to say: "Buy me or my widget"; they want to hear us say: "I like you, I understand you, and I want to try to make things that you will really like. I hope we can grow to trust and depend upon each other. To support this emotional connection, we should strive to thrill our consumers and fulfill their deepest needs. We need to deliver the kind of experiences that evoke brand passion, instill brand trust, and create the desire for an enduring relationship. "Good enough" is not nearly good enough for this consumer group.

In a sense, these interpersonally oriented consumers are looking for products and brands that are "like them." Interestingly, multiple neuroscientific studies have shown that consumers who report feeling a high level of intimacy with products or brands respond to those brands with much the same kinds of neural activity that appears when we respond to other humans. Automobiles are an interesting case in this respect in that they actually display unique and distinguishable "humanoid" physical attributes and very often have unique "character traits" attributed to them. For example, when we look at the front-facing image of a vehicle, we can see the headlights as eyes, the hood and emblem as nose, the grill as mouth, and front fenders as cheeks, and it is easy to see that some models have a happy or friendly "face" and others look fierce or sensual. The image of the car as human is brought to life in Disney's *Cars*, and in Chevron's commercials featuring animated cars. Take a look the next time you pass a Volkswagen, Mazda, or Mini Cooper and see if you detect a grin; look at the front end of an Audi and see if it doesn't seem fiercely poised to leave you behind in the dust.

Sometimes, interpersonally oriented consumers extend their brand relationships to the point of dependence. In that case, they find it difficult to

Our Interpersonal Brain

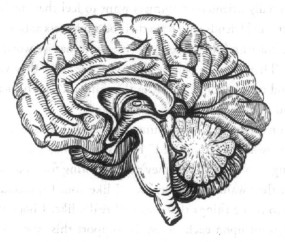

The very size and structure of the human brain has evolved specifically to accommodate our broad and bountiful interpersonal connections.

Biologists refer to us as "hypersocial" animals and point out that our large and multifolded brain enables us to connect with each other better, longer, and in greater detail.

Specifically, our folded brain (the most intricate and complex on the planet) gives us the ability to understand each other and to put ourselves in another's place to see the other person's point of view. The brain also enables us to perceive the subtlest of feelings and emotions in others (even and perhaps especially when they're not spoken aloud), to keep track of more people, to remember the most important ones better, and to be a part of more varied social groups.

We are literally "hardwired to be social."[6]

be without their product and would be bothered if it were no longer available. Manufacturers who "messed with" products that had these kinds of consumer relationships quickly learned from their mistakes. Procter & Gamble (the company that bought Clairol in 2001) reintroduced its Herbal Essences shampoos down to the precise color, scent, and bottle shapes, literally saying to the consumers who lobbied for them: "Have you heard? Herbal Essences are back!" And for those who remember it, it goes almost without saying that Coca-Cola has learned that lesson particularly well through the much publicized New Coke debacle.

In the realm of interpersonal marketing and messaging, some efforts stand apart as truly exemplary, and we'll now take a look at a few.

Federal Express

FedEx demonstrates that, just like a trusted friend, the company understands it is being entrusted with much more than work products. In those packages are their customers' histories, their treasures, their livelihoods, their dreams. Consumers depend on FedEx to understand that the content of those boxes is irreplaceable and that delivering the "precious cargo" inside them is mission critical.

It's the Real Thing

No brand has captured the feeling of belonging and embraced those who belong longer than Coca-Cola. Coke is certainly a product associated with good times spent with friends and family, and since 1892 the company has built a love-love relationship with the friends it invites to share a Coke.

Over the decades, Coke has entertained us with an abundance of innovative campaigns designed to bring us into the fold. One of the most iconic is the "Buy the World a Coke" commercial that aired in 1971. Part of the "It's the Real Thing" campaign, the ad reached out to a war-weary country with a vision of smiling, happy people of all ages gathered on a sunny hilltop to sing about a vision of togetherness and love.

The Pepsi Generation

All of this togetherness at Coke was of course a serious challenge to the folks at Pepsi. After moving gradually to lay claim to being "the modern cola" over the course of the 1950s, and presenting the product as "For those who think young" at the beginning of the 1960s, the marketers at Pepsi developed a famous virtuoso counterplay to the Coke ad campaigns. Aiming to recruit the newly burgeoning generation that would become the baby boomers, Pepsi's marketers decided to forgo marketing the product per se and focused instead on this new population group as target market. The campaign talked about "The Pepsi Generation," and asked everyone to come join it. Millions did. And Pepsi's revenues swelled.

Creative consultant Gordon Plotkin said of this campaign at the time, "There's a sense of freeness to this ad; they really nailed it."[7] He noted that "the campaign also captured a larger audience...encompassed a lot of people." The deeper message from Pepsi's marketers was that joining the "Pepsi Generation" simply required a state of mind, and thus the message was one of inclusiveness. All you had to do was "Come alive!"

A Budweiser Love Story

In the "Brotherhood" commercial Budweiser beer marketing does a great job of demonstrating the power of loving relationships even when the "people" on the receiving end aren't people at all. This commercial comes as close as I've seen any commercial come to capturing what it means to love and, eventually, to let go—a journey all parents know only too well.

The spot begins on a bucolic farm where a man looks in on a newly born foal. The story evolves from the horse's birth until it takes its place on the venerable Clydesdale team, presumably every red-blooded Clydesdale's purpose in life. The ad is bookended by the horse trainer looking through stall bars, first to greet the newly born foal, and then to bid farewell to the beautiful, majestic horse she's become—a Budweiser Clydesdale in all her glory. Between those two markers, Bud delivers a spot-on depiction of fidelity, love, and devotion. We see the trainer feeding the shaky-legged newborn with a bottle, stroking her head during a doctor's visit, and sleeping beside her in the stall when she's sick. Over and over, he trains her and plays with her, and we join him in his pride for her as she takes her first tentative steps on a lead and soon becomes frisky and confident enough for roughhousing in the ring. Finally the full-grown mare races beside the trainer in his truck. She is strong, fast, and breathtaking. Clearly, it's time for her to meet her destiny. The Budweiser horse truck turns the corner into the farm to take her to it.

We then fast-forward three years to the moment when the trainer learns that the Clydesdales will be pulling the Bud wagon in the Chicago parade. Now it's time for him to embark on the same journey she made earlier, and he leaves his farm for the city. The trainer waits among the crowd as the Clydesdales move past. He instantly recognizes his "baby," but she has blinders on and so doesn't acknowledge him. As the trainer walks wistfully away, the blinders are removed and his horse finds him in the crowd and races through the Chicago streets to reach him. He slows her down, and they embrace in evident tenderness and love. His and our last vision of her is through the bars of her stall on the Budweiser truck. She is where she's meant to be.

Throughout the commercial, Budweisers' marketers acknowledge that they know what matters most to us: clearly the beer manufacturer loves what we love and values what we value. Budweiser also expertly crafts the images to appeal to two key demographic targets: first, the cowboy and his farm, truck, and the rugged outdoors are prototypical male ingredients; second, the emotional crescendo of the commercial also hits the mark with female viewers. Guess who most frequently buys the beer for Super Bowl parties? You better believe that the Budweiser people know the answer to that question.

My Car, Myself

When it comes to products that help define us, few are as emblematic as our cars. And one car brand above all hits the hot buttons for interpersonally oriented consumers seeking social esteem. It telegraphs social responsibility and love for the planet; it's the car most frequently bought by prosocial adults with income and education levels that are above par: Toyota's Prius.

How do we explain the dominance of one hybrid car over all others? The fuel-efficient gas hybrid engine of the Prius was certainly on-trend with changing priorities in a growing group of ecologically concerned consumers. But the same is true for several other cars launched around the same time. Prius drivers buy the car and are willing to pay more for it because they are motivated by the position of the Prius brand, which means the purchase will put them at the top in terms of their interpersonal drive for esteem. In purchasing this emblematically eco-conscious car, Prius owners don't just want to be part of the social environmental revolution or even part of the larger green marketing trend. They want to be among the environmental revolution's leaders.

Without doubt, Toyota's Prius is the "poster car" of environmentally minded consumers. Through its ad campaigns across multiple media and online, Prius openly owns the esteem motivation of its drivers: It even projects "Prius envy" onto the drivers of other (presumably less estimable) cars. On the company's website, www.toyotapositive.com, Toyota defines its business model as based on "positivity and optimism." And the company identifies the Prius as a "car that runs on electricity, fuel, and kindness"—sounding a highly interpersonal note.

According to research conducted by Toyota,[8] more than 50 percent of Prius buyers took the leap because they felt their Prius "made a statement about them." And the Prius itself is designed to stand out from the crowd of modern automotive designs with a quirky profile all its own; hybrid models built by many other automotive manufacturers are usually designed to blend into a brand's larger product lines.

The Prius loudly telegraphs the environmental dedication of its drivers. And Prius drivers probably chose their model at least in part because those other, less distinctive hybrids didn't put out the clear message that esteem-oriented drivers were looking for. Prius drivers want everyone to know what their (prosocial) priorities are.

Takeaways

1. The quality of our interpersonal relationships is one of the strongest predictors of our overall happiness.
2. When consumers are motivated by interpersonal longings, they want to feel connected to others, and often this includes connection to the brands and products others use.
3. For interpersonally motivated consumers, the ability to trust you and your product may outweigh considerations of cost or competition.
4. Interpersonally motivated consumers are most devoted to companies that explicitly share their values.
5. Go beyond "satisfaction" to help interpersonally oriented consumers feel connected and appreciated.
6. Make all points of contact for interpersonally motivated consumers warm and inclusive. These consumers are looking for a strong sense of community.
7. Interpersonally motivated consumers often come to consider themselves in a relationship with the brands and products that they feel understand them best. That makes them the most brand-loyal of all the matrix groups.

CHAPTER 12

The Belonging Motive

Remember when "friend" was just another noun? Looking back, I can't help but marvel at how the world has changed since "friending," the verb, arrived on the scene in 2006.

These days the definition of the word "friend" has stretched and expanded far beyond anything we could have imagined just nine short years ago. A portion of our lives is now lived in a virtual world where we measure some degree of success and meaning according to how and with whom we make connections, and who connects with us in return. Social media has ushered us into a whole new world. And this world revolves around the motivation to belong, our basic emotional drive to build connections to others in our world.

One result of the information revolution is that we are all more "connected" than ever. More than two *billion* people now use social media worldwide.[1] I'm not sure how this exponentially expanding practice of making casual virtual connections without some personal interaction will impact how fulfilled we are in our core emotional need to belong. It does seem that we can *maintain* more social connections than ever before over distances in time and space where once our connections might have lapsed. This includes rediscovering former social contacts, such as people we find through social media. Many of my high school classmates from untold decades ago, for example, have begun to connect again as a result of a recent Facebook initiative. Without question, it's a new day for social bonds, expanding our sense of belonging to the virtual limits of society.

I suspect that creating new "virtual friendships" will ultimately be a good thing for our personal emotional fulfillment. These "friends" may not become bosom buddies or indeed ever meet with us in person. But if the goal of connecting with new people online is simply to gather a community for corresponding, casually chatting, or simply following, then the breadth of the social media presents a sea change in social possibilities.

The motivation to belong is a gateway motivation for our interpersonal strivings. Fulfilling this motive means building the social scaffold of acquaintances and friends that lets us exercise our abilities to nurture and to gain esteem from others. A solid sense of belonging also plays a role in the fulfillment of other motives outside the interpersonal realm in line with our fundamentally social nature as human beings. A sense of belonging makes it easier for us to feel secure, for example, because social isolation makes us elementally insecure. And the experience of belonging impacts how we create our own sense of identity, which derives at least in part from feedback we get from our intimates and associates.

As with other motivations that are rooted in species instinct, the drive to connect is apparent very early in life. Babies first reach out to others at a very young age, well before they actually recognize these others as separate, independent people. This drive to connect begins as something not much beyond the curiosity our species naturally displays toward any moving object. But it quickly expands and intensifies as our ability to recognize other people evolves alongside our growing sense of the world. Soon it clearly manifests as intentional reaching out and invitations driven by the emotional urge to connect.

The drive to belong continues to evolve as we grow. It's first evident in our strivings to expand our peer groups as young children and adolescents and continues throughout adulthood as we work to make new friends in the various venues of our lives. At every stage, we focus emotional energy on finding friends, working with teammates, connecting with classmates, developing satisfying work relationships, and meeting prospective partners.

We intensify our efforts to form new and different connections in adulthood each time we face a significant life change. For example, when we move to new cities, we work to establish new connections in our neighborhoods and communities; when we get new jobs, we want to connect with coworkers we feel as if might be somehow like us, and when we become parents, we reach out to other parents at our children's schools and sports events and support our children's growing social networks through the relatively new social institution of the playdate.

Whenever we enter a new life space (a new sport, a new hobby, ownership of a new computer or smart phone), we look for ways to find like-minded enthusiasts in the same circumstances. To satisfy our extensive desire to connect, there are clubs, associations, magazines, and Internet groups for almost everyone: knitters, classic Mustang car restorers, hydroponic tomato growers, devotees of the migratory habits of salamanders, even meditators, and others who practice silence and solitude together.

The drive to belong provides substantial social and physical benefits. Simply being around other people, living our lives day to day in cooperative, interdependent groups, delivers significant benefits mentally, socially, physically, and emotionally.

While the bulk of the emotional rewards from connecting with others arises as relationships grow from our connections, the simple fact of reaching out to another and receiving a positive response is also inherently rewarding: a portion of our self-esteem is based on the social acceptance we receive from others. Indeed, perhaps no social moment is more fraught with the risk of rejection than that initial outreach. When we turn to the companion in the elevator, comment casually to a fellow diner in a restaurant, or strike up a conversation in a bar, we are seeking the positive personal interactions with others that validate our core sense of social acceptability. And when these casual outreaches blossom into relationships, part of the joy is the simple feeling of being connected. As relationships grow over time, an elemental pleasure we get beyond the intimacy of friendship is the more abstract emotional pleasure that comes from simply having enduring stable connections: "I have people, I am known and accepted. I belong." As it turns out, stability is a key component to a successful, enduring sense of "belongingness."

The feeling of being connected, of belonging, can take different forms as a function of the socioemotional distance between us and our social connections. This degree of belonging begins at the center with our closest relationships and ripples outward in concentric circles. For example, I belong first to my wife and children, next to my brother and friends, then to my company and colleagues and coworkers. After that, I'm a part of the larger research community that focuses on human motivation, and then I'm a part of the marketing community, and so it goes throughout my state, my country, and my global connections.

The social distance between me and my connections regulates expectations about emotional nurturance I can expect from these people and the expectations they will have for nurturance from me. My very closest connections of family and friends rightfully expect to interact with me regularly and to be loved, liked, and cared for. At the greatest social distances, a sense of connection can mean nothing more than an agreement about potential, a sense of social permission: I *could* talk more with my distant, casual connections; I *could* choose to visit them; I *could* ask them for help, or respond to a request for it.

Social Animals

You've heard it before, and you'll hear it again: we human beings are social to the very cores of our being. The characterization of humans as social animals goes all the way back to Aristotle. In about 380 B.C. he said, "Man is by nature a social animal.... Society precedes the individual."[2]

In saying that society precedes the individual Aristotle was on to something very important. We are not just social in the sense that we like to be with each other, we are social in our very being. And the emotional value of connection—of the basic fact of knowing and being known—is significant. Substantial research shows that once our basic needs are met, additional income doesn't increase our level of happiness. And happiness doesn't derive from being smarter or wiser. Neither education nor IQ changes our basic level of happiness. Youth? No again. In fact, the Centers for Disease Control, which track these kinds of things, find that people under the age of 25 are less happy than those of us over 60. With marriage, we get a small bump in happiness, mostly for men (although there is some discussion around the possibility that happier people are more likely to marry as opposed to the conclusion that marriage makes people happier). But friendship? Bingo! Studies by one of the founders of the study of optimism, Martin Seligman,[3] show a clear and predictive similarity among the top 10 percent of the happiest people. They all had lots of social ties. "Word needs to be spread," says the study's coauthor Edward Diener. "It is important to work on social skills and to form a network of social support to be happy."[4]

Sociability helps define who we are and who we think we are. Psychologists writing about the "social construction of reality" tell us that our sense of the world—what's true and what's not, what's real and what's imaginary, what makes sense and what is nonsense—relies upon interactions we have with others, in which we collectively agree on the "reality" that surrounds us.

The drive to belong is shared with other social animals that adapt to the world partly through forming social groups or coalitions. Coalition-building is a key evolutionary advantage: animals that pool their resources and work together are generally more effective and better able to advance their interests than animals that do not. For social animals of all types, including our hunter-gatherer ancestors, "strength in numbers" enhanced the ability to get and keep food, the ability to defend against predators, the ability to raise and protect young, and many more lifesaving advantages in a complex and dangerous world. Of course, humans took this belonging drive a lot further than other social animals. Consider this: human beings are the only species where an individual's food and resources are most often provided by someone else.

The human drive to belong and form social groups has led to the development of highly elaborate social structures we create and inhabit together. As our social interactions regularly include strangers, we have everywhere created informal "signs of belonging"—modes of dress, dialects of speech, a particular form of a surname—these and other identifiers are all ways of signaling where and with whom an individual belonged.

We also have formal rituals of belonging, countless ceremonies and customs, codes of manners, and a lexicon of social signals that told others where we belonged. Many of these symbolic signals are imbued with great meaning rooted in the emotional strength of our motivation for belonging. From flag raising to funerals, in many religious and secular ceremonies we advertise that we share in the values, customs, priorities, attitudes, and behaviors that make us feel we were a precious and irreplaceable component of something bigger and more important than ourselves.

All this social complexity in our worlds also shapes the demands of parenting. We need to invest considerable time to teach our children the complex signals of belonging in society. And so the length of time the young are in training has steadily increased, and childhood and adolescence were prolonged to a process that's now often more than nearly two decades long.

The need to function in our complex social worlds has turned us into experts at monitoring and adjusting our own behavior to fit the rules we believed society imposes. Freud claimed that we "internalized" the examples of our parents into a portion of our psyches that monitored social rules and the restraints they call for, and called this psychological structure, the superego. He suggested that it provides internal parameters and imposes limits on our behavior in society, telling us what is acceptable behavior and what is not.

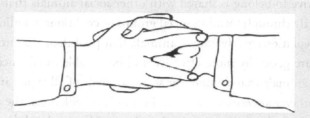

The Secret Handshake

Another way we pursue our need to belong in a vast and largely anonymous population is by forming cliques, clubs, and secret societies. The secret handshake emerged as one way for members of an exclusive group to signal to one another that they belonged.

The Masonic Society employs one of the most well-known and longstanding secret handshakes; it distinguishes at least 12 secret handshakes that subtly signal the level each Freemason has attained in the society.

Scholarship on the Need to Belong

Our motivational drive to belong first got serious scholarly attention from Abraham Maslow. In his seminal theory of the hierarchy of needs, first published in *A Theory of Human Motivation* in 1943, Maslow asserts that "belongingness" is critical to our development. His hierarchy of needs, often represented as a pyramid (although Maslow never used a pyramid as an illustration himself), describes belongingness as the very first emotional need we strive to fulfill. Maslow suggests that the groups people belong to (e.g., neighborhood, family, sports team or club, etc.) help to create our identity in the social world, and are an important source of pride and self-esteem.

Contemporary scholars Roy Baumeister and Mark Leary take Maslow's premise about the importance of belonging a step further and argue that most of what we do proceeds from an intense yearning to belong. According to them, our needs for power, intimacy, approval, achievement, and affiliation are all driven by a powerful underlying urge to belong.

Development of the Belonging Motive

To see evidence of the early expression and development of the motivation to belong, we can visit any playground for toddlers and observe the exquisitely complex dance of inclusion and exclusion, the subtle signs of acceptance and rejection that make up an average day for a child at play in any group of children. And parents will remember when—generally in the middle-school years—their child came to them with a burning need to acquire some sign of group belonging: a special pair of shoes, a hat, or a particular brand and style of shirt.

The drive to belong becomes a serious force when children enter adolescence, and the more fundamental questions of identity (see chapter 5 for more on the identity motive) become intertwined with desires to define oneself in terms of group membership. Adolescents famously operate atop a constantly shifting platform of styles and values, experimenting continuously and trying on different social identities as they move with astonishing speed from one look to another in the attempt to balance their search for individual identity with their urge to belong.

The Sporting Life: An Incubator of Social Belonging

When it comes to the thrill of belonging, few pastimes can match the fervor or the dedication that many of us have for sports. Over 90 percent of Americans watch sports at least occasionally, and more than three-fifths of Americans, consider themselves sports fans. Among the top ten sports in America—which are football, baseball, basketball, hockey, soccer, golf, tennis, motor sports, pro wrestling, and martial arts—fans pump millions of dollars into the economy to support their teams, and to visually present their allegiance through purchases of posters, pennants, memorabilia, and clothing.

On occasion, our devotion to sports rises to almost mythic proportions. To proclaim our belonging, we tailgate, paint our faces, wear team clothes, set out our flags, and stick bumper stickers on our cars. We tune in and hunker down with gusto, joined by a family of fans who are "just like us" in their dedication to our team.

That dedication to our team is formidable and often unwavering. Boston Red Sox fans in my town—and they are legion—waited 86 years, from 1918 until 2004, for the Curse of the Bambino to be lifted and a World Series win to be delivered. As any Bostonian will tell you, we never gave up hope (though most of us didn't wait the whole 86 years).

And let's not forget the Olympic Games. An almost *3 billion* fans from 124 countries around the world watched and cheered as "their" athletes competed on the world stage in London at the 2012 Olympic Games. And by the way, you can expect that almost every one of the 300 distinct events in the 2016 Summer Olympic Games has an enthusiastic fan group (Google the sport of competitive canoeing if you'd like proof).

In all of these cases, belonging is its own reward. We don't receive any-thing in return for our activities in the arena of sports fandom (except per-haps the occasional sports pool winning). And we don't personally know the vast majority of the fans who watch with us, cheer with us, and unite with us to support the team. The thrill of the game is certainly not to be discounted in all of this, but at the bottom of it all, the core emotional fulfillment of rooting for the team comes from a sense of belonging, the elemental pleasure of uniting with others around a common cause.

Leveraging the Energy of Belonging: Team Sports for Kids

Since the passage of Title IX of the Education Amendments in 1972, girls and boys can equally reap the many rewards of belonging to a sports team or club. And it turns out that all of these sports teams are more than just child's play. There is overwhelming evidence that the emotional experience of team sports can offer significant, even life-changing, advantages. And those advantages have their most significant impact on at-risk kids who often live in circumstances where they feel very little sense of belonging.

Literature in the field confirms a direct correlation between sports-based youth development programs and a decrease in crime rates among juve-niles. Kids involved in sports are also less likely to take drugs or to smoke. Academically speaking, kids who play team sports have better grades and higher scores on standardized tests. They attend school more regularly, and they are less likely to drop out of school. Moreover, as the Women's Sports Foundation reports year in and year out, female high school athletes are 50 percent less likely to become pregnant than non-athletes.[5]

Surely some of these benefits arise from simply providing kids with a pro-ductive outlet for all that youthful energy. There is an influence as well from learning about hard work and discipline. Sports teach kids about how to set goals and then work to achieve them. Kids on teams can come away with an idea about how they can accomplish the things they want if they're willing to work hard.

But I am here to tell you that the chance to belong—really belong—and to have a definite role in a group and to work with this group on something larger than the self is the foundational emotional benefit that comes from kids' involvement in sports.

Belonging and the Pressure to Conform

Situations of belonging usually carry with them an element of social pressure. Membership in social groups usually involves conforming to the beliefs and customs that define the culture of the group. To signal our membership and unity with other group members, we may change our actions and our attitudes (or at least the public presentation of them) to match the spoken or unspoken rules of the group. Conformity with group values and mores is evident everywhere groups form, whether this involves school uniforms or the right way of speaking in a political party or those top secret Masonic handshakes. An outward appearance of uniformity can work to strengthen the sense of belonging among group members, showing them that they are all "as one" in a situation.

While we all feel the need to connect and belong, it may put this motivation in sharper contrast if we look at a (fictional) portrait of one person who has an especially strong drive to belong.

Consumer Portrait: The Drive to Belong

Barb likes to view her world as an almost limitless place for connecting with others. She lives for the social connections she makes and the social networks she calls home. Being part of an extended family, part of a women's group, part of a softball team, and part of a community at large create a lot of the pleasure in her life.

Barb and her husband Jeff live in the town where she was born and socialize with the many friends they've made over the years and some of whom they've known since grade school. Barb is generally "good with people" and loyally maintains her connections. Barb and Jeff's house is a kind of drop-in social scene where neighbors and friends feel free to visit any time. Regular dinner parties also keep the expanding circle of friends connected. Barb is also very active in her daughter's school and is frequently one of the organizers when school activities are planned.

Barb and her friends enjoy shopping together. For everyday needs, she tries to frequent small merchants who know her by name. The grocer, the hardware store, the laundry are all run by people who know Barb and ask after her family members when she visits to shop, and she asks in turn about the families of "her" merchants. She has little interest in exploring new retailers just for the sake of something new.

When it comes to shopping alone, Barb turns to her online connections to help her choose products when she doesn't already have a preference. She also looks to connect to the brands she buys. She is likely to visit the brand Facebook pages and connect with the brand, and likely to offer her suggestions and comments when these are solicited. Brands that reach out to Barb have a better chance of gaining her loyalty than those that do not connect with their consumers. Barb also expresses her belonging motive directly in her consumer behavior, seeking out products that can help her connect with others. To recruit Barb to your franchise, begin by making an overture toward a social connection with her.

Marketing to the Need to Belong

Marketing to the motivation to belong primarily involves promising/implying that the product will bring the consumer a sense of community, an opportunity to feel connected, or a chance to create and maintain expanded social connections.

Some well-known examples of marketing to this motivation simply portray a large and diverse group of users with the implication that "everyone can belong." Coca Cola's "I'd like to Teach the World to Sing" television commercial is a perfect example of this. AT&T's famous "Reach Out and Touch Someone" campaign implied that the company could help fulfill the desire to create an emotional connection. The large and growing variety of social networks on the Internet also plays to the belonging motive. Facebook lets us keep connections, however briefly initiated ("friend me!") or however deeply buried they might lie in our past (find your high school classmates!). Pinterest lets us look at things that others find interesting or exciting, and share the things that excite us, Houzz lets us look in on others' home renovation projects, LinkedIn encourages us to grow our networks of professional colleagues, to create a feeling of "strength in numbers," and to build business connections between perfect strangers.

Political ads frequently involve marketing to the belonging motive, with candidates' messages often boiling down to: "I'm just like you (and you, and you)," "I know your struggles," and "We are all connected by common values, fears, and goals." These appeals all essentially say: "We belong to the same group; we have the same values; let's work together."

Marketing to Conformity

Another element of the belonging motive that can be useful for marketers is the pressure to conform that can be felt by those who want to belong.

Portraying the users of a product as a very cool group, as the in-crowd, can be persuasive in two ways. First, in the typical interpretation, the advertisement says to consumers "use this product, and you can be like these guys." But a second and more compelling emotional message is: "if you want to belong in a group like this, you should be doing what they are doing." This type of marketing is prevalent in campaigns for a wide range of food and beverage products, whenever a "cool crowd" appears to coalesce around a favorite brand and having the kind of great time the viewers wish they were having.

Sample Marketing Messages: Belonging

Messaging to consumers who are driven by the desire to connect and belong can be effective when it takes the form of an overture or an invitation. Promises to behave in a connected way—to take care of consumers, to serve their needs and interests—will also resonate with people focused on the motivation to belonging. Examples of phrasing that can do the job include the following:

- Let us help you take great care of your family/home/lawn/laundry.
- We've got your back.
- You're always welcome here/we'll help you feel at home.
- You can connect to your world with us.
- We know what you love, because we know you.
- Your friends endorse this product. /Everybody agrees...
- Make us part of the family.
- Make new friends.
- Be a part of the family.
- Join us!
- Send them a hug. Share/show the love.
- Because you're the glue that keeps it all together.

Belonging Case Studies

Green Homecare Products

One of our clients had long been dedicated to environmental responsibility. But the company was challenged in this pursuit because it made cleaning products that sometimes required potentially harmful chemicals to do the job.

Early green home care products were often not quite as effective as their less environmentally friendly cousins, so creating a compelling emotional benefit of "being green" to complement the basic functional use of the products was critical to getting consumers interested.

Over years of working with this client—and as concerns about the planet grew—we saw that the motives behind this lifestyle choice had changed. In the beginning, when talking to the early adopters of green products, an emphasis on the motive of esteem—"setting a good example"—seemed to be the best emotional benefit to highlight in relation to being green. But as environmental issues have become more of a mainstream interest and levels of concern about the planet have risen, the optimal emotional promise shifted to one of *belonging*, of the desire to "join hands" as consumers and work together to save the planet.

Realty

A realty company developing a home relocation product wanted to create a program to address both the logistical and the emotional needs of people leaving their current community and entering a new one. In their research with us, the company identified an emotional dimension underlying what they had previously considered a logistical concern: new homeowners weren't just worried about the logistical hassles of finding new bankers, grocers, auto mechanics, and so on, they also felt a great deal of trepidation concerning the emotional risk of feeling "rootless" in their new homes and communities.

With that insight in mind, the company examined its existing catalogs of local retailers and service providers to highlight those who were interested in providing *individualized, welcoming services* to new members of their community. The realty company then alerted these interested business collaborators about the presence of their new neighbors, encouraging them to create a sense of belonging for new homeowners in their communities.

Financial Services

Making decisions about how to grow our savings while keeping our hard-earned money safe is challenging for almost all of us. We don't want to lose control of decisions about our money, but we also know that investing is a complicated activity we might need help with.

Our client in the financial services industry asked us to do deep-dive emotional research to better understand how clients wanted to feel about their financial services company. Our research revealed one finding that we had expected—namely, that customers in transition had an emotional need for achievement; they needed to feel they were getting somewhere in life with the help of their financial advisor. The research also uncovered consumer frustrations and insecurities we had expected to hear about: people felt overwhelmed by the complexity of financial products and thus found it difficult to manage their own money.

However, most important, the motivational profiles of these consumers indicated a need to belong. Clients wanted to feel a meaningful connection with their financial services advisors. They wanted to feel the advisor understood them, their personalities, lifestyles, and aspirations for the future. Once they had this sense of connection to an advisor, consumers could then delegate the complex task of financial management with some confidence that the advisor would have their interests in mind.

Based on this research, we developed a service approach the clients called "trusted advisor." The trusted advisor combined high levels of financial expertise (the basis of being an advisor) with high levels of knowledge about and personal involvement with the client (the basis of being trusted). To deliver on this concept, our client instituted a customer awareness program that required advisors to maintain a detailed log about customers' family names and occupations, significant anniversaries (birthdays and so on), and most important, with a summary of answers that the client had provided regarding priorities for saving and investing. The result was a significant uptick in reported levels of satisfaction among clients.

Takeaways

1. The need to belong is likely instinctive for our species given humans' overwhelmingly social nature.
2. More than other good fortune, having friends is what makes us happiest.
3. A portion of our self-esteem derives from our interactions with others.
4. Belonging-focused consumers want to feel connected to the brands they choose and use; in marketing to them reach out to them as your "user community."

5. Belonging-focused consumers want to be part of groups of like-minded others, and they may adopt products and brands used by these others.

6. These consumers also desire brands and products they believe are "just like them." Connect with them around choices in values, tastes, and styles.

7. Entering new life stages can destabilize our sense of where we belong and magnify our longing to connect and bond with others—and with brands that are iconic of this new life situation.

CHAPTER 13

The Nurturance Motive

My favorite Beatle, John Lennon, is a fitting ambassador for the nurturance motive; through his lyrics, John Lennon was a great champion of the transformative power of love. In the portion of my life's soundtrack he inhabits, Lennon offers the assurance—and the plea—that "love is all you need."

The nurturance motive is indeed about love just as Lennon would have had it, but it's also about a lot more than romance, hearts, and flowers. Psychologists have long recognized that we can express our desires to care in a wide range of circumstances and toward a broad range of recipients, and all of these fall within the purview of the nurturance motive.

As it turns out, we humans have the ability to "have heart" in many ways and for many different objects of affection. Taking care of the neighbors' dog while they're on vacation is nurturance twice over, for instance, directed as it is at both the neighbor and the dog. In similar fashion, our desire to stop to help a stranded motorist we don't even know is a reflection of our desire to nurture. And we can actually direct our nurturant emotional energies toward inanimate objects as well—for example, think of a treasured keepsake from a favorite grandparent left to you.

Like belonging, nurturance is a psychological force in humans with analogues in the animal world, a good indication that it's rooted in instinct. Like most other animals, we are driven—compelled, really—to nurture our offspring, helping our children reach maturity and pass down our genes. Darwin would tell us that, from an evolutionary perspective, this activity is our chief purpose in life, the central mission we are pulled toward from our earliest days.

The Nature to Nurture

Like a great number of animal species, it is our nature to nurture. As a part of our drive to propagate our species, we experience an instinct to make sure our offspring make it to the age where they too can propagate. And nurturing by nature goes further than the local gene pool. Animals famously "adopt" the orphaned young of other species. This phenomenon might be simply an overexpression of the instinct to nurture our own. I think that the forces of evolution may have created the instinct to take care of the small and helpless.

The drive to nurture seems at times as if it trumps other elemental drives for self-interest. Taking in orphaned infants and children and protecting and nourishing them could clearly be a disadvantage for the tribe in many ways. Helpless children and infants consume copious amounts of resources—food, shelter, transportation, energy—that all would have been precious commodities in the hand-to-mouth world of hunting and gathering. But the early human instinct toward altruism, almost certainly an emotional cousin of biological nurturance, pays off in a broader sense, strengthening the gene pool and expanding the genetic variability in the tribe. This adoptive "crossbreeding" allowed us to enhance our abilities to adapt and evolve in response to our surroundings even more quickly. Put another way: Kindness is a formidable evolutionary advantage.

As powerfully social animals we are also drawn to nurture our *society*, to take care of all the collective cultural accomplishments of the group, including our social relationships and connections, our material culture, our intellectual creations—the ideas, stories, and legends that ground and connect the group. We are uniquely tied, emotionally if not biologically, to the artifacts and ideas with which we have filled our environment, caring for and cherishing them almost as if they were our children.

In this larger view, nurturing behavior is good for our groups or communities and, ultimately, really good for our species and our collective culture. And it's also good for us—literally, physically, and in real time.

Oxytocin: The Cuddle Chemical

Nature has a vested interest in our ability to nurture and love. One of the most famous of her tactics is the production and release of oxytocin. Important in generating uterine contractions and stimulating lactation, oxytocin also works beyond the birth process and encourages bonding of all sorts, including sexual rapport, social recognition, and pair bonding. It also brings about a peaceful, happy state of mind that moves us to feel cozy and close to those around us, a feeling that's magnified with the added ingredient of touch.

Scientists have found solid evidence of the hardwiring that's behind our gestures of caring and cooperation. Studies show that the level of oxytocin, the soothing feel-good hormone produced in our brains, rises when we feel compassion and care for others. And recent studies show that those who volunteer have lower mortality rates, greater functional ability, reduced heart rate, lowered blood pressure, increased endorphin production, enhanced immune system, lowered feelings of stress, and lowered rates of depression.

More than Cookies and Milk: How Grandmas Saved the World

One beautiful expression of the importance of nurturance is what has come to be called the grandmother hypothesis. Our species is one of the few whose females live many years beyond their ability to reproduce. According to the grandmother hypothesis,[1] grandmothers and the care and protection they provide are a "central determinant" of the long life spans humans enjoy. That contribution is only possible because of the adaptation of menopause, which allows human females to have long, productive lives after their ability to reproduce comes to an end.

Living decades beyond their fertile years gives grandmothers the opportunity to help, protect, teach, and feed the children of their daughters. After their grandchildren are weaned and continuing through their long adolescence (another beneficial adaptation we share with whales), grandmothers are instrumental in passing on the wisdom and survival strategies that allowed them to live as long as they did. Go Grandma!

Development and the Nurturance Motivation

The first experiences each of us has with nurturance are passive; as infants we *receive* love and protection in the arms and at the hands of parents or caretakers who watch over us. At this point, we are best viewed as only modestly intentional actors; we are literally unable to control our physical actions. Still, children in infancy clearly become emotionally attached to their caretakers, seek them out if they are available, and become upset if they disappear for any length of time.

Not surprisingly, and not too long after we can hold a rattle, active expressions of affection toward others becomes apparent, and by the age of two toddlers spontaneously pat the back of another child who has started to cry. This phenomenon is mediated by cognitive development, that is, the child has to first understand that others *have* feelings and then must learn to infer what these feelings might be. It is also a direct expression of the motivation to nurture.

As toddlers, children can be seen playing at caretaking with dolls, pets, and one another. Our motivations to nurture, in all their complex manifestations, grow and develop quickly after that; for example, just watch a group of teenage girls react to someone pushing a baby carriage or walking a dog. The timing here is not accidental; once upon a time adolescence was typically the age when we were recognized as adult members of the tribe and were expected to become independent and raise families of our own. It is, interestingly, also an age at which many of our religious practices—such as bar and bar mitzvahs at age 13—recognize the transition to adulthood.

Father (Sometimes) Knows Best

In almost all of nature, fathers, though playing a big part in conception have only a relatively small part in postnatal care. But nature, as is often the case, offers some lovely exceptions to this "love 'em and leave 'em" rule. Seahorse dads incubate their babies for a month and a half before giving "birth" to them (complete with contractions) all at once. Many bird dads share in the care and feeding of their chicks. There's not much of a learning curve when it comes to flying, so chicks must be well-fed, fit, and fully developed before taking that first big leap.

The "Best Dad" award in the animal kingdom certainly goes to the emperor penguins of Antarctica, the subject of the beautiful 2005 National Geographic film *March of the Penguins*, which shows how penguin parents take a tag team approach to bringing their chicks into the world.

After laying their eggs, the females march (70 miles!) to the sea to find food. For the four months that round-trip journey takes, penguin papas don't eat or drink, and they remaining standing to incubate their chicks in the cozy warmth of their feathers.

Closer to home, scientists have begun to document shifting gender roles in human couples.[2] In a study by Pew Research, nearly 9 in 10 respondents indicated that sharing in-home responsibilities was important to long-term marital harmony. This was true regardless of the age or gender of the respondent and represented an increase of about 30 percent over results in a previous study conducted in 1990.

Maternal Nurturance in Focus

We have already talked at some length about research on the importance of creating and enjoying social connections in the introduction to interpersonal motives, and the research on happiness mentioned there can be considered as a part of the nurturance scholarship story. The work of Martin Seligman[3] will provide the interested reader with a very solid background in the scholarship on nurturance in its broader sense—including everything from affiliation, cooperation, and trust, to companionable liking and romantic loving. But there are a number of other scholars whose contributions to our understanding of the nurturance motive focus directly on maternal nurturance. This expression of the nurturance motive is likely the evolutionary essence of its reason for being, as nurturance is the motivational expression of our biological drive for reproductive success. It is clearly also the place where we all learn how good nurturance feels, and have our first chances to practice giving and getting it. A brief account of some of this research follows.

John Bowlby pioneered the idea that emotional attachment of child to mother was a critical factor in the child's later mental health and social/intellectual functioning. In the aftermath of World War II, during which many children were orphaned and others separated from parents during the Blitz, Bowlby was commissioned to write a report for the World Health Organization (WHO) on the experiences of homeless children in post-war Europe. In the document that resulted,[4] Bowlby presented his conclusion that children needed a warm and stable relationship with a parent or parents starting in early infancy in order to avoid mental health problems in later life. Bowlby continued his work for decades, and is considered the father of attachment theory as well as a seminal student of separation anxiety.[5]

Mary Ainsworth, a colleague of Bowlby, extended the theory of attachment with her experiments using the "Strange Situation Procedure," where children experience systematic separations from their parent over a 30-minute period, in a series of situations of gradually increasing separation stress. Ainsworth used this procedure to classify the security of attachment between infants and mothers. Through ongoing study of infants showing different levels of security in their maternal attachments, Ainsworth advanced our understanding of how attachment between mother and infant proceeds, and how it can go awry. She published work on this topic with Bowlby in 1965.[6]

Harry Harlow[7] conducted perhaps the most famous experiments on the importance of nurturance in his famous study of rhesus monkeys. Harlow's experiment involved giving young rhesus monkeys a choice between two different "mothers." One was made of soft terrycloth, but provided no food. The other was made of wire, but provided food from a baby bottle attached through the back of the wire frame. Harlow removed monkeys from their natural mothers soon after birth and left them with the mother surrogates. The results were remarkable: baby monkeys spent significantly more time with the cloth mother than with the wire mother—seeking the physical comfort of soft maternal surfaces over actual nourishment from cold metallic mothers.

More recently[8] researchers at the University of Pennsylvania extended Harlow's idea to humans. They conducted a longitudinal study of 110 children in which they correlated observed parental interaction in home with formal tests of cognitive function over the period from age 4 to age 8. Their results demonstrated empirically that children who received more parental nurturance developed better cognitive abilities.

Surely all of this research points to mothering and being mothered as fundamental to the levels at which we experience, and the styles with which we express, the nurturance motive. Marketers would do well to consider the imagery of mothers and mothering whenever they are crafting a nurturance promise.

Let's take a look at the (fictional) lifestyle of a consumer who is especially oriented to being a nurturant in all dimensions.

Consumer Portrait: The Drive to Nurture

Susan likes to view her world as a warm and loving place where people care for and support each other. She is very motivated to help others feel good, and she enjoys it when others are also kind to her. She doesn't have a huge network of friends, but the close friends she has share bonds with her and with each other that are as deep and as constant as those with family. She's protective, supportive, and compassionate with those she loves. She remembers birthdays, shows up at games, and high-fives her patients and her staff throughout the day. Susan's friends and family know she'll always "have their backs," and she often looks after the interests of others before her own. She has a gift for always seeing the best in people and tends to give everyone, including strangers, the benefit of the doubt.

Susan knew she wanted to be a doctor from the time she time she was a young girl. Unlike some members of her profession, though, she is not primarily motivated by the financial rewards or the status being a physician accords; what motivates her is the satisfaction she gets from helping others. As her habits and pastimes outside of work also show, Susan is a tireless advocate for the vulnerable in our midst. She supports those causes in her heart and with her wallet, as a card-carrying member of organizations such as the World Wildlife Federation and United Way. Susan is a great target for your prosocial marketing effort.

When Susan goes shopping, she is often thinking about how the things she buys will make the people in her life feel. She buys brands of products that she notices her family members like, and she often asks for requests. She is also very interested in the companies that make the products she buys. She is likely to be willing to pay a little more for a product from a company that seems to care about its customers and about the world. Generic customer outreach that seems to just "go through the motions" of connecting with consumers will be worse than nothing for Susan. Nurturant consumers have well-developed radar for signs of authentic caring as well as for inauthentic posturing. If you actually care about her business, you can win it.

While most of her emotional energies are focused outward, Susan also spends some of her nurturing energies on herself, caring for her hair and skin and working out regularly at the gym. And if you watched her lovingly washing and waxing her vintage MG, you would be convinced you were looking at another facet of Susan's nurturant nature. And you would be right.

Marketing to the Nurturance Motive: Have Your Customers Felt Loved Today?

Marketing to consumers with a strong need for nurturance involves promising that your product will help satisfy their desire to care. This message can be conveyed head-on, as has traditionally been the case with food products ("Just like mom's"; "'nothing' says loving…"). Or the message can be more subtle, such as messages of protection, consideration, or thoughtfulness. Hallmark (which literally built a business on our desire to nurture) ran a 2009 campaign with the tagline: "A card. It's the biggest little thing you can do."

Nurturance messages can be found in marketing related to practically any product or service connected to caring or caretaking, including self-care. In the health and beauty industry, we don't have to look far to find messages that focus on pampering, renewing, or strengthening us. Olay skincare products do a good job of playing on our motivation to nurture our bodies when they encourage women to "love the skin you're in." Hair care marketing is rife with nurturance messages: fortify your hair with vitamins and nutrients and give it tender loving care to produce a lustrous, healthy "cared-for" look.

Although many marketing messages from financial service companies lead with security ("you can be confident that we know how to make the most of your money") or empowerment ("you can have the knowledge and insight to invest well"), it turns out that a strong nurturance need motivates consumers' choices in this service category. Consumers often feel a need to be cared for and to trust in the professionals and institutions that help them manage their money. And the potential symbolism of savings as a "gift to your heirs" is also a significant force in this category—linked to nurturance motivation through the idea that saving or preparing for your child's future demonstrates how much you love him or her today.

Sample Marketing Messages for Nurturance-Oriented Consumers

Consumers with nurturance motives seek to show their love to friends and family, to themselves, and even to beloved possessions. Examples of nurturance-oriented marketing messages include the following:

- We agree that the important things in life aren't things at all.
- Show (them, yourself, it) a little love.
- We can help you show how much you care.
- Help us help others.
- Part of our proceeds will go to children in need/breast cancer research (or similar causes).
- The makers of this product know that you are a generous and thoughtful person.
- Let us take care of the details so you can focus on what really matters.
- We'll help you spend more time with those you love.
- Feel closer to those you love.
- We understand and appreciate the beauty in life that you see.
- We're/they're so lucky to have you.
- Thanks for always seeing the best in others.

Case Studies for the Nurturance Motive

Frozen Food

The drive to nurture manifests itself most strikingly in the context of mothering and, not surprisingly given the roots of our word for this motive (*nūtritus* is Latin for "to suckle"), specifically in the realm of food preparation for the family.

Convenience foods pose interesting benefits for consumers seeking to care for families while leading demanding modern lifestyles, but they also pose challenges. On the one hand, these products free up time and help consumers get a hot meal on the table. On the other hand, the level of convenience and lack of hands-on effort can feel almost like a cop-out to nurturant consumers whose self-image is to be good mothers or fathers, husbands, etc.

Our client wanted to understand the best ways to talk to consumers about frozen entrées. The client offered a range of frozen products and wanted to give each product its own identity. We discovered that the different products in the line emerged with different associations for the company's primary consumers; some products were geared to mastery ("here's gourmet eating at its best"), some to identity ("set your imagination free with an exotic new cuisine"), and some to security ("you can count on this product every time").

One product emerged as an optimal candidate for enhanced nurturance positioning. It had two important qualifications: it came in a single family-sized portion and was designed to be baked in the oven rather than the microwave. Images for the product focused on steaming casserole-sized meals emerging from the oven—which carried the nurturant emotional associations to grandma's dinnertime meals—updated for our modern lives.

Breakfast

A breakfast food manufacturer was developing a new line of breakfast products for adults. We explored the atmosphere of breakfast time and the feelings that typically accompany eating breakfast, and we conducted a motivational analysis to uncover consumers' unmet emotional needs and wants right at the moment when they are deciding what to have for breakfast.

Data from this analysis indicated that consumers often felt as if their awakening each morning was almost like being reborn. They experienced an urge to "care for their inner infant" at breakfast time and to send themselves off to work with a warm, loving, fortifying meal. An appetite for self-nurturance was clearly on the table at breakfast time.

Based on this insight, our client developed and tested a range of new hot cereal concepts that focused on self-nurturing ideas such as providing "a little hug for your tummy" first thing in the morning. Responses to these ideas were extremely strong, and these ideas remain in the brand promise of that client's products today.

Insect Repellent

The motivation to nurture can also manifest in other less intimate forms of social behavior. A client in the insect repellent business came up against an unusual challenge. A bath oil marketed by a leading cosmetic company was rapidly encroaching on the market on the coattails of a grassroots movement for consumers to use the oil as an insect repellent for themselves and their kids.

Our client's scientists tested this bath oil extensively and found its effectiveness as a repellent to be marginal at best. Our client's products, on the other hand, contained the proven ingredient DEET and were shown in the same tests to be highly effective.

The client had always used a "problem/solution" model to illustrate how its repellent would solve users' insect troubles. That implied emotional benefits focused on needs for security—"keep my kids and me safe from these bugs"; "let us enjoy the outdoors with confidence that we won't be covered in bites."

But the results of our motivational research established that the true consumer motivation in this product category was about nurturance, not security: parents used repellents on their children because they wanted to take good care of them and to be good parents. Hosts at barbecues and pool parties provided insect repellents to their guests because they wanted those guests to be relaxed and happy and because they wanted to be good hosts.

And the fact was that offering an oily, petroleum-scented DEET-based repellent simply didn't feel like an act of nurturance. The bath oil, by contrast, went on like a lotion and smelled fabulous, and it came in a package that looked as if it were intended for skin care; it featured a lot of white and soft, flowing cursive lettering. Our client's products, on the other hand, came in packaging that looked like it belonged in an auto repair shop, complete with harsh colors, and large, black block lettering—altogether not something you'd reach for to express your love.

Once our client recognized the need to speak to the nurturance motivation, the company developed new products with a lotion-like feel, attractive fragrances, and packaging that resembled that of skin care products. The public response was resoundingly positive, and the bath oil craze gradually disappeared.

Furniture Care

One of our more intriguing projects demonstrated that even when surrounded by a world of loved ones, friends, children, and pets, we still have a reserve of nurturant energy that can be directed at the inanimate objects in our lives.

A client in the furniture polish business wanted to explore motivation in the furniture care category. This client had been experiencing some challenges to its business when a competitor's "dusting aid" claimed that its products left nothing behind on the furniture and so avoided any "unsightly buildup."

Our motivational research revealed that wood furniture, because it came from trees, continued to possess a certain "life" in the minds of consumers that needed to be nurtured. In this way, care for the wood furniture took on many of the emotional qualities of caring for living things. Deep in their subconscious, consumers felt as if their wooden furniture needed "feeding" or it would be starved and become dry and "dead."

Repositioning the product promise away from dust abatement to "giving your furniture the care it deserves" activated the nurturance motivations in the target group of homemakers.

Takeaways

1. The drive to nurture and be nurtured is clearly hardwired. We share the instinct with most other animals, but have evolved its expression far beyond its biological roots.
2. Altruism and compassion strengthen the bonds within social groups and thus reinforce the powerful evolutionary advantage of "strength in numbers."
3. We can direct our nurturing behavior to children, family, social groups, strangers, ourselves, and even inanimate objects.
4. Nurturing, including preserving traditions and artifacts, is one basis for the structure of our family and our culture.
5. Emphasis on nurturing benefits is an appealing way to market a wide range of products from food products to childcare, skin care, and even furniture care.
6. Cause marketing has a natural target in consumers who are motivated to nurture.
7. Our ideals of nurturing behavior are often linked to childhood memories, to sentimental and nostalgic images of when and how we felt particularly nurtured ourselves. The images of "the way mom/grandma did it" are the pinnacle of nurturing imagery.

CHAPTER 14

The Esteem Motive

Rodney Dangerfield built a career around his lack of it; Aretha Franklin got us on the dance floor with her demand for it; teen-agers sometimes commit mayhem in pursuit of it. And "ordinary heroes" earn it day in and day out through their acts of integrity, authority, grace, and kindness.

To borrow from Ms. Franklin, that elusive but much desired quality is often called *R E S P E C T*, but the academic term, the one we use in the field of psychology and in this book, is esteem.

Like the other motivations in the interpersonal triad, esteem has our inherently social nature at its core. And like the other motives in the bottom row of the matrix, it is focused on *outcomes*, in this case, on the outcome we seek from socializing and social interactions, including the approval, respect, and admiration of others.

If the intrapsychic need for security is the most developmentally basic motivation in our matrix, then esteem is arguably the most developmentally evolved. We become capable of desiring esteem only when we are able to view ourselves objectively, that is, with a view from the outside in. We are only able to evaluate our traits, skills, and accomplishments, to apply what we think is the perspective of others, and to develop the feeling that we deserve their approval, respect, and admiration when we have a solid, objective point of view of ourselves.

Like the other domains in the interpersonal column of the Forbes Matrix, the domain of esteem is quite broad. It covers the gamut of aspirations from the desire to be seen as prosocial, doing the right thing, to the drive for status, power, and influence. All of these aspirations rest on the foundation that a positive evaluation from others is a satisfying end unto itself.

Striving for Esteem

The deepest root of the drive for esteem is likely based in instinct as evidenced in the form of male preening that takes place among most animal species in mating season. Here we see a focused attempt to compete for social status with the aim of specific positive social outcomes. However, once we look for status seeking outside the context of reproductive attraction and once we move beyond other jousting for status among males that is also rooted in sexual competition, the drive for esteem emerges as quite developmentally evolved.

The drive for esteem appears early in childhood. Child psychologists mark the onset of esteem motivation at the point of toilet training when a child first shows an interest in "getting it right" for the encouraging and coaching parent, and experiences both pride and shame on the journey to that developmental milestone. Strivings for esteem continue to grow and take root as childhood progresses. Kids bring their school work home to show their parents and grandparents, and galleries of juvenile accomplishment soon adorn refrigerators as signals of parental pride and in turn make their children feel very proud in seeing them there. And of course, these galleries are made public in part on behalf of the strivings of the parents themselves: "Look how talented little Matt has become; isn't my gene pool fabulous?" and/or "aren't I doing a wonderful job raising him?"

At a fairly early age kids begin to show off to one another on playgrounds and in schoolrooms. Monkey bars and tetherball mastery become a venue for some to earn esteem on the playground; gold stars and test scores attest to the esteem goals of others expressed in the classroom.

The stakes around striving for esteem rise when puberty ushers in the agonies and ecstasies of adolescence: who gets invited to the "cool" birthday parties, who's included in which sleepovers, who sits where for lunch. And while esteem is on the face of it something earned by standing out from the crowd, the drive to gain respect from peers in adolescence can also generate a kind of conformity, particularly with respect to style and appearance.

It may not always be possible to know if one is measuring up to some invisible standard of "cool," but it is certain that the worst possible situation to find oneself in at this age is to be caught doing something that's "uncool." Like a flock of birds that seems to move in magical synchrony, teens look eagerly to one another to discern the direction of the next style, the next trend, and the newest definition of "cool." Conversely, striving for esteem by standing out from the crowd in adolescence can lead to a dangerous kind of brinksmanship, as teens indicate to one another how little they fear (lack of fear seems very cool at this age).

The Pecking Order

This familiar colloquial term has been around for nearly 200 years. It refers, as you might guess, to the method chickens use to express dominance. The most dominant chicken gets to peck all of the others; the least dominant chicken—you guessed it—gets pecked by all the rest.

In adulthood, strivings for esteem take forms as diverse as the social groups to which we eventually belong. And most of us belong to a range of groups, each with its own values against which we can earn esteem. Esteem in the workplace has different rules than esteem in a neighborhood, which has different values regulating it than those prevalent in a men's club or even those that prevail in the neighborhood bar. Diversity of esteem strivings also develops based on individual differences in character and personal ability. For example, the strong or the fast leverage their athleticism, the smart work to produce feats of intellect, and the artistic work to create their paintings or poetry, and so on.

An important distinction we should make clear at the beginning of our discussion about the esteem motive is that between two kinds of esteem: the striving for attention/envy and the striving for admiration/respect. The first type focuses on acquiring personal objects and attributes that may evoke attention or envy from social reference groups. It's a competitive striving, where esteem is linked to comparative accomplishment. The second type focuses on displaying personal excellence as measured against a metric of the sociomoral values we share. This type of striving is not necessarily competitive or comparative; instead, it's aimed at shaping personal behavior in a direction that will evoke *admiration and respect* across the spectrum of society.

The Scholarship on Esteem

Abraham Maslow[1] offers one of the most inclusive analyses and definitions of esteem. Maslow views psychological maturation in terms of movement through a series of stages, each characterized by the types of needs we focus on in each stage, as follows: physiological needs (warmth, food, etc.), safety needs; the need for belongingness and love, the need for esteem, and the need for self-actualization.

Maslow viewed the drive for esteem at the peak of the fulfillment of physiological, safety and belonging needs. He was the first to propose a distinction between two types of esteem motivations, a "lower" version (what we term esteem as envy) and a "higher" version (our esteem as respect). Maslow noted that both these ideas of esteem reflect our strong need to be accepted and valued. In the "lower version," esteem focuses on renown, fame, and flattery. These needs are fulfilled by external social reinforcement or reward and on positive feedback from others in one's social groups. In the "higher" version, esteem fulfillment becomes implicit and internalized, relating almost entirely to how we feel about ourselves. It is thus really a striving for "self-esteem," the respect and admiration we feel we deserve from others or that we imagine we would get from those we know and respect if only those people were aware of our actions.

More recently, the work of Daniel Batson,[2] a social psychologist, has focused on the "higher" form of esteem seeking through acts of prosocial helping behavior. Batson's work on the forces that trigger helping behavior has become known as the "empathy-altruism hypothesis." According to his hypothesis, altruistic helping behavior requires a kind of empathy for the person(s) in need. Batson suggests that the degree of emotional empathy we feel for another person who needs help regulates the level of prosocial action we take on that person's behalf.

Batson's theories suggest that this subset of self-esteem behaviors may be anchored in judgments we make about how we would feel if we were the person who needs help. In his view, the motivation to help another person may be a case where benefits to the self (i.e., a feeling of self-esteem) are not the ultimate goal of helping but are instead an unintended consequence of it. How much of our internalized striving for self-esteem may be a function of empathy for others is a subject for future study.

Strivings for "Low" Esteem: Attention/Envy

A great number of esteem-seeking behaviors are strivings of the "low" type of esteem, where we seek to acquire visible evidence of our superior levels of success or our prowess as signaled in the status symbols, awards, possessions, and fame we gain in our lives. Our beautiful lawns, our beautiful children, even the brand of refrigerator we choose all provide strong signals to others that we have "arrived." Our status symbols often attest to our financial standing and can include the attention we pay to our cars, our clothes, and that panoply of toys we accumulate in the belief that he who dies with the most, wins. The instinct to compare yourself with others and to have them appreciate your quality and that of your possessions is a more primitive element of esteem motivation. Indeed, it is probably an extension of the energy originally focused on that original competition for a sexual partner.

In modern times, the level of our attention to the social comparison of our material circumstances has reached new and extreme heights. This kind of striving for esteem is rooted in the possibility that we can control and change our material circumstances. It rests on the idea of upward mobility, which is, in many ways, a by-product of the Industrial Revolution.

When life still revolved around agriculture and animal husbandry, access to arable land and workers to tend it was pretty much the only route to wealth and status. And land was for the most part an inherited commodity that was the sole province of aristocrats and landed gentry. Prominent families held the same lands for generations, and that land was farmed by successive generations of tenant farmers.

Wealth accumulated and increased in the aristocracy generation after generation. But the successive generations of farmers didn't really do much better than their parents and grandparents had before them. This arrangement was widely understood to be the "natural order" of things, and as such it was considered a manifestation of "God's will."

Horatio Alger Jr. was a prolific nineteenth-century American author best known for his many popular children's books featuring a rags-to-riches narrative, wherein boys rose from humble beginnings to the upper echelons of American society through hard work and personal virtue. Alger's writings were especially influential in the Gilded Age of the late nineteenth and early twentieth centuries when real-life rags-to-riches stories were evident in the breathtaking success and accompanying wealth of the legends of contemporary entrepreneurs, such as Andrew Carnegie, the son of a weaver who became one of the richest and most influential men of his age.

Interestingly, Horatio Alger is often invoked incorrectly today as if he himself rose from rags to riches. He did not. Harvard-educated, Alger had been born into what we'd now call the upper middle class.

In this historical context, one's social and economic position was largely predetermined, and the idea of significantly improving one's lot in life was rarely a consideration. Of course, even then people compared themselves with others in their social rank, but the notion that they could qualitatively transcend their class would have been quite foreign at the time.

This all changed with the advent of the Industrial Revolution. As older, more rigid social hierarchies fell away, new options for social mobility took their place. Manufacturing innovations created a new working class that functioned in a new social stratum of its own making, beneath nobility but above peasantry. This group succeeded largely on each individual's personal merits. Increases in production and commerce soon created a merchant class that was the foundation of the middle class most people belong to today. For the first time ever, if people worked harder and smarter, they could accomplish—and possess—almost anything. This new vista was particularly clear and compelling in the United States, where the Constitution expressly forbids aristocracy by insisting that "no title of nobility shall be granted by the United States."

Within this new environment of social and economic mobility, "captains of industry" arose. Great entrepreneurs like Carnegie, Melon, and Hearst amassed almost incomprehensible fortunes, complete with lavish lifestyles and possessions. They were not royalty; they had no titles or heraldry. Instead, their possessions became the testament to their status. And the middle and working classes, understanding that these men rose from humble beginnings, selected their own dreams to strive toward. Along the way, material possessions became the status symbols of the post aristocratic social structure.

Later, with the advent of television, it became possible for the first time for the public to be regularly and broadly exposed to how the other half lived and to see what rich people had for dinner, what cars they drove, what clothes they wore. And our appetites for material goods were stoked by all of this material possibility. Naturally, forums for displaying wealth and success have expanded greatly with the advent of the Internet and our ubiquitous computers and smartphones. And all this gave rise to the desire to "keep up with the Joneses."

Keeping up with the Joneses

The long-running comic strip *Keeping up with the Joneses* (see sidebar) helped spread the idea of measuring ourselves by comparison against the outward

Still Keeping Up[3]

The cartoon *Keeping up with the Joneses* ran nationally from 1913 to 1939, and its influence is still felt today. In fact, given our fascination with celebrities and reality TV, such as the similarly named show *Keeping Up with the Kardashians*, the concept of social comparison promoted by the cartoon has likely even increased in prevalence.

signs of the success of others. At the end of World War II, this form of social competition, this striving for the "low" variety of esteem, reached new heights in the United States where a vigorous postwar economy helped the average person craft a new life, a new prosperity, with new benchmarks of material success.

Fame and Fortune

Alongside the material strivings for the low variety of esteem, we should also mention those who seek celebrity or fame. In some cases, this element of the esteem motive manifests through vicarious fulfillment as we identify with famous people in order to share their esteem. Fan clubs and fan magazines allow us to follow the lives of our sports or media heroes and imagine ourselves living like that. We might wear clothing associated with that person or adopt our idol's hairstyle to be a part of the legend, and we do all this as a means to get a small, reflected connection to fame.

Meanwhile, our modern connected world now offers a host of venues for the pursuit of actual personal celebrity. Post your music on YouTube, for example, and you may become the talk of the town or even of the globe. Or you can put your images on Instagram, or Pinterest, and they may wind up in various print media sources. Organized commercial conduits to fame also abound. There are more reality shows than scripted programming today, each offering a chance for ordinary citizens to be plucked from obscurity and elevated to stardom.

Of course, the rise of the online social network has created even more opportunities to seek esteem and to measure whether we have it. Film celebrities, politicians, and other newsmakers are celebrated, vilified, judged, and

Friend or Frenemy?

New research confirms what many of us in my field may have suspected: Constant exposure to the "perfect" families, awesome vacations, and adorable pets of our Facebook universe may be making some of us miserable. A German study found that one in three people felt worse after visiting Facebook and felt more dissatisfied with his or her own life. Researchers noted that these negative feelings left users feeling, lonely, frustrated, and angry even after they logged off.[4]

compared, for example, according to the number and temperament of their Twitter followers.

Social media continues to transform what it means to be esteemed by others. We can tell in an instant who's viewed our profile and who shares a first connection with us in LinkedIn. We can participate in an endless variety of online forums and see who recommends us, and we can make decisions about whom we should recommend in turn. We'll probably never meet many of the members of our LinkedIn groups in person, but our association with them allows us to earn and grant esteem through our virtual interactions. We collect virtual esteem today much as we counted the Valentines we received in second grade.

We should note that we always have very specific social reference groups in mind when we engage in our strivings for this low variety of esteem. What might get us a lot of attention and envy from one group (e.g., a fabulous tattoo or a Harley-Davidson motorcycle) is very different from what would get us esteem from a different reference group (e.g., that Louis Vuitton Bag or a Rolex watch). And of course, what might make us famous within one particular reference group (the ability to eat 60 hot dogs at one sitting) is very different from what may create fame in another group (an encyclopedic knowledge of Shakespeare's sonnets).

Strivings for "High" Esteem: Admiration and Respect

Besides our yearnings for fame and fortune, we also desire the high variety of esteem. This type of esteem motivates drives us to engage in prosocial activities and to seek sociomoral esteem by doing the right thing, setting an example, or standing up for what is right. The urge to do the right thing may have its roots partly in our instincts to nurture and the altruistic behavior that can arise from nurturant instincts. It may also have roots in the instinctual drive to connect and belong by doing good for others.

Those seeking the high variety of esteem are not locked into a circumscribed reference group context as a source of validation. Instead, the search for this kind of esteem revolves around social values and evaluations that cut across lines of class and subculture. Doing the right thing—demonstrating honesty, integrity, loyalty, dependability, selflessness, and other social virtues—can be a path to the higher kind of esteem for any of us and can also earn us admiration and respect from a wide range of people. In these situations, strivings for esteem are really strivings for self-esteem: when we do the right thing based on our internalized personal value code, we can imagine the positive judgments of others, and we experience the fulfillment of our esteem needs when we conclude that others would hold us in esteem if they knew what we'd done:

An internalized sense of healthy self-esteem provides a constant source of fulfillment for our esteem strivings. It allows us to have ongoing pride in our actions and ongoing faith in our values and principles even when

> We collect our "virtual" esteem much as we counted the Valentines we received in second grade.

they're challenged by others. We trust our convictions, and feel free to voice an opinion on matters of values or ethics, and we're also confident enough to have an open mind about new ideas. We can respect others' points of view without a reflexive need to challenge them. We can also enjoy the company of diverse types of people even if they hold opinions very different from our own.

Furthermore, several studies clearly link healthy self-esteem to both greater mental and physical health. In adolescents, self-esteem is related to lower incidence of anxiety and depression. Adults with higher self-esteem tend to be more productive, can talk about successes in life without overinflating them, and can accept criticism of their actions without shame or embarrassment.

Meanwhile, we should note that not all of what appear to be esteem strivings are rooted in selfless desires to do the right thing. Politicians and other social servants, for example, strive for this type of esteem because they hope it will become a basis for broad support of their political aspirations.

Striving for Esteem in Consumer Behavior

In consumer behavior, the search for the validation of external esteem and the striving for internal self-esteem can be widely observed. Just like our adolescent selves, many of us continue to search out the "cool things" in life with the hope that this will boost our social esteem.

Consumers driven by desires for more internal self-esteem and a prosocial image of themselves may buy products they feel represent good social values and then feel fulfilled by the social respect and/or personal self-esteem this behavior generates. Some examples for this version of esteem-building could include buying products from small merchants we want to support, buying only recycled paper goods to help reduce waste and care for the planet, and avoiding processed foods at the grocery store that may be bad for humans in general. These behaviors and others like them are driven by our needs for self-esteem that arise from the morals and values we internalize from our social groups. In these cases we do not require the explicit positive social judgment of others.

In consumer behavior as in behavior generally, we may find the low variety of esteem masquerading as the high type, and we may see apparently prosocial behavior that is actually driven by the desire to gain the attention or envy of others. The writers of South Park famously portrayed Toyota's hybrid Prius sedan as the "Pious" in an episode poking fun at drivers who may purchase this car in part for the politically correct image the purchase gives them.

Andy Warhol Was Right[5]

Andy Warhol once commented that in the future we will all be famous for fifteen minutes. Our superconnected lifestyle and our ability for self-promotion may be making Warhol's future a reality. Increasingly, our media are becoming populated with visually familiar faces of people who have done nothing special—but are "famous for being famous."

Consumer Portrait: The Longing for Respect

Maria likes to view her world as a place filled with chances for her to do the right thing. She is a valued and active member of the large Hispanic community in which she lives. She supports a variety of causes and participates actively in the community political action group. Maria will always do her best at whatever she is doing. She has little time for the "faux-lunteers" she meets who seem more interested in getting credit for good deeds than in actually doing them. Over the years, Maria has learned a lot about local government and has met and earned the respect of everyone from town manager to town clerk. As a result, she is the go-to person for friends, neighbors, and other community members who need help navigating the intricacies of local politics.

Through a decade and a half of solid, high-quality work, bolstered by referrals from happy clients, Maria has developed a successful real estate business. She has a reputation for honesty and trustworthiness, and people feel safe putting their property in her hands, knowing she can be counted on to get the best deal for them.

Maria's motivational orientation is also evident in her family life. She's taught her kids that one key to success in life is doing your best and honoring your commitments. Though they're still young, Maria's son and daughter already know the importance of self-respect and respect for others. And of course, she takes pride in them for that reason.

As a consumer, Maria is a great a fan and advocate of recyclable or earth-friendly products; she reads the ingredient lists and packaging. She tries to learn about the political and social orientation of the companies whose products she buys. She is a loyal customer for products and services that embrace a prosocial agenda, and tries to stay away from brands whose manufacturers don't have such a prosocial position. She will choose the socially responsible product option even if it means paying a bit more for it. She is committed to shopping locally and feels strongly that small businesses should get support from their local communities. You can recruit Maria to your brand franchise by adhering to sound business ethics and creating products that are good for your customers and, when possible, also good for the planet.

Marketing to Needs for Esteem

Marketing to consumers seeking the low variety of esteem in the form of social competition is very hard to distinguish from the old-fashioned marketing approach of telling people: "look how cool my widget is." That is, one needs only to combine romancing the product as the best with an implied (or even explicit) promise that "you'll be the envy of your neighbors" to carry the day with consumers seeking esteem as attention/envy.

Adopting celebrity spokespeople for your product can also enhance its appeal to those seeking the low kind of esteem because the spokesperson certifies that the product is desirable. Will wearing JLo's perfume or Jessica Simpson's clothing line really imbue consumers with these star's qualities? Likely not, but the marketing for these products is intended to suggest that how people regard JLo is exactly how they will regard another woman wearing her perfume. Likewise, wearing a jersey with LeBron James's number won't really improve your basketball game, but it may give you a small cachet of stardom on the gym floor. Touting an award-winning status for your product or claiming that 98 percent of consumers prefer it can also bolster the idea that your product is the one others wish they had. We should note that this version of marketing to the esteem motive is most appropriate for products that have the potential for status value in the target market. Paper towels or trash bags will likely not be good candidates for this type of marketing.

Marketing to consumers' desires for high esteem involves promising or implying that a product will reflect or help develop their image as individuals with values and attitudes that are respected and admired by others. One of the most prevalent forms of this type of esteem marketing is that of nonprofits; their advertising plays directly on our desires to do a good thing for people in need, to set a good example with our actions to be caring, selfless, or generous. The campaign to go pink in support of breast cancer is an example of cause marketing that succeeds because of its ties to the mainstream products that identify the consumer as someone who is doing good.

The advent of social responsibility as a spotlight issue in recent years provides a host of opportunities to market products to those who seek respect and admiration for their product choices. If a product choice supports an admirable basic values lifestyle (artisanal goat cheese or clothing made locally)or if it is good for the planet (green home care products, hybrid automobiles) or if it works to conserve resources that are now deemed to be dwindling (recycling, bicycling), marketers can benefit from concentrating on a message highlighting the benefits of esteem. "Buy and Give" products can also take advantage of consumers' strivings for high esteem. Tom's Shoes and 2 Degrees Food are recent examples of this marketing approach, which had its roots in Paul Newman's "Newman's Own" food products started in 1982.

Sample Marketing Messages: Esteem

Since esteem motives occur in two forms, the low and high varieties of esteem, marketing messages geared to this motivation also need to take two forms. Ideas that will likely play well for a marketing strategy aimed at consumers seeking the low variety of esteem. Low include the following:

- You've arrived.
- Be the envy of your friends.
- Imagine the look on their faces when they see you have this.
- You're going to look like a million bucks.
- This is the one for discerning consumers who know what quality looks like.
- Not just anyone can carry this off, but you can.
- You know quality when you see it.
- Good taste is its own reward.
- It's perfect for [your celebrity role model] and perfect for you too.
- Show them who's boss.

Ideas that will likely play well for marketing messages aimed at consumers seeking the high variety of esteem include the following:

- Set a good example.
- You have a right to feel proud.
- Because it's the right thing to do.
- There's more to life than toys.
- We trust you: you always do the right thing.
- Your good opinion matters most to us.
- No wonder others look up to you:
- Your vision—a path to follow.
- We applaud your conviction.

Esteem Case Studies

Fine Dining

A prominent national steakhouse wanted to explore ways to enhance customers' perception that the restaurant was a place for very special (that is, highly esteemed) patrons. The company's business was focused on those dinner occasions when executives brought clients, prospects, or vendors to the steakhouse. The company knew this customer group represented a high-value target and wanted to identify ways to stand out more from the competition.

In our motivational analysis, we discovered that the hosts of those special dinners were highly motivated by the desire to gain the admiration of their guests. They wanted the restaurant to provide a service experience that communicated that they were indeed high-status customers, and this would then increase their guests' admiration of their hosts.

Management understood that this esteem-focused service strategy—the prestige of the exclusive restaurant and the highly personalized experience of dining there—would increase both the loyalty of the restaurant's primary clients and the positive word of mouth among the guests of these primary clients. We worked with the company to design an exceptional service program called VIP for a day.

In that program, the business hosts of steakhouse dinners could provide the restaurant with important details about their preferences, including seating, service details (such as servers calling them by their name), and meal selections. The VIP hosts were always warmly greeted, welcomed, and recognized by restaurant managers and servers.

A trial of this program at selected locations was very successful and senior management at this restaurant chain is planning similar affinity programs across the country.

Home Decorating

Our client, a manufacturer of decorative items for the home, wanted to understand what the company's high-end clients were truly searching for when they selected objects for decorating their homes. These homeowners were able to afford just about anything they wanted, so the opportunity for our client to stand out from the crowd of exclusive home product offerings would be crucial to the firm's success in this marketplace.

Motivational analysis showed that these homeowners had a strong interest in responsible design. This design vision included one-of-a-kind objects from the third world or other disadvantaged areas. These décor choices gave the impression that these women were not only cultured and successful but were also outstanding stewards of the world, forward thinkers who made choices that advanced the causes of vulnerable populations—that is, they were making décor choices that were worthy of esteem.

Our client's marketing people realized that offering socially responsible decorating choices that were much more interesting and "socially evolved" could indeed set them apart from the typical luxury home goods stores. This approach could potentially get them off the treadmill of searching for *de rigueur* items that were always at risk of becoming stale.

Vaccines

As those of us who regularly market to physicians know, they are a marketing challenge unto themselves. They're busy, they're excessively marketed to, and they tend to be not interested in many of the product promises made by pharmaceutical manufacturers. Our client was a major maker of vaccines, whose marketing people knew that a small fraction of doctors accounted for most of the vaccinations given. The client wanted to understand more about what moved these doctors to be vaccine enthusiasts.

Our motivational research for this client confirmed one assumption and yielded two big surprises. We were not surprised to learn that one of our groups of heavy vaccine users saw the vaccinations as a way to protect and care for their patient base; that is, they acted on the nurturance motive.

But two other groups came to their enthusiasm about vaccines from less expected motivational sources. The first outlier group saw vaccines as a very efficient way to generate income for their practices—a somewhat surprising dynamic, given the typical self-presentation of doctors as selfless servants of the public good. This group showed very high scores regarding the achievement motive.

The second outlier group saw vaccination primarily as a way to set an example for their medical colleagues. Vaccination for this last group was an important public health issue, and a lack of vaccination was a trend in medical practices they felt a need to improve. Often these doctors were in a group identified by pharmaceutical researchers as KOLs (key opinion leaders). The aspirations of these doctors to lead a public health charge for vaccination appeared to be driven by a desire to gain the respect and admiration of others for the examples they were setting (a high esteem motive).

We also discovered that the doctors in these three different motivational groups tended to practice in three distinct types of medical settings (probably appealing to these different medical personalities). As a result of this research, our client had three distinct approaches to discussing vaccination with doctors, each targeting one of the three different practice contexts where different motivational dynamics were likely to be found. This tactic allowed our client to adopt the best approach to persuading doctors for vaccination in each type of medical setting, a winnowing tactic that's proven very successful.

Takeaways

1. Consumers' drives for esteem are broad in focus, from generally prosocial behavior to striving for influence and power.
2. Esteem drives have been organized into two levels of esteem striving:
   - Low esteem goals focus on competitive striving. Attention and envy from others are the goals of low esteem.
   - High esteem goals focus on moral/ethical desirability, such as by means of setting a good example and behaving in an exemplary manner.
3. Low esteem rewards are usually defined in the context of a social reference group (e.g., what my kind of people would envy or admire).

4. By contrast, high esteem goals focus on broader and often internalized social and moral values.

5. Successful marketing to consumers motivated by seeking the low variety of esteem includes romanticizing the products and positioning them as something others will envy or admire.

6. Traditional status symbols, including clothes, homes, cars, and other possessions, appeal to those seeking the low type of esteem. They signal financial standing and support consumers' efforts to gain attention and envy from others.

7. Celebrity endorsements and designations like "award-winning" or "unanimously preferred" are great methods for reaching consumers motivated by seeking the low type of esteem.

8. Consumers most often satisfy their desire for the high type of esteem implicitly, by imagining what others would think of them if they knew of their actions.

9. Marketing to those seeking the high type of esteem requires that a brand conforms to the dominant moral or ethical goals and standards of society.

10. Seeking the high variety of esteem drives consumers to align with products or brands that give voice to their strongly held prosocial values.

11. Affinity and cause marketing are very effective tools for reaching consumers motivated by the drive for the high type of esteem.

This page intentionally left blank

CHAPTER 15

The Scholarship on Motivation

Throughout these pages, you've discovered nine core motivations that drive *all* consumer behavior. I've attempted to map these ideas out in a way that makes it easy for you to think about how to incorporate some of them into your own business almost immediately—as soon as you close the covers of this book, if not sooner. I also hope that your new viewpoint on consumer motivation brings you great success.

But I would be remiss if I left you without at least a summary glance at the great students of motivation that have illuminated this topic since antiquity. It is upon their shoulders that my work has been constructed.

The Ancients

Discussions on the nature of motivation began over 2,000 years ago, with the works of the great Greek philosophers. The ideas of Plato, Socrates, and Aristotle about how and why things happen provided the basis for the motivation theory implemented in the nineteenth century. They continue to inform our theories today.

Aristotle[1] in particular explored the relationship between cause and effect. Of the four types of causality Aristotle explains (material, formal, efficient, and teleological) two influence modern psychological tenets of motivation theory. First, efficient causality looks at human behavior in terms of what has happened before. A modern-day application of this idea is behaviorism—the concept that explains behavior in terms of the conditioning we experienced in our past and were molded by.

Aristotle's doctrine of teleological causality, on the other hand, looks at human behavior in terms of the outcomes we want to bring about as a result of the things we do. In other words, it looks forward to the future to see what we hope will happen as a result of our actions.

This last notion is the foundation for the idea of striving toward a goal, which underlies most of current theories on motivation. So, for example, "John started the opinion page in the newsletter because he wants to become president of his organization" demonstrates that the processes that lie behind this type of goal-oriented (or "teleological") behavior *push* us to make the choices in the present we hope will help us reach our goals in the future.

Along the same lines, the ancient concepts also provide the foundation for understanding motivations as forces that *pull* us to strive in our behavior— again toward outcomes we hope to make happen.

Medieval Writers

Medieval thinkers such as Augustine and Thomas Aquinas brought a greater interest in religion to the discussion. Augustine[2] was interested in establishing a basis for free will in human action because he wanted to demonstrate that God was not responsible for evil in the world. Like the Greeks, Augustine saw our behavior as the result of an interplay between the forces of virtue or spirit and those of desire or passion, which were mediated by intellect and rationality. But unlike the Greeks, Augustine posited the potential for an "immoral act of free will." He felt that immoral behavior could fully be a result of the operation of the intellect, which could freely decide to give in to passion and the appeal of temporal pleasures.

Thomas Aquinas created one of the most complex and detailed accounts of human motivation in his writings, with a fully articulated vision of the process through which psychological forces interact to control intentional behaviors. The process begins when the human will creates a goal for an individual. Aquinas viewed the human will as fundamentally focused on a desire for the good. Once a person has a goal in mind, a process of intellectual deliberation takes place and forms a plan for reaching the goal. Once the behavior is chosen by intellect and executed, the outcome is experienced as the joy of achievement by the virtuous will.

Aquinas also thought there were forces of passion in the human psyche, and he acknowledged that these forces could push one toward actions that were not a pursuit of the good. However, unlike Augustine, Aquinas saw human beings as fundamentally virtuous, and he believed that the forces of passion could never entirely overwhelm the force of intellect as long as it was functioning properly. Thus, evil action became a form of psychological malfunction for Aquinas, giving us the first notions of an "abnormal psychology."

The Fathers of Modern Motivational Psychology

In the eighteenth and nineteenth centuries, with the Industrial Revolution in full swing, writers turned away from purely spiritual questions about human motives to adopt a more practical line of inquiry and so the idea of "applied motivation theory" was born. Understanding that no amount of factory automation could function without the stewardship of a workforce, these social scientists and writers turned their attention to how an understanding of motivation might help manufacturers succeed in the brand-new and bustling world of factories and manufacturing. Front and center in these efforts was the task of understanding the motivation to work and of developing ways to increase motivation in the workforce so as to improve profitability. These efforts in applied motivation were of great interest to the rising class of factory owners with employees they wanted to motivate to work as long and as hard as humanly possible.

Jeremy Bentham (1746–1832)

Jeremy Bentham, writing at the end of the eighteenth century, was the father of a school of ethics called utilitarianism, an ethical and social doctrine that advocated, among other things, that the best solutions were those that served the highest good of the greatest number of people.

Within Bentham's larger body of work is the first appearance of "the carrot and stick" as twin motivators of human behavior. Through this lens, motivation theory exhibited both a positive and a negative face. Human behavior could be described as attempts to avoid or reduce negative outcomes while trying to attain or strengthen positive ones.

Bentham's philosophy of carrot and stick motivation is expressed in *An Introduction to the Principles of Morals and Legislation*, in which he argues that "nature has placed mankind under the governance of two sovereign masters: pain and pleasure."[3]

In the dehumanizing atmosphere of the "factory age it was perhaps a natural consequence—if not a particularly admirable one—that Bentham's work focused as it did upon using motivational theory to drive worker productivity. To his credit, Bentham was also a strong opponent of slavery, a strong advocate for religious freedom and social tolerance in general, and an energetic campaigner for improvement of working conditions in the factories.

William James (1842–1910)

William James is widely considered the father of American psychology. In his *Principles of Psychology*,[4] James integrated insights into positive and negative motivation into a formal theory of motivational psychology. He called motivations the springs of action in human behavior.

James also separated his vision of motivation from conscious decision making, deliberation, and even conscious goal setting. Instead, James proposed that inherited instincts serve as motivations for behavior. He believed that we act in ways that enhance or protect our survival and did not think it necessary to add a layer of conscious control or decision making to this account of the causes of human behavior.

James created a list of human instincts that included attachment, play, shame, anger, fear, shyness, modesty, and love. In all, he identified 20 physical instincts, and 17 mental instincts that he felt explained human behavior. In many ways, James's vision of behavior laid the foundation for Freud, who also talked of behavior as being driven by instinctual forces.

James is also well known for what's widely called the James-Lange theory (developed independently James and Carl Lange, a Danish physician working independently in Europe).[5] Both James and Lange argued that emotions begin with a stimulus and a reaction, which then trigger the corresponding emotion. For example, James invited us to consider, in part, whether we run away from a bear because we fear it, or whether we experience fear because we are running away?

Sigmund Freud (1856–1939)

Sigmund Freud's contributions to psychological theory almost all derive from his therapeutic interactions with and reflections about patients he took on in order to cure their neuroses. His therapeutic work led him to become very interested in the insights into the human psyche that can be gained by looking at behavior that is unintentional ("Freudian slips") or that is unconscious (*interpretation of dreams*).[6] Freud's explanations of the role of the unconscious in his therapies provide the first insight into why explicit question-and-answer examinations of human behavior do not reveal much about the causes of our actions. To learn what really moves us, Freud would suggest, we must reach below conscious reasoning and touch the powerful drives of the subconscious.

Freud saw the human psyche as dominated by two primary drives or motivational forces, both of which were evident in the unconscious: life (Eros) and death (Thanatos). Depending on which drive is dominant at the time, our actions constantly move us either toward life or toward death. The drive of Eros pulls us toward life-affirming actions and beliefs, including eating, reproducing, and exercising. The drive of Thanatos is manifest in dangerous or risky behavior such as starting fights or driving dangerously.

Sigmund Freud took motivational theory to the next level with his theory that the human psyche is made up of three components: the id, the ego, and the superego. In his view of human behavior, what we do arises from an interplay among what our emotional urges push us toward doing, what our rational consciousness tells us is reasonable or possible to do, and what the judgmental faculties of our superego tell us we *ought* to do. Looking at the influence of unconscious emotional forces in motivating us, Freud laid the groundwork for current theories and research regarding unconscious motives.

David McClelland (1917–1998)

David McClelland took Bentham's concept of applying motivation theory in the workplace to a much higher level. He studied the forces of human motivation as a way to help corporations understand the distinctive motivations of different kinds of employees and to build work environments that were distinctively rewarding to workers with different motivational dynamics. McClelland identified three types of motivating needs in the workforce: the need for achievement, the need for affiliation, and the need for power.

The need for achievement was McClelland's first and most prolonged focus of study. He identified the striving for achievement as the drive to create, to solve problems, and to accomplish tasks. He noted that employees with a high need for achievement tended to focus on the achievement itself rather than on the accolades, rewards, or pay they might receive as a result of it.

McClelland described the need for affiliation as a drive toward harmonious relationships with others, including a need for approval. He noted that people with a high need for affiliation were usually "conformists" in the workplace who would do well in jobs with high levels of public contact.

Finally, McClelland discussed a need for power among workers. He saw this need in two forms—a need for personal power, involving directing others and being in charge, and a need for institutional or social power, involving the desire to organize others on behalf of a company or an organization.

McClelland's work on striving for achievement and affiliation[7] is one of the main building blocks of modern motivational theory and explicitly reflected in the Forbes Matrix.

Abraham Maslow (1908–1970)

Abraham Maslow's theory of the hierarchy of needs[8] famously describes the developmental sequence of human needs that moves from the most basic through to the most evolved. Maslow's theory posits that we are motivated by unsatisfied needs and that each level of needs, once satisfied, leads us up to the next. Maslow's account begins with the most fundamental physiological needs and progresses to the abstract need of feeling actualized as a person.

At the most basic level, we first strive to meet our metabolic and survival needs—food, water, air, warmth, shelter—and our reproductive needs. Only after our physiological needs are met are we able to move to the next level of the hierarchy and strive to satisfy our safety needs. After our physiological and safety needs are met, we can then consider our social needs; primarily, these consist of the need to feel a sense of belonging with others that could include love, friendship, and acceptance. When those belonging needs are met, we can address our drives for esteem, both self-esteem and the esteem of others. Finally, at the pinnacle of Maslow's hierarchy is our drive toward self-actualization, the opportunity to realize our full potential in every respect.

Maslow's model of the needs hierarchy is still among the systems taught to marketers as a basis for developing marketing strategy and one of the theories taught to business executives to help them manage and motivate employees. The model remains a valued resource in the workplace, particularly in human resources, even today.

Maslow has received some criticism from motivational theorists for his preoccupation with the pinnacle of the human condition he calls self-actualization. His premise that all of us are actively striving for actualization in real time ignores a vast range of behaviors whose energies have nothing to do with how we feel about ourselves. And his stipulation that actualization is the endpoint of everyone's strivings in life ignores the vast majority of us whose attainments may fall far short of self-actualization. In short, Maslow's theory is a very potent vision of how we *ought to* lead our lives and what we *ought to* be striving for in our behavior, but it is less accurate as a description of what people *are actually* striving for in their day-to-day behavior. We might say that Maslow's motivation—to build an account of how people become self-actualized—led him to pay less attention to the varieties of motivation that drive most of us most of the time.

The other theorists whose work on motivation has shaped the perspective I've offered in this book are far too numerous to summarize here. In a review of motivational theory I published in 2011,[9] I identified 106 writers on the topic, and I would commend that article as a starting point for those interested in a more granular view of the history of this topic.

Takeaways

1. Great thinkers have been fascinated by the question of "why we do what we do" for thousands of years.
2. The concept of doing things *because of outcomes they will create* appeared in philosophical literature as far back as the Greeks and formed the foundation for thinking about motivation as a drive to create outcomes through actions.
3. The idea of *unconscious motives* made its appearance in the nineteenth century, most notably in the writings of Sigmund Freud.
4. The study of motivation for use in business appeared at the onset of mass production and factory work when owners sought ways to motivate their workers to increased productivity.
5. Scholars in great numbers have sought to enumerate a catalog of human motives over the past hundred years, but none has tried to integrate the totality of past efforts into a unified theory before now.

This page intentionally left blank

CHAPTER 16

MindSight: Learning to Talk to the Emotional Brain

You've spent a good bit of time reading this book and learning how to view the world through the lens of emotional motivation. In this chapter I turn to the challenge of actually accessing insights about those emotional motivations in order to better understand and market to the emotions of your consumers.

But here's the rub: having an emotional conversation with our consumers is not nearly as easy as recognizing the need to have it. By far the biggest barrier to opening an emotional dialogue with our consumers is that they are very often unaware of the emotional forces driving their actions. Even if they wanted to talk about these emotional forces, they often can't because they themselves don't have access to them.

The Can't Say Barrier: The Role of the Subconscious
in Consumer Emotions

For the researcher seeking to learn how people feel, the unconscious nature of emotional activity creates what has been called the "can't say" barrier, which means that in most circumstances, consumers truly "can't say" what they are feeling because they cannot access that information.

We can only speculate about the reasons why emotions reside primarily in the unconscious, but we do know that conscious, rational thought is only the tip of the iceberg of brain activity. As Dr. Emmanuel Donchin of the Laboratory for Cognitive Psychophysiology at the University of Illinois writes: "An enormous portion of cognitive activity is non-conscious.... It could be

99 percent; we probably will never know precisely how much is outside aware-ness."[1] And this makes intuitive sense. Even our rational processing takes place in large part below the threshold of consciousness. If we had to consciously formulate and sequentially perform every element of a complex task, such as driving our car, for instance, we'd never get beyond our driveway, let alone navigate freeways, enjoy chatty companions, sing along to our favorite songs, or use our conscious brain to think about and plan the strategy of our day. And thus it falls to our subconscious to perform the myriad small judgments and calculations that make up many of the things that we do. Add to those tasks—and they are just a tiny sliver of what's really going on within us—the incredible network of subtle social judgments and assessments we perform in the course of a day, and it's easy to see why nearly everything we do or think happens beneath the edge of our conscious awareness.

And so it is with emotion. The limbic system, identified as the seat of emo-tional brain activity, acts and reacts independently of the frontal lobes where consciousness resides. And many of these emotional processes never reach the level of consciousness. This situation has of late spawned a variety of books on our "irrationality," on the fact that we often act under the sway of emotional biases of which we are unaware.[2] In recent years, an entire discipline called "Behavioral Economics" has undertaken the study of how decision making is influenced by irrational emotional forces. I recommend an excellent book by Daniel Kahneman, *Thinking Fast and Slow*, for readers who want to begin at the beginning of this important theoretical work.[3] There is still another bar-rier to emotional learning that prevents us from simply asking people about their feelings: the "won't say" barrier. Here's how that works.

The "Won't Say" Barrier: Roots inEvolution

Our ability to say one thing and mean another is what scientists call "strat-egizing behavior," a somewhat euphemistic moniker for what preschoolers might call being "sneaky" or a court of law might label outright "fraud." Evolutionary biologists and cultural anthropologists tell us that concealing or misrepresenting our true feelings and motives is a distinct evolutionary advantage and a defining characteristic of higher-order primates, particu-larly those whose gaze we meet in the mirror each day. People quite regularly censor facts about how they feel to lubricate the process of social interaction (have you ever opened a present you didn't really like in front of the person who gave it to you?) Learning to conceal our less acceptable or laudable feelings from others is a part of attaining social maturity. And it's not too surprising that sometimes people just don't want to discuss their even slightly awkward or intimate emotions with a stranger from the business world.

Overcoming the Barriers: The Search for a New Way

With all of the barriers between us and the information we need to have to understand our consumers, it's clear that we need a new way to discover emotional information. Since we don't seem to be able to get anywhere talking directly to the rational brain of the conscious consumer, we have to change our conversation. We need to develop ways of going behind what the consumers are willing or able to tell us.

Meanwhile, marketers and marketing researchers have not stood idly around lamenting the inaccessibility of consumers' emotions. Development of alternatives for accessing this information has been underway for some years, and a variety of options have arisen for bypassing the rational brains of our consumers to access information about emotions. Some of those methods simply avoid the brain entirely and seek to discern or impute emotional states by looking at observable physiological states that we know accompany emotional arousal. Other methods have capitalized on the emerging field of neuroscience to look directly at areas of the brain known to be involved in emotional reactions and experience. Here are a few highlights of that research.

Physiological Measures of Emotion

For quite some time marketing researchers seeking measures of emotion have turned to autonomic physiological measures associated with emotional response; typically, these involve readings taken from the skin, cardiovascular system, and eyes. LaBarbera and Tucciarone studied skin conductance as a measure of "motivation to buy" in response to advertisements in 1995,[4] and they reported that this measure is a better predictor of purchasing than self-report measures. Cuthbert and a team of coworkers looked at increases and decreases in heart rate in a 1996 study also trying to measure physiological responses to advertising stimuli. Most recently, in 2012, Laeng and colleagues[5] used measurements of pupil diameter to infer the intensity of mental activity, particularly changes in attention.

There are at least four good things about using physiological measurements like these to uncover emotional responses of consumers. First and most important, this kind of passive physiological response doesn't require consumers to be consciously involved in "answering" questions; their responses are thus free of conscious distortions. Second, physiological responses don't require consumers to interpret or explain their emotional states (to which we know they have no access). Third, physiological responses are measured in real time, and this means researchers don't have to rely on consumers' often inaccurate, incomplete. or embellished memory of a feeling state. Finally, real-time data collection of physiological responses at the moment consumers experience advertising content, eliminates any contamination of the stimulus from imperfect memory.

At the same time, there are some shortcomings to working with physiological measures to understand emotion. The biggest is that physiological methods can't tell the difference between *types* of emotion. Skin conductance and skin potential measures can't tell the difference between positive and negative feelings; heart rate measurements can distinguish positive from negative emotions, but they stop there and are unable to distinguish "anger" from "fear," for example. Measuring pupil size can tell us about the amount of mental activity in the emotional brain, but pupil size is also affected by conscious rational brain activity, and so it can be hard to tell the difference.

Behavioral Measures of Emotion

Using nonverbal behavior as a clue to emotional states has a long history in emotion research, dating all the way back to Charles Darwin's descriptive accounts in *The Expression of the Emotions in Man and Animals* over a century ago.[6] In the century and a half since Darwin, researchers have gotten more scientifically precise. Gross and Levenson linked facial expression and body posture to specific emotions in a 1993 study; others (e.g., Brickman in 1976 and 1980, Backhaus, Meyer, and Stockert in1985) have tried to measure the vibration frequency of the voice (voice pitch analysis) to measure emotional response to advertising stimuli. Another widely used approach has looked at facial expression as evidence of emotional state. The Facial Action Coding System (FACS), developed by Paul Ekman and Wallace Friesen in 1978, gathers data on how individual facial muscles change the appearance of the face. A newer version of this system called the EMFACS technique (Emotional FACS) has been used to identify the emotional character of facial expressions.

The most useful aspect of measuring emotion through expressive behaviors is its accessibility and scalability in our era of near-universal webcam access. Today's providers of facial coding analysis (notably Affectiva in Cambridge, MA) offer access to facial coding online for users to implement as needed. Facial coding has been especially useful in judging subjects' reactions to a stimulus they are viewing as an online camera tracks their changing facial expressions. Key measures delivered through the facial coding of subjects as they view a stimulus (most often an advertisement or a product description) are focused on their level of attention and overall liking. The main drawback of this technique is that accuracy in judging more subtle emotional states based upon facial expressions is not yet well developed.

Neurological Measures of Emotion

Studies of the brain itself as it reacts to stimuli are another fast-growing approach to uncovering the subconscious emotions of consumers. The earliest efforts at direct measurement of brain responses to advertising used electroencephalography (EEG) to measure variation in brain waves (alpha versus beta waves)[7]. Brain wave analysis has also been used to correlate brain activity to consumers' states of arousal and pleasure.[8] However, critics of this approach have questioned the validity and reliability of direct measurement of brain responses. Some note that lateral location of brain activity has only a weak relationship to other emotional measures; others emphasize that EEG has not been shown to correlate with any particular emotional or rational process and that laboratory variables (such as where electrodes are placed on a subject) can have significant influence on the results produced. Given that EEG is inherently imprecise in inferring the experience of specific emotions, ad testing firms have typically relied on it only as a measure of an "overall emotion" score.

The advent of additional brain imaging techniques such as functional magnetic resonance imaging (fMRI), positron emission tomography (PET), and magnetoencephalography (MEG) marks a major development in the neuropsychological study of emotion. These techniques detect magnetic activity or radioactive patterns in the brain and have shown promise in predicting the overall consequences of emotional states, such as product preferences, advertising effectiveness, and brand loyalty[9]. Helliker [10]did a study in 2006 in which he used fMRI to demonstrate that brain regions associated with pleasure, self-identification, and reward were activated by a well-known brand whereas an unfamiliar brand activated brain regions associated with displeasure.

Neuropsychological approaches to understanding emotions also offer the compelling advantage of seemingly going directly "to the source" for information. However, the ability of neurological measurement methods has been very limited thus far in the ability to distinguish much detail about emotional states—beyond negative and positive arousal, and evocation of attention and memory. Clearly, this promising field of research will only grow in value as we learn more and more about the human brain. President Obama's well-funded initiative to map the human brain, for example, and a similar initiative in Europe promise to give us an increasing amount of detail from which to make inferences from brain activity to emotional states.

A New Approach: MindSight®

My colleagues and I at the Forbes Consulting Group have been working for several years to overcome the persistent and sizeable difficulties in studying emotion. The result of this is development of the emotional research technology we call MindSight.

The foundational element of MindSight is a technique for "talking in pictures" with consumers' emotional brains. This conversation in images utilizes a rapid exposure/response technique that we developed based upon neuroscience research as reported by Antonio Damasio[11] and others. Looking inside the brain to document the microgenesis of perceptions, emotions, and thoughts formed in reaction to visual images, David Rudrauf (with Damasio and others)[12] used magnetoencephalography—an alternative to fMRI especially suited to documenting sequences of neural events—to follow the brain activity related to processing of visual stimuli. Starting from the moment a visual image was presented to a subject, the first 100 milliseconds or so of brain activity were occupied with visually processing the stimulus; processing next shifted to the emotional brain, and only after about 700–800 milliseconds did activity begin to appear in the frontal lobes, signaling rational thought about the stimulus. Damasio writes:

> From the moment the stimuli were processed in the visual cortices to the moment the subjects first reported feelings, nearly 500 milliseconds passed, or half a second. Is this a little or a lot? It depends on the perspective.

In "brain time" it is a huge interval...in "conscious mind time," however, it is not very much. It sits between the couple of hundred milliseconds we require to be conscious of a pattern in perception and the seven or eight hundred milliseconds we need to process a concept.

On the basis of this research, we envisioned an "emotional discovery window" that exists in a 300–800 millisecond time frame, starting from the moment consumers first perceive a visual stimulus presented to them and lasting until the moment of their first conscious rational thought about the stimulus. Data from a task where respondents are shown images and constrained to respond in this time frame should, we surmised, be primarily linked to emotional brain activity and so would be substantially free of the distortion that arises from conscious editing, self-presentation, and general "rationalizing" linked to conscious conceptual processing. MindSight uses this rapid presentation/rapid response technique to open a "dialogue of imagery" with the emotional brains of consumers.

This technique circumvents the difficulties of self-reports and all of the conscious distortions those involve. At the same time, it accesses the richness and nuance of activity in the emotional brain to assess a much wider range of emotions than purely physiological or neurological measures have done.

The MindSight Image Library

To create an emotional measurement task where subjects respond in the sub-one-second time frame of the "emotional discovery window" we needed to confront the fact that consumers couldn't do much more than provide "yes/no" feedback in this short response time. For feedback gathered this quickly to be meaningful, MindSight needed to present images whose emotional meanings were well-established in advance of consumers' exposure to them (so that a "yes/no" response indicated a specific emotional state being accepted or rejected by the subject). Accordingly, we created a library of images that were each validated to be linked to the emotions created by fulfillment (or frustration) of one of the nine motivations of the matrix.

MindSight Case Study: The Subtle Emotions behind Fragrance Choices

To illustrate how this technique works, consider an interesting case where a large, international women's cosmetics company was asking for help predicting the success of potential new fragrance introductions. Management at this company understood very well that their fragrance products succeed in the marketplace primarily by creating appealing emotional experiences for the women who wear them. Managers were convinced that information about the nature and magnitude of emotional responses to new product concepts could help them to predict their success.

Prior to the MindSight Matrix study, this company had judged the likely emotional impact of a fragrance through informal qualitative research using traditional projective testing techniques. The company's marketers were continually on the lookout for a better way, for a more structured scientific technique. As a global business, the company wanted an emotional research tool whose results could be statistically reliable and would be valid across the many cultures in their global markets. Let's take a look at how MindSight fulfilled these goals.

Overview of Methods

A total of 300 respondents were presented with one of two new fragrance concepts. Each subject first completed a brief battery of established evaluation measures (e.g., self-reported judgements of purchase interest, uniqueness, and value).

Subjects were then introduced to the MindSight task and told that this exercise was intended to help the company understand how they felt wearing the new fragrances might make them feel:

- The first MindSight task was a positive image exercise, using the priming sentence "I'd be excited to wear this new fragrance because I think it might make me feel a little more _____."
- This was followed by a negative image exercise, using the priming sentence "I'd be hesitant to wear this new fragrance because I think it might leave me feeling a little bit _____."
- The third task presented the participants with a range of phrases they could select to expand on the feelings they got from the images selected.

The fragrance concept stimuli (which we've disguised completely to protect the client's proprietary information) were as follows:

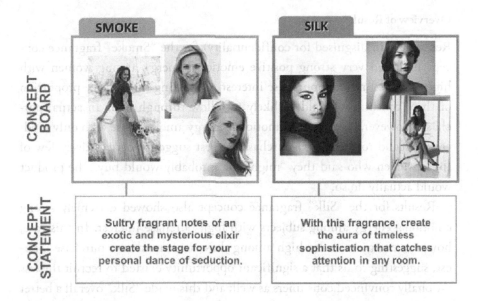

First, each concept was evaluated for rational appeal using a traditional five-point purchase interest scale. Subjects who were deemed "potential prospects" for the new fragrance were selected for further assessment. One group consisted of those who indicated high purchase interest (top box rating), and a second group consisted of subjects who reported moderate purchase interest (second and third box ratings).

Then, for each interest group, emotional energy was assessed for each concept, including:

- Total motivational energy: a weighted combination of the number of images selected and the speed with which they were picked.
- Net emotional energy: total positive motivational energy score minus total negative motivational energy score.
- Emotional drivers and emotional barriers: based on the distribution of emotional energies across the nine motivational dimensions in the MindSight Matrix. Positive emotional drivers of the most rationally convinced (highest purchase interest) group were identified, as were potentially negative emotional barriers among the less rationally convinced group (moderate purchase interest).

Overview of Results

Results (again disguised for confidentiality) for the "Smoke" fragrance concept indicated very strong positive emotional energy among women with high (top box) rational purchase interest, suggesting that a large proportion of these consumers would be likely to follow through with an actual purchase. However, very limited emotional energy among those with only moderate (second to third box) purchase interest suggests that relatively few of those women who said they "might" or "probably would buy" the product would actually do so.

Results for the "Silk" fragrance concept also showed extremely strong emotional energy among subjects with high purchase interest. In this case, however, energy was also high among those with moderate purchase interest, suggesting to us that a significant opportunity existed to recruit the less rationally convinced consumers as well; and this made "Silk" overall a better opportunity.

When we looked in detail at the profile for "Silk" across all nine motivational domains, it appeared that the emotional hesitation among the less convinced respondents was more an issue of lower enthusiasm than of greater resistance. Accordingly, we recommended marketing that emphasized the positive emotional forces that were stronger among those with highest purchase interest: empowerment, engagement, achievement, and nurturance (indicated by bars with scores circled next).

We used these results to create an "emotional infographic" presenting the images most often chosen by consumers in the exercise along with words most often chosen in a follow-up exercise to further explicate imagery. These materials were used to assist the company's creative efforts during concept development.

To apply those learnings worldwide, this company is now using MindSight to develop normative benchmarks for their fragrance concepts in markets around the globe. Our shared goal is to create a mathematically calculated motivated purchase interest measure, or MPI, that integrates rational purchase interest with emotional purchase drives to deliver a psychologically valid and predictive measure of actual purchase behavior.

We are encouraged by the results of our emotional research this far using MindSight, and we hope that this tool may help us make a contribution

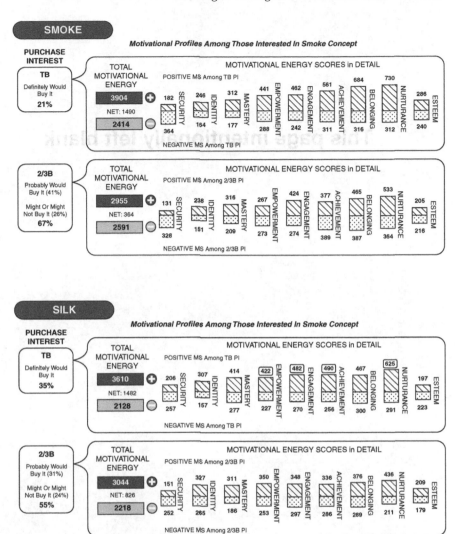

to the understanding of how emotions influence decision making and behavior in the marketplace. Those wishing to learn more about MindSight or wanting to explore more details of this case illustration, can visit www. mindsighttechnologies.com.

This page intentionally left blank

CHAPTER 17

Epilogue

Now that you have finished this narrative journey along the pathway to motivational marketing, I trust that your head is spinning with new ways to approach the business problems you face every day. You now have, I hope, new ways of thinking about your consumers, their lives, and their emotional needs. You should also have new ways of thinking about your product and the benefits it can deliver to truly fulfill consumers' innermost emotional frustrations and aspirations. It is my sincere hope that each and every one of you has emerged from this book with a new and different perspective on the dialogs that take place between businesses and consumers.

But before you set to work reanalyzing and changing things in your business, I would ask you to spend some time thinking about how you have succeeded thus far. Think about how the consumer insights that your business already has may actually speak to the inner motivations of those consumers. And work to discern how the messages your brand has been sending to its consumers all along may have implicitly carried the promise of deeper emotional fulfillment. Successful brands have succeeded for good reasons, and typically those reasons include an intuitive understanding of what motivates consumers.

Once you have conducted a thorough review of your brand as it exists today, I would recommend you take a few initial steps toward making good business even better.

1. Take a good hard and fresh look at your consumers. Conduct new qualitative or quantitative research or simply conduct a careful review of research

that you've done recently. Ask yourself which of the kinds of aspirations and frustrations you've learned about here are likely to be operating in the lifestyle moments in which your products are at work.

2. Take a similar hard look at the messages you've been sending to your consumers about your product. This includes your explicit messages in advertising and promotional material as well as the messages you send implicitly with your package design and any other sensory elements involved in your product. Try to decode" the emotional messages that come through with all of this communication and think about ways you might bring your message content closer towhat you think your consumers really want.

3. Think also about the tone and style of your messaging. If you decide the benefits of your product really are intrapsychic ones, then your communications, implicit or explicit, should be telling the consumers about how they will feel about themselves. By contrast, if the benefits of your product appear to be interpersonal in nature, then your communication should be focusing more on what people close to the consumer will think or feel about them. Similarly, if you think the benefits of your product focus on expanding life's possibilities (like the motives in the first row of the matrix), you should focus on the promise of the future. And if your product's benefits appear to be focused on getting great results (like the motives in the third matrix row), then you need to be showing those results.

4. No matter what decisions you make about a motivational marketing strategy for your product, remember that executing this type of communication will require a good amount of thought. Emotional promises are usually better delivered implicitly than explicitly and can often be delivered more effectively by tonality than by text. And getting it right may take a few tries—as you work to evoke an emotional response without engaging in hyperbole or just plain schmaltziness. Find a good creative agency and work closely with them. And make sure that they're thinking and working in the same emotional terms that you are.

I'd like to finish by offering a few predictions of how business and consumers may evolve as we all become more and more motivationally aware. I believe that we are standing at the brink of great change. I'm even comfortable calling it a revolution: a quantum leap that fundamentally alters the relationship between businesses and their consumers. Just as the steam engine first made large-scale distribution of goods possible, for example, and as communications innovations—radio, TV, the Internet—transformed how we relate to goods, services, and the people who consume them, so our new era of consumer-based, emotionally aware communications will change the way business works.

As the emphasis on marketing messages shifts to focus on consumers' emotional experiences and the emotional fulfillment that results from them, as we increase our ability to measure and understand those emotional needs and to build pathways to nurture and sustain them, as consumers increasingly influence the products, services, and messages they bring into their hearts and homes, and as our consumption of products and services becomes more and more personalized and fulfilling, we will witness a sea change in what we do, how we do it, and how it all feels.

Here are some examples of what I see on that horizon:

1. I predict that the products in our lives will get better and better at making us happy—they will go beyond a job well done to deliver truly meaningful emotional experiences.
2. I predict that consumers will speak more and more loudly and make their voice heard with more impact. The time is not far off when you will be able to get the product you really want, not just the one that's on offer.
3. I predict that we will see a design-driven revolution in the look and feel of virtually everything in our product universe. These changes will make the objects in our lives more pleasing to all of our senses and the performance of those objects more fulfilling of our innermost needs.
4. I predict that companies everywhere will spend more time with consumers—watching, listening, consulting, and learning. This will transform the process of production into a cybernetic loop, where consumers' needs and wants directly inform the nature of the products in their lives, and those products in turn directly impact the needs and wants of consumers.
5. I predict that a growing gap will develop between those companies who truly commit to learning about and fulfilling consumers' emotional needs and those companies that refuse to embrace the power of motivational marketing. The difference between the companies that "get" the new perspective versus those that don't will be as great as the difference between companies that adapted to and adopted emerging

information technologies and those who failed to do so over the past two decades.

6. And finally, I predict you, dear reader, will have a significantly greater amount of fun going about your business on the platform of an ongoing and authentic emotional connection with your consumers. I wish you luck!

Notes

2 Introducing the MindSight Motivational Matrix

1. Paula Niedenthal, Silvia Krauth-Gruber, and Francois Ric, *Psychology of Emotion: Interpersonal, Experiential, and Cognitive Approaches* (New York: Psychology Press, 2006).
2. C. P. Snow, *The Search* (New York: Scribner's, 1958), 58.
3. David Forbes, "Toward a Unified Model of Human Motivation," *Review of General Psychology* 15:2 (2011): 85–98.

3 Introducing the Intrapsychic Motivations

1. Rene Descartes, *Principles of Philosophy*, translated by John Cottingham, Robert Stoothoff, and Dugald Murdoch. *The Philosophical Writings of Descartes*, volume 1 (Cambridge: Cambridge University Press, [1644] 1985).
2. Plato. Rouse, W.H.D., ed., *The Republic Book VII* (New York, Penguin Group Inc. 2008), 365–401.
3. *Motivation and Personality* (New York: Harper, 1954). *Contents.* Second Ed. (New York: Harper, 1970.) *Contents.* Third Ed. (New York: Addison-Wesley, 1987).
4. R. Franken, *Human Motivation* Third Ed. (Pacific Grove, CA: Brooks/Cole, 1994).
5. C. R. Rogers, "A Theory of Therapy, Personality, and Interpersonal Relationships," in S. Koch (ed.), *Psychology: A Study of a Science*, vol. 3 (New York: McGraw Hill, 1959), 184–256.
6. Sigmund Freud, *The Ego and the Id*, translated by Joan Riviere and newly edited by James Strachey (New York: Norton, 1962).
7. John Donne, *John Donne's Devotions* (Cambridge: Cambridge University Press,1923).
8. "The Harley-Davidson Experience—Living by It," on www.youtube.com /watch?v=jyocDeGh7Qs, uploaded by infernorulez August 6, 2008.

4 The Security Motive

1. Abraham Maslow, "A Theory of Human Motivation," in *Psychological Review* 50 (1943): 370–396.
2. William James, *Psychology: The Briefer Course* (New York: Harper, 1961), 408.
3. R. C. Kessler, W. T. Chiu, O. Demler, and E. E. Walters, "Prevalence, Severity, and Comorbidity of Twelve-month DSM-IV Disorders in the National Comorbidity Survey Replication (NCS-R)," *Archives of General Psychiatry* 62, no. 6 (2005): 617–27.
4. "Twelve-Month Prevalence of World Mental Health Composite International Diagnostic Interview," *Diagnostic and Statistical Manual of Mental Disorders*, 4th ed., downloaded from http://jama.jamanetwork.com on December 14, 2014.
5. WHO World Mental Health Survey Consortium, "Prevalence, Severity, and Unmet Need for Treatment of Mental Disorders," in *Journal of the American Medical Association* 291, no. 21 (2004): 2581–90.
6. Eric Fromm, *Escape from Freedom* (New York, Henry Holt and Company, 1994).
7. *Oxford English Dictionary*, 2014. www.oed.com.
8. R. C. Kessler et al., "Lifetime Prevalence and Age-of-onset distributions of DSM-IV: Disorders in the National Comorbidity, Survey Replication" *Archives of General Psychiatry* 92, no. 6 (2005): 593–602.
9. David Chase, "How Brands Thrived during the Great Depression," MediaConnection.com, downloaded on December14, 2014.
10. David Rhodes and Daniel Stelter, "Green Shoots, False Positives, and What Companies Can Learn from the Great Depression," Boston Consulting Group White Paper June 12, 2009.
11. Tuttle, Brad, "Warren Buffett's Boring, Brilliant Wisdom," *Time Magazine, Business Section* March 01, 2010.
12. Kim Witte, "Extended Parallel Process Model," in *Communication Monographs*. 61 (June 1994): 113–134.

5 The Identity Motive

1. Erik H. Erikson, *Childhood and Society* (New York: Norton, 1950).
2. P. T. Costa Jr., and R. R. McCrae, "Revised NEO Personality Inventory (NEO-PI-R) and NEO Five-Factor Inventory (NEO-FFI) Manual" (Odessa, FL: Psychological Assessment Resources, 1992).
3. K. T. Tian, W. O. Bearden, G. L. Hunter, "Consumers' Need for Uniqueness: Scale Development and Validation," *Journal of Consumer Research* 28:1 (2001).: 50–66.
4. Ayalla Ruvio, "Unique Like Everybody Else? The Dual Role of Consumers' Need for Uniqueness," *Psychology & Marketing* 25:5 (May 2008): 444–464. Published online in Wiley InterScience (www.interscience.wiley.com) © 2008 Wiley Periodicals, Inc. DOI: 10.1002/mar.20219.

6 The Mastery Motive

1. The Urban Child Institute, "What drives Kids' Curiosity?" in *News and Articles,* www.urbanchildinstitute.org, June 2014., Downloaded December 16, 2014.
2. Robert W. White, "Motivation Reconsidered: The Concept of Competence," *Psychological Review,* 66:5 (September 1959): 297–333.
3. Albert Einstein, "About Education," in *Ideas and Opinions* (London: Souvenir Press, 2005), 55–67.
4. Susan Harter, "A New Self-report Scale of Intrinsic versus Extrinsic Orientation in the Classroom: Motivational and Informational Components," *Developmental Psychology* 17:3 (1981): 300.
5. Michael Jordan by Nike. www.youtube.com/watch, February 16, 2012. Downloaded December 16, 2014.
6. Malcolm Gladwell, *Outliers: The Story of Success* (New York: Back Bay Books, 2011).

7 Introducing the Instrumental Motivations

1. Unilever Press Release, Unilever Media Center, May 20, 2013, http://www .unileverusa.com/media-center/pressreleases/2013/doverealbeautysketchesmost viewedonlinead.aspx, accessed December 16, 2014.

8 The Empowerment Motive

1. Jose Ashford and Craig LeCroy, "Human Behavior in the Social Environment," in *Brooks/Cole Empowerment Series* (Boston: Cengage Learning, 2012).
2. Albert Bandura, "Toward a Psychology of Human Agency," *Perspectives on Psychological Science* 1:64 (New York: Sage Publications, 2006).
3. Albert Bandura, "Self-efficacy," in V. S. Ramachaudran (ed.), *Encyclopedia of Human Behavior,* vol. 4 (New York: Academic Press, 1994), 71–81.

9 The Engagement Motive

1. H. D. Thoreau, [1906] *The Journal of Henry David Thoreau.* Edited by B. Torrey and F. H. Allen (New York: Dover Books, 1962).
2. Mihaly Csikszentmihalyi, *Flow: The Psychology of Optimal Experience* (New York: Harper Perennial Modern Classics, 2008).
3. C. Tavris, "Contentment Is Hard Work," *The New York Times,* March 18, 1990.
4. Bill Utterback, "Athletes Savor Being in 'the Zone,' But No One Has Yet Figured Out How They Can Stay There Forever," *The Seattle Times,* March 3, 1991, downloaded December 16, 2014.
5. "The Promise Is All Bruce and the Band," *Winston-Salem Journal,* December 12, 2012.
6. Mihaly Csikszentmihalyi, "Finding Flow: The Psychology of Engagement with Everyday Life," in Robert E. Quinn (ed.), *Change the World: How Ordinary People Can Achieve Extraordinary Results* (San Francisco: Jossey Bass, 2010), 210, 272.

7. Roberto Verganti, Design Driven Innovation: Changing the Rules of Competition by Radically Innovating What Things Mean (Boston: Harvard Business Press, 2009).

10   The Achievement Motive

1. David McClelland, *The Achieving Society* (Princeton, N.J.: Van Nostrand, 1961).
2. "Where Are They Now? Past Spelling Bee Champions," in *Business Insider*, online at http://www.businessinsider.com/lives-of-national-spelling-bee-champs-2013–5?op=1#ixzz3NzmDnHev; downloaded on December 29, 2014.

11   Introducing the Interpersonal Motivations

1. Jack N. Rakove, The Annotated U.S. Constitution and Declaration of Independence (Cambridge: Belknap Press of Harvard University Press, 2009), 7–22.
2. Martin Seligman quoted in Claudia Wallis. "Science of Happiness: New Research on Mood, Satisfaction," *Time Magazine*, January 9, 2005.
3. Harvard School of Public Health Newsletter, "Happiness and Health," Winter 2011, 1.
4. Dan Gilbert, *This Emotional Life*, PBS documentary series, 2010.
5. Thomas Hobbes, *Leviathan*, Chapter 13. "Of the Natural Condition of Mankind as Concerning Their Felicity, and Misery" (Seattle: Pacific Publishing Studio, 2011).
6. James Coan, "Human Brains are Hardwired for Empathy," cited in *UVA Today*, https://news.virginia.edu August 21, 2013, posted by Fariss Samarra, downloaded December 15, 2014.
7. Cited in AdWeek.com, November 10, 2011.
8. Rudi Halbright and Max Dunn, "Case Study: The Toyota Prius: Lessons in Marketing Eco-friendly Products," *Managerial Marketing* (SUS 6060), March 3, 2010, 5.

12   The Belonging Motive

1. Simono Kemp, "Global Social Media Users Pass 2 Billion" in News on We Are Social Blog, http://wearesocial.net/blog downloaded August 8, 2014.
2. Aristotle, *Politics*: Second Edition (Chicago: University Of Chicago Press, 2013).
3. E. Diener and M. E. P. Seligman, "Beyond Money: Toward an Economy of Well-being," *Psychological Science in the Public Interest* 5: (2004): 1–31.
4. E. Diener and M. Seligman, "Very Happy People," *Psychological Science* 13:1 (January 2002): 81–84.
5. T. Dodge and J. Jaccard, "Participation in Athletics and Female Sexual Risk Behavior: The Evaluation of Four Causal Structures" *Journal of Adolescent Research* 42 (2002).

13 The Nurturance Motive

1. G. C. Williams, "Pleiotropy, Natural Selection, and the Evolution of Senescence." *Evolution* 11:4 (1957): 398–411.
2. "Modern Marriage: 'I Like Hugs. I Like Kisses. But What I Really Love is Help with the Dishes.'" In *Pew Research Social and Demographic Trends*, July 2007.
3. Martin Seligman, *Flourish: A Visionary New Understanding of Happiness and Well-being* (New York: Free Press, 2011); Seligman, *Authentic Happiness: Using the New Positive Psychology to Realize Your Potential for Lasting Fulfillment* (New York: Free Press, 2004).
4. J. Bowlby, *Maternal Care and Mental Health* World Health Organisation (1951).
5. J. Bowlby, *Separation: Anxiety & Anger. Attachment and Loss* (vol. 2); (International psycho-analytical library no.95) (London: Hogarth Press, 1973).
6. M. Ainsworth and J. Bowlby (1965). *Child Care and the Growth of Love* (London: Penguin Books).
7. Harry Harlow, "The Nature of Love," *American Psychologist* 13 (1958): 673–685. Washington, DC: American Psychological Association
8. Martha J. Farah, Laura Betancourt, David M. Shera, Jessica H. Savage, Joan M. Giannetta, Nancy L. Brodsky, Elsa K. Malmud3, and Hallam Hurt, "Environmental Stimulation, Parental Nurturance, amd Cognitive Development in Humans," *Developmental Science* 11:5 (2008): 793–801. Malden: Blackwell Publishing.

14 The Esteem Motive

1. Abraham Maslow, "A Theory of Human Motivation," *Psychological Review* 50 (1943): 370–396.
2. C. Daniel Batson et al., "Empathic Joy and the Empathy-altruism Hypothesis," *Journal of Personality and Social Psychology* 61:3 (September 1991): 413–426.
3. http://chroniclingamerica.loc.gov/lccn/sn83045462/1921–09–12/ed-1/seq-24. Downloaded December, 16, 2014.
4. Peter Buxmann and Hannah Krasnova, "Envy on Facebook: A Hidden Threat to Users' Life Satisfaction," summarized in the newsletter of Humboldt Universität zu Berlin, posted by Constanze Haase, January 21, 2013.
5. Andy Warhol, in the program for a 1968 exhibition of his work at the Moderna Museet in Stockholm, Sweden, cited in Jeff Guinn and Douglas Perry, *The Sixteenth Minute: Life in the Aftermath of Fame* (New York: Tarcher Penguin, 2005).

15 The Scholarship on Motivation

1. Aristotle, *Physics* David Bostock (ed.), Robin Waterfield (trans.) (Oxford, Oxford: Oxford University Press, 2008).
2. Augustine, *On the Free Choice of the Will, On Grace and Free Choice and Other Writings*, Peter King (ed.) (Cambridge: Cambridge University Press, 2014).

3. Jeremy Bentham, *An Introduction to the Principles of Morals and Legislation* (Mineola, NY: Dover Publications, 2007), chapter 1, section 1.1, 1–8.
4. William James, *Principles of Psychology,* Kindle edition (Seattle: Amazon Digital Services, 2011).
5. Lange, Carl, "Ueber Gemüthsbewegungen: Eine psycho-physiologische Studie" (1887), Benjamin Rand, (ed.) (Boston: Houghton Mifflin, 1912), 672–684.
6. Sigmund Freud, *Interpretation of Dreams,* Kindle edition (Seattle: Amazon Digital Services, 2010).
7. David McClelland, *Human Motivation* (Cambridge: Cambridge University Press, 1988) Part III, Sections 7–9.
8. Abraham Maslow, *A Theory of Human Motivation* (Eastford: Martino Fine Books, 2013), 66–102; Abraham Maslow, *Motivation and Personality,* Third Ed. (New York: Addison-Wesley, 1987).
9. David Forbes, "Toward a Unified Theory of Human Motivation," in *Review of General Psychology* 15:2 (2011): 85–98.

16   MindSight: Learning to Talk to the Emotional Brain

1. Daniel Goleman, quoting Emmanuel Donchin, director of the Laboratory for Cognitive Psychophysiology at the University of Illinois, in "New View of Mind Gives Unconscious an Expanded Role," *New York Times,* science section, February 7, 1984.
2. Daniel Kahneman, *Thinking, Fast and Slow* (New York : Farrar, Straus and Giroux, 2013).
3. Ibid.
4. P. A. LaBarbera and J. D. Tucciarone, "GRS Reconsidered: A Behavior-based Approach to Evaluating and Improving the Sales Potency of Advertising," *Journal of Advertising Research* 35 (1995), 33–53.
5. B. Laeng, S. Sirois, and G. Gredeback. "Pupillometry: A Window to the Preconscious?" *Perspectives on Psychological Science* 7:1 (2012): 18–27. Web doi: 10.1177/1745691611427305.
6. Charles Darwin, *Expression of the Emotions in Man and Animals* (Chicago: University of Chicago Press, 1965).
7. H. E. Krugman, "Brain Wave Measures of Media Involvement," *Journal of Advertising Research* 11:1 (1971): 3–9.
8. S. Weinstein, "A Review of Brain Hemisphere Research." *Journal of Advertising Research* 22 (1982): 59–63;S. Weinstein, C. Weinstein, and R. Drozdenko,"Brain Wave Analysis: An Electroencephalographic Technique Used for Evaluating the Communications-Effect of Advertising," *Psychology & Marketing* 1:1 (1984): 17–42.
9. M. Carmichael, "Neuromarketing: Is It Coming to a Lab Near You?" *PBS Online,* November 9, 2004.
10. K. Helliker, "This Is Your Brain on a Strong Brand: MRIs Show Even Insurers Can Excite," *Wall Street Journal* (2006) *p. b1-b4.*

11. A. Damasio, *Self Comes to Mind: Constructing the Conscious Brain* (New York: Pantheon, 2010).

12. D. Rudrauf et al., "Rapid Interactions between the Ventral Visual Stream and Emotion-Related Structures Rely on a Two-Pathway Architecture," *The Journal of Neuroscience* 28:1 (2008): 2793–2803; Rudrauf et al., "Enter Feelings: Somatosensory Responses Following Early Stages Of Visual Induction of Emotion," *International Journal of Psychophysiology* 72:1 (2009): 13–23.

This page intentionally left blank

Image Permissions

Index